KYOTO-CSEAS SERIES ON ASIAN STUDIES
Center for Southeast Asian Studies, Kyoto University

LIBERALISM and the POSTCOLONY
THINKING THE STATE IN 20TH-CENTURY PHILIPPINES

KYOTO-CSEAS SERIES ON ASIAN STUDIES
Center for Southeast Asian Studies, Kyoto University

LIBERALISM and the POSTCOLONY
THINKING THE STATE IN 20TH-CENTURY PHILIPPINES

LISANDRO E. CLAUDIO

NUS PRESS
Singapore

in association with

KYOTO UNIVERSITY PRESS
Japan

The publication of this book is financially supported by the Kyoto University President's Special Fund.

© 2017 Lisandro E. Claudio

All rights reserved. No part of this publication may be reproduced or transmitted in any form or by any means, electronic or mechanical, including photocopy, recording, or any information storage or retrieval system, without permission in writing from the publisher.

NUS Press
National University of Singapore
AS3-01-02, 3 Arts Link
Singapore 117569
http://nuspress.nus.edu.sg

ISBN 978-981-4722-52-0 (Paper)

Kyoto University Press
Yoshida-South Campus, Kyoto University
69 Yoshida-Konoe-Cho, Sakyo-ku
Kyoto 606-8315
Japan
www.kyoto-up.or.jp

ISBN 978-4-8140-0067-8

National Library Board, Singapore Cataloguing in Publication Data

Names: Claudio, Lisandro E.
Title: Liberalism and the postcolony: thinking the state in 20th century Philippines / Lisandro E. Claudio.
Description: Singapore: NUS Press; Kyoto, Japan: in association with Kyoto University Press, [2017] | Series: Kyoto-CSEAS series on Asian studies. | Includes bibliographic references and index.
Identifiers: OCN 961835980 | 978-981-47-2252-0 (paperback)
Subjects: LCSH: Liberalism--Political aspects--Philippines--20th century. | Philippines--Politics and government--History--20th century.
Classification: DDC 320.5109599--dc23

Cover photograph: Salvador P. Lopez and Carlos P. Romulo
(From *Manila Times* Photo Archive, Rizal Library, Ateneo de Manila University, n.d.)

Cover and book design by R. Jordan P. Santos
Printed by Markono Print Media Pte Ltd

For Jojo, Jun, Carol, and all my teachers

Contents

ACKNOWLEDGMENTS	ix
INTRODUCTION **LIBERALISM ASKANCE**	1
CHAPTER 1 **CAMILO OSIAS AND THE NATIONALIST INTERNATIONAL**	23
CHAPTER 2 **SALVADOR ARANETA AND THE FILIPINO NEW DEAL**	45
CHAPTER 3 **CARLOS P. ROMULO AND THE ANTI-COMMUNIST THIRD WORLD**	81
CHAPTER 4 **SALVADOR P. LOPEZ AND THE SPACE OF LIBERTY**	111
CONCLUSION **POSTCOLONIAL LIBERALISM, A GLOBAL IDEA**	147
AFTERWORD **A FIFTH LIBERAL**	157
NOTES	165
BIBLIOGRAPHY	204
INDEX	221

Acknowledgments

I wrote most of this work during a two-year postdoctoral fellowship at Kyoto University's Center for Southeast Asian Studies (CSEAS). I have never intellectually benefited so much in so short a time as in these two years, and this is due to the wonderful sensei, staff, students, and visiting fellows at CSEAS, including: Center Director Yasuyuki Kono, Hiromu Shimizu, Julius Bautista, Masako Akedo, Chiaki Abe, Michiyo Ide, Marites Vitug, Hope Sabanpan-Yu, Kimiya Kitani, Narumi Shitara, Mario Lopez, Nate Badenoch, Narumi Shitara, Masao and Jackie Imamura, Zenta Nishio, Natsuko Shiraishi, Tran Van Do, and the world's best officemate, Jafar Suryomenggolo. Vice Director Yoko Hayami not only served as my faculty counterpart while in Kyoto but also coordinated the co-publication with NUS and Ateneo. My deepest gratitude is reserved for CSEAS's Carol Hau, who brought me to Kyoto, carefully read every page of this work, bought me numerous dinners, and forced me to think about macroeconomics and the Philippine elite.

My thanks as well to other Japan-based colleagues: Jenny and Jamie Coates, Wataru Kusaka, and Yusuke Takagi.

I remain indebted to my two Ph.D. supervisors from the University of Melbourne, Kate McGregor and David Goodman, who have continued to take an interest in my work.

My home base in Manila was the Ateneo de Manila University, where I benefited from the support and friendship of colleagues and friends like Jayeel Cornelio, Jowel Canuday, Ambeth Ocampo, Melissa Lao, Arjan Aguirre, Mary Racelis, Niño Leviste, Von Totanes, Sally Llanes, Melissa Mar Reyes, Shyl Sales, Marichi Guevara, Ram Balubal, Tey Ilagan, Angelli Tugado, Nandy Aldaba, Benjie Tolosa, Emma Porio, Fr. Jose Cruz, Fr. Luis David, Karl Cheng Chua, Mike Pante, Rowie Palacios, and the ever chatty Melay Abao. I am most grateful to Jun Aguilar, a pioneering scholar and a fount of career advice.

Outside Ateneo, I thank colleagues from down the street at the University of the Philippines: Ed and Tesa Tadem, Natsy Verceles, Maya Tamayo, Eric Manalastas, and Mitch Ong. For helping me dig through the papers of Salvador P. Lopez, my thanks to UP's Aaron Mallari.

Two of my heroes in Philippine arts and letters were of immense help. Manong Frankie Sionil Jose personally knew the characters in this narrative and provided me with tips on how to represent them. Resil Mojares, whose work on 19th-century intellectuals inspired this book, likewise provided me with leads. Outside Philippine studies, I also received critical feedback from Roland Burke and Tom Larsson.

The dreaded social media and email have allowed me to stay in touch with colleagues from all over the place: Nicole Curato, Ronnie Holmes, Sharmila Parmanand, Clark Alejandrino, Nicole CuUnjieng, Vina Lanzona, Bobby Benedicto, RC Cruz, and Jonathan Ong. Then there is my original sensei, Jojo Abinales, who kindly passed me on to his "achi" in Kyoto for safekeeping and likewise read the full manuscript.

Apart from Kyoto University Press, publication of this book was made possible by NUS Press under Peter Schoppert and Paul Kratoska. My thanks as well to Lena Qua for coordinating manuscript preparation. In the Philippines, I thank Karina Bolasco and the Ateneo de Manila University Press for continuing to be my publisher. Tina Castro, in particular, was on top of the production process.

This book is being published amid my transition to a new post at De La Salle University. I thank July Teehankee and Rene Escalante for the warm welcome.

For their friendship, thank you to Vinny Tagle, Glenn Tuazon, Mara Coson, and Christine Herrin.

As always, I am thankful to my family. My Aunt Cynthia Estrada was the source for much information in the afterword. My parents, Rafael and Sylvia, remain my anchors, and my brothers, Basil and Redd, my favorite comedic diversions.

Introduction
Liberalism Askance

Liberalism is in crisis. Once thought to be the pinnacle of political development—the end of history—it is now under siege by resurrected forms of authoritarianism and populism. I write these words shortly after the election of a racist as President of the United States, amid the continued erosion of a cosmopolitan Europe, and the ever-increasing influence of a warmongering autocrat in the Kremlin. This trend of global illiberalism is not limited to Europe and America. India is undergoing a resurgence of communalism and ethnic intolerance. The Philippines is degenerating into a warzone as its new strongman president terrorizes the country's poor with an ill-conceived war on drugs.

Liberalism's crisis impels us to both its criticism and its defense. We must criticize it because its inadequacies have led us to this perilous interregnum—not quite Weimar, yet bearing the promise of more violence to come. Liberal smugness—optimism in previous times—cannot survive a world riddled with uncertain economic crises. What is more, liberalism's goal of considered, deliberative, and slow progresses is rendered emotionally barren by populism's capacity to stoke public ire.

One thing is obvious: if liberalism fulfilled its promises, it would be safely ensconced in modern polities. Still, one of liberalism's key attributes is its capacity to evolve. From a credo of bourgeois elites in the late 18th century, it slowly became the language of mass electoral democracy in the 19th and 20th centuries. It also became the language of many anticolonial movements that sought a grammar for representation and rights. Liberalism does not die because it is never completely born.

If liberalism is to reinvent itself, it must seek inspiration in unlikely places. This book hopes to make a modest contribution to the quest for a new liberalism. It contends that narrating a history of liberalism outside the so-called "liberal-democratic West" will allow us to view it askance. From this strange vista, we may yet infuse creativity into a tiring political credo.

THE WHIPPING BOY OF ANTI-IMPERIALISM

LIBERALISM IS A dense idea—a plenitude of concepts about freedom and liberty that has been applied, assessed, and corrected in various political and historical contexts. Yet it is also a simple notion: it restricts abuses of power, and it advocates openness to different values and truths. In liberal education, argues Arjun Appadurai, we find the "germ of the sense of cosmopolitanism"[1]—a "principle of self-expansion through engagement with the other."[2] This openness makes liberalism the blueprint for governance, for, as Dipesh Chakrabarty notes, "we do not, in modernity and as yet, know of *desirable* institutional arrangements in public life that could be seriously built on principles other than those of liberalism."[3] An openness to dissent and the willingness to compromise must remain the lowest common denominator of democratic societies.

None of this should sound controversial for those who profess a bare minimum of open-mindedness. And yet, given the vitriol directed at liberalism by contemporary "progressives," one sometimes wonders if they are talking about the same thing. Liberalism, a fleeting concept that operates more as a blueprint than as an ideology, is difficult to grasp and easy to caricature. "It may be hard to define," explains Adam Kirsch, "because it is the air we [in the West] all breathe and the lens through which we see all political issues."[4] Moreover, since liberalism is the default code of Western states, it is quickly equated with the global status quo—a world of Western domination. Therefore, if one believes that another world is possible, liberalism is an easy target, especially for critics who view themselves as "postcolonial."[5]

Anti-liberals see liberalism as "universalizing," imposing its will on worlds and peoples with different traditions. It was precisely the large claims of Enlightenment liberalism, they argue, that informed the creation of empires. As Uday Singh Mehta contends, imperialism was not a contradiction of liberal thought.[6] Rather, in colonialism, liberal thought "found a *project*, with all the grandeur of scale, implicit permanence, purposefulness, and the absence of a need to negotiate what is extant." Colonialism was an Enlightenment vision, a "clear philosophic horizon" for liberals.[7]

Empire is thus the end-point of universal liberal dreams, and the postcolony (or the Global South) serves as liberalism's most immediate repudiation, a reminder of its inherent hypocrisy. Hence, the decolonizing process represents a slow movement away from the liberal tradition. As Jean and John Comaroff note, "liberal modernism" is "an artifact of a particular epoch in the Euro-American past" and "parochial cultural form," which is undergoing a "theoretical incursion from the south."[8] From this perspective, the inherently more radical south can only challenge and revolt against liberal modernity, precluding the possibility that poor countries may also recreate and participate in this very modernity.

Similarly, for Boaventura de Sousa Santos, "the main traits of the epistemologies of the South," in contrast to those of the liberal North, are "ways of knowing born in the struggle against capitalism, colonialism, and patriarchy."[9] Liberalism, on the other hand, is a tired creed. "Indifference," he notes, is the "hallmark of political liberalism" and, in response to this, "it is necessary to revive the friend/foe dichotomy."[10]

Many of these critics write from the global north and project their hopes for radical change on societies that cannot even partake of the basic freedoms they enjoy in their liberal societies. In this regard, they are part of a first-world tradition that wishes radicalism on others before themselves.[11]

But if liberalism is "indifferent," as de Sousa Santos would have it, it is because of its history—a history of inoculating political communities against various extremisms. If liberalism does not have steady friends or foes, it is because it negotiates those categories through constant praxis. The catastrophes of the 20th century prove this point. Eric Hobsbawm describes the 20th century as "the age of extremes," where "secular ideologies of a nineteenth century vintage" became "militant and bloodthirsty."[12] It was in this century that socialism begot communism and nationalism begot fascism. Though Hobsbawm, a lifelong Marxist, demurs from admitting the point, these extremes had a common target. The genesis of the 20th century's extremes, as Francois Furet argues, was the 19th-century belief that "modern liberal democracy was threatening society with dissolution because it atomized individuals, made them indifferent to public interest, weakened authority, and encouraged class hatred."[13] Communism and fascism were twin ideologies, born from the same anxieties, whose "great secret," according to Furet, was "the existence of that common enemy which the two opposing doctrines would downplay or exercise with the idea that it was on its last legs: quite simply, democracy." This democracy is one Furet understands in liberal terms as "the philosophical definition of modern societies, constituted by autonomous and equal individuals, free to choose their activities, beliefs, and life-styles."[14]

This liberal freedom becomes necessary if we are to avoid the ideological wars of religion of the past century. Our present century, like all other eras, remains plagued by a plurality of competing ethical norms, requiring a politics of mediation. As John Gray reminds us, liberalism "originated in a search for *modus vivendi*," and the task of contemporary liberals "is refashioning liberal toleration so that it can guide the pursuit of modus vivendi in a more plural world."[15] Both communists and fascists understood that their absolute mastery of political life clashed with liberalism's modus vivendi and sought to crush it. If liberalism is so totalizing, as its critics argue, how did it become the self-proclaimed enemy of totalitarianisms? Is it simply because liberalism, despite its claims to tolerance, ultimately falls back on universal principles often derived from the Enlightenment?

The moderation of postwar European liberal thought, manifested in a resurgent social democratic movement, reflected the lessons learned from the global catastrophes of the early 20th century. But the postcolony, apparently, cannot partake in this, for it needs to live up to its revolutionary image. My contention is that if we are to stop patronizing postcolonies, we must accept that moderation has a role in their histories, too.

A LIMITED ENLIGHTENMENT FOR THE POSTCOLONY

THE ELEPHANT IN the room lies in the history of the Enlightenment and its articulation within Eurocentric thought. Postcolonial theory, as Neil Lazarus eloquently argues, shares with "the West's" defenders an equally blurred and ahistorical conception of the West.[16] Both those who wish to spread "Western values" and those who resist them produce a West that is "dematerialized through personification," such that "divisions within are flattened out entirely," creating a "Manichean divide between 'West' and 'Rest.'"[17] Similarly Vivek Chibber criticizes Indian subaltern theory for insisting on a fundamental East-West dichotomy, precluding "the possibility that the theories emerging from European experience might well be up to the task of capturing the basic structure of Eastern development in the modern epoch."[18]

A first step in examining liberalism in the postcolony, therefore, must be to extricate it from the haze of anti-European caricature. And a major facet of that caricature relates to liberalism's relationship with the Enlightenment and its attendant universalism.

What critics of liberalism fail to discuss are the tensions within the liberal tradition, the tug of war within an open-ended form of thinking that safeguards it from being "universalizing." To quote Gray again:

> Liberalism has always had two faces. From one side, toleration is the pursuit of an ideal form of life. From the other, it is the search for terms of peace among different ways of life. In the former view, liberal institutions are seen as applications of universal principles. In the latter, they are a means to peaceful coexistence. In the first, liberalism is a prescription for a universal regime. In the second, it is a project of coexistence that can be pursued in many regimes.[19]

The first face is often associated with the social contract tradition in political philosophy, grounded in the works of Hobbes, Rousseau, Kant, and, in contemporary times, most articulately championed by John Rawls. These works are premised on abstractions: in the case of Rousseau and Hobbes, they detail institutions of governance that transcend the chaos of "man in the state of nature," and, in the case of Rawls, they derive ethical principles from an "original position" bereft of one's positions in society, what Thomas Nagel famously labeled "the view from nowhere."[20] The result of this thinking, as Amartya Sen argues, was the development of "theories of justice that focused on transcendental identification of the ideal institutions."[21] It thus becomes more concerned with "identifying the nature of 'the just,'" rather than comparing which situations are less just than others.[22] Similarly, Michael Sandel argues that this form of liberalism only "provides a framework of rights that respects persons as free and independent selves, capable of choosing their own values and ends," precluding debates concerning "the good life." Sandel adds that "this liberalism asserts the priority of fair procedures over particular ends," and so, "the public life it informs might be called the procedural republic."[23]

The second face of liberalism is what Gray refers to when he sees liberalism as modus vivendi, a contextual aggregator of real-life interests and conflicts and a way to open up political debate. It is this liberalism that Sen considers when he advocates for "an accomplishment-based understanding of justice" premised on "the argument that justice cannot be indifferent to the lives that people actually live."[24] Similarly, for Sandel, a departure from the procedural republic requires viewing liberty as it is exercised in the everyday acts of public deliberation. His defense of liberty, derived from Aristotle, "sees civic virtue and political participation as *intrinsic* to liberty; given our nature as political beings, we are free only insofar as we participate in the public life of a free city or republic."[25]

A civic, deliberative liberalism is necessary in the postcolony, for postcolonies are, like other polities, venues where multiple value claims are debated. Moreover, many countries of the former Third World are negotiating gradual, ground-up transitions to democracy. Such gradual transitions may be sparked by seemingly "radical" events like the Arab Spring, but they are deepened by bureaucrats and state builders, who navigate the shades of grey inherent to democratization. In other words, they are sustained by liberals.

A PROVISIONAL DEFINITION AND A DEFENSE OF BORING POLITICS

THIS BOOK IS about a liberalism for the postcolony, the developing world, the Global South, the Third World—related but distinct terms that, broadly, gesture towards inequality between states and global marginality.[26] In particular, it will focus on this postcolonial liberalism using the case study of the Philippines.

It begins with a simple question: What if, in certain postcolonial contexts, liberalism is a good idea for nation-builders? What if it is practical? Not revolutionary, not utopian, simply practical. In postcolonial contexts where economic and political problems are immediate, this practicality may be more apt than ivory tower utopianism.

To understand this practicality, we must first attempt a definition. Liberalism is a large assemblage of ideas, and this rules out pithy summaries. This entire book, as such, will be an inductive unfolding of postcolonial liberalism via intellectual history, culminating in an *a posteriori* definition in the final chapter. But for now, let us begin with a few broad attributes, which we will nuance as we progress through our story. Liberty, as Alan Ryan notes, "is in general a negative notion—to be free is to be *not* in jail, *not* bound to a particular occupation, *not* excluded from the franchise, and so on—and the history of liberalism is a history of opposition to assorted tyrannies." Thus, "[o]ne way of understanding the continuity of liberal history in this light is to see liberalism as a perennial protest against all forms of absolute authority."[27]

This critical attitude towards absolute authority led liberalism—once a creed of elites within empires—to embrace democratic governance as a way to tame the revolutionary fervors of the 19th century, forging what we now recognize as liberal democracy. "Politically," explains Edmund Fawcett, "it involved liberal acceptance that their [liberals] aims and ideals applied not just to a worthy, propertied elite but to everyone regardless of how lowly, useless seeming to society or poor."[28] This new liberalism focused on processes aimed at gradual change. No longer was liberalism a "governing creed of a progressive elite," but "a set of neutral procedures for brokering conflict and managing bargains."[29] In other words, liberalism became bureaucratic, a boring pencil-pushing process.

How has this bureaucratic liberalism been applied in postcolonial contexts? Since liberalism is anathema to many contemporary accounts of decolonization, this question is rarely answered. An important exception is Ramachandra Guha's essay on Indian liberalism—a liberalism remarkably similar to its Philippine counterpart. As with the Philippines, Guha argues that liberalism in India was the dominant discourse of the immediate postwar period, despite its present obscurity. Rather than "principles laid down on canonical texts," Indian liberalism was "a sensibility rather than a theory, a product of empirical engagement."[30] Eschewing both leftwing and rightwing radicalism, it created a "capacious" "middle ground."[31]

It had three attributes—attributes we will also apply to our Philippine case study. First, it evinced "hopefulness about the future" of the state. "Liberals were convinced that the idealism nurtured by the national movement would find constructive expression in free India, with scientists, civil servants, politicians and scholars working unitedly to eliminate poverty, disease, and illiteracy, thus allowing India and Indians to take their place with honour in the modern world."[32] Second, Indian liberals were, consciously or unconsciously, patriotic. Many went overseas to study, but did so to contribute to the project of "nation-building."³³ Finally, consistent with liberalism's pencil-pushing ethos, "Indian liberals paid close attention to the promotion of institutions of civil society such as the law courts and universities, and to the fostering of rule-bound procedures within them."³⁴

The India that emerges from Guha's account is not the India of postcolonial theory: It is an image of the postcolony comfortable with modernity. I hope to do the same for the Philippines. This book is about postcoloniality, but a very different version thereof. I am not concerned with jungle guerrillas, millenarian proto-nationalists, or anarchistic mountain peoples. Instead, this book is about bureaucratic writers and pencil-pushers, who aided the transition of a nation from colonial rule to independence.

A SHORT HISTORY OF 19TH-CENTURY PHILIPPINE LIBERALISM

THE PHILIPPINES IS simultaneously an obscure, untenable, and ideal case study for a history of postcolonial liberalism in the 20th century. For, as I hope to show, it was liberalism, as opposed to Marxism or radical nationalism, that allowed the Philippines to transition from colony to independent nation-state. When the United States colonized the incipient nation after the brutal Filipino-American War (1889–1902), it did so under the subterfuge of democratic tutelage. Thus, the promise of American exceptionalist imperialism was a peaceful transition to democratic self-governance. This formal commitment to decolonization blunted the appeal of the revolutionary nationalism that had emerged in the 1896 revolution against Spain and continued in the war against the Americans. It also meant that a new generation of nationalists developed a congenial nationalism premised not on struggles against a colonizer but on the peaceful building of a new nation-state.

These reformers would draw from two sources of liberalism: First, the American liberalism, which is the primary concern of this book, and second, an older tradition of liberalism from the *ilustrados* (enlightened intellectuals) of the late 19th century. This liberalism was clustered around a group of fin-de-siècle exiles in Spain known as the "Propaganda Movement," its most famous member being national hero Dr. Jose Rizal.

Nationalist historiography has often attempted to foist a binary between the liberal Enlightenment ideas of the ilustrados and the aspirations of the 1896 Philippine revolution, which is commonly portrayed as both proletarian[35] and religious/millenarian.[36] Yet, as this short history will show, the revolution is best seen as a continuation of the ilustrado liberalism, not so much because it was an upper-class phenomenon, but because of the strong influence of intellectuals from the middle class, or *el elemento medio* on its politics.[37] As Caroline Hau argues, it was precisely this in-between class position of the ilustrados that allowed them to develop a critical but evolving stance that could bring together divergent and even conflicting interests.[38] Despite its tensions, however, we can glean three prominent characteristics of turn-of-the-century ilustrado liberalism that would eventually filter into the 20th century:

1. The desire to form and govern a rule-based nation-state in the European tradition;
2. A critical stance towards Spanish institutions of power like friar orders and the colonial government;
3. A belief in open and progressive education (defined in various ways).

Where did these ideas come from? Nick Joaquin, the greatest Filipino public intellectual of the 20th century, traces the roots of the Propaganda Movement to the last decade of the 18th century, when a group of *creoles* (Spaniards born in the colony) "imported to the islands the ideas of the Enlightenment and the French Revolution."[39] The main figure of this early liberalism was Luis Rodriguez Varela, the "Conde Filipino," who was the first Spanish creole to call himself a "Filipino."[40] A supporter of Spain's liberal constitution of 1812,[41] Rodriguez Varela and other Creole liberals advocated what we now recognize as the main tenets of the late 19th-century Propaganda Movement: secularization of Catholic parishes,[42] hispanization of the colony (mostly through intermarriage), educational reform, and Filipino representation in the Spanish Cortes.[43] Though the Conde would eventually gravitate to more rightwing politics, his liberal ideas survived into the mid-19th century, promoted by prominent Creole families like the Zobels, Palmeros, Regidors, and Pardo de Taveras (more on this family below).[44]

By 1837, Spanish liberalism was once again ascendant as a result of the tensions of the Carlist wars. To fend off the reactionary followers of Don Carlos (the deceased king's younger brother), the regent Maria Cristina—representing her daughter Isabel—was forced to compromise with liberals, resulting in a new liberal constitution.[45] The succeeding years would find Spain vacillating between moderate and progressive governments until Queen Isabel II was overthrown in the "Glorious Revolution" of 1868.

These events had a number of consequences for the Philippines. First, as John N. Schumacher speculates, "[t]he deportations consequent upon the various coups prior to 1868 had brought a certain number of Liberal and Republican exiles to the country, who were, one may suppose, not completely silent about their ideas."[46] Second, the revolution brought to the Philippines its first liberal governor in Carlos Maria de la Torre, who was "anxious to institute the new democratic practices of the Peninsula in the Philippines as well."[47] As Megan Thomas explains, de la Torre's brief period in power "left a legacy not so much of long-lasting change but of the unforgettable taste of promise." Under the governor general, "press censorship was relaxed and the overseas ministry decreed significant educational reforms," including reducing Church control over major educational institutions.[48]

This liberal promise, however, would eventually be denied, and the frustrated hopes of liberals is best symbolized by the aftermath of the 1872 Cavite mutiny—an uprising of Filipino soldiers in a Spanish arsenal about thirty miles from the Bay of Manila. Though there was "little convincing evidence that more than a mutiny over local grievance was involved (one quickly put down by Filipino troops), the authorities took advantage of the hysterical atmosphere to arrest all who were suspected of liberal leanings." Those arrested included Father Jose Burgos, a Creole leader of the secularization movement, and two other priests (Mariano Gomez and Jacinto Zamora), who were publicly garroted for conspiracy in the rebellion.[49] (Rizal would eventually dedicate his 1891 novel, *El Filibusterismo*, to these martyred priests.)

According to Joaquin, "the struggle and the reprisals" brought by the events of 1872 "would generate the idea of Filipino, through the violent fusion of societies that had hitherto thought themselves distinct from one another."[50] The persecution after the mutiny targeted native indios, mestizos, and Creoles—all of them lumped together for holding liberal beliefs. In this sense, therefore, the very genesis of "Filipino" is tied to the persecution of so-called "filibusteros," a blanket term for anyone who sought Enlightenment and modernity within the strictures of a colonial and religious political system.[51]

The "Creole libertarian movement" that peaked in 1872 had a filial link to the Propaganda Movement; many members of the latter generation had parents or older siblings who were implicated in the mutiny.[52] And despite confused debates about what it meant to be a "pure Filipino," the expatriates in Spain, like the victims of 1872, united under what Filomeno Aguilar calls "a grand political project shared among a group divisible into indios, mestizo, and Kastila."[53] They also continued the same liberal agenda of representation in the Spanish cortes and educational reforms, as evidenced by Rizal's novel *Noli me Tangere* and their newspaper *La Solidaridad*. Abroad, the propagandists consorted with liberals and even anarchist libertarians from other Spanish colonies like Cuba.[54] Moreover, their ties to Masonry, explains Schumacher, connected them to the "centers of the Liberal conspiracies in Spain" and the colonies.[55]

Though the propagandists themselves advocated gradualist reform within Spanish colonialism, it is widely acknowledged that their creation of a national "self awareness"[56] inspired the anti-Spanish-revolt of the revolutionaries known as the Samahang Kataastaasang, Kagalanggalang Katipunan ng mga Anak ng Bayan (Supreme and Most Honorable Society of the Children of the Nation), or simply, the Katipunan. Though the group was previously conceived as lower class,[57] Michael Cullinane's rigorous profiles of its conspirators establish that it was "an organization composed of representatives of Manila's urban middle sector and leading members of the municipal elite (*principales*) of the provinces contiguous to Manila."[58] "Close to the centers of power, but unempowered," Cullinane explains elsewhere, "they found common cause in their critique of the colonial condition."[59] It was thus a revolution led by a "middle element" educated enough to continue advocating the changes sought by the Propaganda Movement. Indeed, Jim Richardson has effectively argued that, far from being a millenarian, proto-socialist sect, the Katipunan's avowed program was that of uniting the nation through "Reason and Enlightenment."[60]

The consistent undercurrent of liberalism within 19th-century anticolonial discourse explains why many earlier critics of Spanish colonialism became open to American annexation after Spain "sold" the Philippines to the United States in 1898 Treaty of Paris. The ilustrados bifurcated into those who wished to continue the anticolonial war against the Americans and those who advocated various forms of compromise with the colonizers (from statehood to protectorate status).[61] Gradualism within an American system became the response of some liberals, who had begun to fear the internecine conflicts within the Philippine liberal revolution. Some lacked confidence in the leadership of Philippine President Emilio Aguinaldo,[62] while others feared the emergence of a strong military bloc within Aguinaldo's congress.[63]

By the early 20th century, many ilustrados were beginning to view the country's Americanization as part of a broader narrative of national development—a fulfillment of the 19th century's liberal promise. Trinidad Pardo de Tavera, who belonged to one of the most prominent liberal Creole families, was the first to articulate this view. He saw the country's Americanization as the fulfillment of the liberal dreams of 19th-century Creoles. According to Resil B. Mojares, Pardo depicted the "Spanish colonial period as a tragedy of friar misrule," sketched "the formation of a national spirit in the dynamic of assimilation and resistance," assigned "to the elite a leading role in the creation of nationhood," and assumed "a benign view of U.S. rule as a way towards progress and freedom."[64] Pardo also carried forward the secularist impulse of the previous century, contrasting a benighted era of Spanish religiosity, focused on producing pious and docile citizens, with the potential for enlightenment under American-style secular pedagogy.[65] In this regard, Pardo is the link between the Propaganda Movement and the liberals to be discussed in this book, as he established the mode of reformism that would be the norm for most of the 20th century.

At the dawn of the 20th century the country had gone full circle. Among the diverse tendencies within the ilustrado tradition, gradualism had won out. Mojares explains:

> The country had, in a sense, returned to the ideology of gradualism that characterized the pre-revolutionary Propaganda Movement, although this time the policy and structures for constructive collaboration were in place, the mood was optimistic, and the primary instruments were no longer those of cultural and political agitation by intellectuals operating outside the system, but of state-sanctioned propaganda and education and through parliamentary and diplomatic action by politicians within the system.[66]

Liberalism had become official. Hitherto excluded and even persecuted, liberal intellectuals began assuming the towering heights of a new state-building project and articulating a liberalism for the postcolony.

Twentieth-century Philippines, therefore, presents us with a different way to think about decolonization and the actors that facilitate it, as its post-independence nation-builders were not the same as its founding nationalists. Instead of learning the martial virtues of a revolutionary movement, they would imbibe the moderation of the bureaucracy. The "fathers" of Philippine nationalism, from Rizal to Katipunan Supremo Andres Bonifacio, were not the leaders of the post-independence state, like, for instance, Nkrumah in Ghana or Sukarno in Indonesia.[67] The generation of 20th-century nation-builders was socialized not in a period of war or agitation. Their intellectual heritage, moreover, could be traced to a Spanish-era liberal tradition that was unthreatening and even congenial to the new colonizers. No doubt this generation mouthed radical nationalist rhetoric and stirred populist sentiment. But they did so in the halls of power, from the chambers of the colonial state and not on the streets or battlefields. What they achieved in these halls is the topic of this book.

EXCLUDING LIBERALISM

DESPITE LIBERALISM'S CLOSE connection with Philippine nationalism, it has largely been excluded from the historical record. To explain this, we need to briefly examine a turn in nationalist historiography, which began in the 1950s and solidified into a form of orthodoxy in the 1970s—a tradition that I will call the "Diliman Consensus." The term is a slightly facetious label referring to the origins of this thinking in the Diliman campus of the University of the Philippines.[68] The key figure of the Diliman Consensus is University of the Philippines historian Teodoro Agoncillo, who published the seminal work *The Revolt of the Masses: The Story of Bonifacio and the Katipunan* in 1956.[69] Ostensibly, the book was about Andres Bonifacio, represented as a proletarian leader (inaccurately, as we now know) of the Philippine revolution, who is eventually betrayed by elites.

The book was published amid rising social tensions. It was a period that saw the rise of the Comintern-aligned Hukbong Mapagpalaya ng Bayan (HMB or People's Liberation Army), which many intellectuals viewed as the heir to the "unfinished revolution" of the earlier Katipunan.[70] According to Reynaldo Ileto, "the reader" of that time "would not have failed to connect the Katipunan to the HMB," "the wealthy landlords of the past" to those of the present, "and the (Spanish) friar suzerains to the American suzerains in a supposedly independent nation."[71] The book was, therefore, a polemic amid debates that pit Communist fellow travelers against their anti-Communist critics. Beyond endorsing a revolutionary movement, however, the book altered the way Filipinos spoke about the nation.

Methodologically, Agoncillo made an explicit link between "true" nationalism and one's class position. Rommel Curaming contends that

Agoncillo's tome, along with the polemics of fellow UP Diliman historian Renato Constantino (see next chapter), changed the definition of "Filipino" from mere citizenship into a belonging to a "socio-economic class."[72] The true Filipinos and "bearers of history" became the masses (an ill-defined concept), who were now "the proprietary claimant" to the nation and its identity.[73] Postwar leftwing nationalism, then, conjoins the nation with the lower class—a viewpoint that Agoncillo mainstreamed through the popular history textbook, *History of the Filipino People* (1960), which remains the standard collegiate textbook in Philippine history.[74] Moreover, the nationalism espoused by this historiography was inward-looking and defined "Filipino" against foreign influence.

The legacy of the Agoncillo/Constantino School was broad. I have previously discussed how their views filtered into Maoist leftwing activism and nativist trends in the Philippine social sciences, the effect of which was to conflate "foreign" Enlightened thought and elitism.[75] Thus, the political impulse of the Diliman Consensus has been to purge the national narrative of its Western heritage, including the Enlightenment project of liberalism.

In its rejection of the "West," the effect of the Diliman Consensus has been to obscure the long history of Philippine liberalism and the intellectuals associated with it. In its eyes, immediate postwar liberals were not nationalist enough, or, for the Maoists, not Marxist enough.[76] And since they failed the nationalism test, they were, in effect, elitist. Effete liberal bureaucrats had no role in the muscular nationalist history that the Consensus sought to promote. As Yusuke Takagi explains, Filipino nationalist historiography has "paid sympathetic attention to rebellion or symbolic leaders of the opposition party rather than to the politicians and bureaucrats within the government."[77]

The burying of liberalism in Philippine scholarship, then, stems from a caricatured version of "elite"-led political projects. As Caroline Hau notes of Philippine literature and political writing:

> "Elite vs. masses" has been an important symbolic and ideological weapon for mobilizing segments of the population, providing critical ammunition for a succession of political movements—most notably from the Left—that challenged the American, Commonwealth, and Philippine state. Its political value is incontestable, but its conceptual underpinnings have long been subject to debate.[78]

This elite vs. masses demonology is a simplification that assumes the given interests of two ill-defined groups. However, Hau argues, elites have "tended to be socially coherent, culturally ascendant but not hegemonic, and politically divided and vacillating."⁷⁹ Moreover, while the elites have "readily claimed and exercised political leadership in various political movements for and against the state, they remain ideologically divided, and their political effectiveness depends on their ability to forge often temporary, issue-based, and fragile coalitions with other classes."⁸⁰

This in-between position of the middle class, the elite, the bourgeois, the ilustrado, and so on, imbues it with political potentiality, because it may channel heterogeneous intellectual currents. Unfortunately, this potency is easily dismissed, since any form of "elite politics" gets read as hypocrisy, opportunism, or predation. In contrast to revolution, the grey areas of ilustrado politics are effete and ineffective. The immediate suspicion of any political project "from above" filters even into work more sophisticated than the reductive Diliman Consensus.

A recent critique in this vein is historian Vicente Rafael's critical assessment of the Philippine revolution and the Katipunan. Having reviewed the recent scholarship on the revolution, Rafael correctly concludes that, since the movement stemmed from Rizal, it was, "from the outset," "liberal in orientation"—a liberalism "articulated in the language and symbols of Freemasonry and bits of the French Enlightenment."⁸¹ Because of this orientation, the Katipunan did not have a vision for social change, since it did not seek to "democratize social relations" or advocate the redistribution of property.⁸² "Its revolutionary aims," Rafael contends, "were thus limited to replacing the Spaniards on top with male Filipino revolutionary leaders, and limiting, but not banishing, the Church's power by neutralizing the influence of Spanish friars (again, a standard liberal goal)."⁸³ In asking "just how revolutionary was the revolution?"⁸⁴ Rafael observes that its impact was minimal:

> The Philippine Revolution was thus nothing like the French Revolution. There was neither regicide nor mass slaughter of Spaniards. To my knowledge, only a handful of friars, the real "kings" of the country, were executed, and usually to the great reluctance of both leaders and common people. It was certainly not like the Russian or Chinese revolutions with their emphasis on social leveling (though keeping the Party on top).⁸⁵

Rafael's assessment of the revolution is thus the postcolonial critique of liberalism applied to the Philippines—a critique similar in tone and substance to the work discussed earlier. It therefore warrants sustained scrutiny. In the process, I will touch on certain elements of the liberal critique that I make against postcolonial theory in the chapters to come. I offer three replies to Rafael's aporia concerning the Philippine liberal revolution.

First, Rafael homogenizes the ilustrado leaders of the revolution, distilling their goals to simply "the rule of private property alongside formal legal and racial equality with the Spaniards, then later with the Americans."[86] Rafael thus views the "middle sector" that led the Katipunan as operating similarly to the late 19th-century European bourgeoisie, which, according to Rafael's epigraph drawn from the *Communist Manifesto*, forces nations "to adopt the bourgeois mode of production."[87] As such, "there was nothing at all proletarian about the leadership of the revolution."[88]

The *elemento medio* that constituted the Katipunan and parts of its leadership, however, cannot be confused with the Marxian bourgeoisie. The latter prioritized the campaign for private property because of their relationship to capital: they owned the means of production and extracted surplus from wage labor. However, as Rafael himself observes, the former were either "salaried urban *empleados*" or "provincial *principales*" (regional elite). The former, in particular, included "printers, office workers, court transcribers, warehouse clerks, book keepers and the like."[89] This is a broad category. And based on Marxian criteria, *empleados* could not have been bourgeoisie because, as salaried employees, they were wage laborers, not capitalists. By strict Marxian criteria, they would, in fact, be closer to proletariat than bourgeoisie.

A comparison with Russia is instructive. Prior to the Russian Revolution, notes Manfred Hildermeir, the Socialist Revolutionaries viewed a similar lower urban middle class as "proletarian intelligentsia" that, "like real proletariat, lived from the sale of its labor and hence occupied a position between the bourgeoisie and the workers."[90] The point here is less to quibble about the details of Marxian terminology than to argue that the middle sector of the Katipunan carried with it a political potential that transcended the immediate goals of the revolution. Although the revolution itself did not advocate for redistribution, the critical position it nourished within the urban middle sector would, in fact, give birth to more class-conscious forms of politics. For example, in the same work on the heterogeneity of the ilustrado "middle class" cited earlier, Hau also argues that 20th-century Philippine socialism stemmed from the same ilustrado milieu born from the liberal revolution.[91] One crucial point I will continually return to is that liberalism never views itself as an end, as it enables other forms of emancipatory politics that may transcend it.

A second response concerns Rafael's conflation of liberal thought with the impulses of capitalism. Rafael correctly argues that material interests informed the revolutionaries' defense of property rights. However, it should be possible to disentangle liberalism as a political and cultural credo from the material impulses of the bourgeoisie. Vivek Chibber, in his critique of a similar argument concerning the bourgeoisie from Ranajit Guha (the doyen of Subaltern Studies), argues that "Guha does not entertain the possibility that the spread of cultural and political forms he associates with the British and French bourgeoisie [that is, liberalism] might have issued from other sources; hence, while they might have become established in the capitalist *era*, they would not have been brought about by capitalist *design*."[92] Indeed, as we delve into the capaciousness of liberalism as political ideal (particularly in Chapter 3), we explore how its multiple impulses, though not negating capitalism and the accumulation of property, prevent us from seeing it simply as capitalism's handmaiden. I will argue that a class-sensitive politics can emerge from the liberal tradition.

Finally, we must assess Rafael's definition of "revolutionary." For a revolution to truly be revolutionary in Rafael's eyes, it appears it must have promoted the violence of the French revolution ("regicide and mass slaughter") or espoused socialist redistribution like the Russian and Chinese revolutions. On the topic of the French revolution, one must reject Jacobin bloodletting and executions, thereby celebrating Philippine revolutionaries for not succumbing to such bloodlust (although one must still insist that both wars against the Spaniards and the Americans remain valiant acts of *armed* resistance.) As for the comparison to socialist revolutions, one cannot assess the Philippine revolution based on the criteria of another era. Socialist internationalism was in its infancy in the late 19th century and there had been no socialist revolutions in Asia, let alone Europe, in that period. The revolutionary causes of that time were liberalism and nationalism. Thus, based on the standards of the time, the Katipuneros were true liberal revolutionaries.

THE LEGACIES OF LIBERAL REVOLUTIONS

HOW THEN DO we assess the legacies of liberal revolutions? Here we may find germane comparisons between the European and the Filipino liberal revolutions. It is incorrect to insist on a fundamental dissimilarity between the French and Philippine revolutions. Though one was, indeed, more violent than the other, both were liberal revolutions, with similar defects, yet important legacies. As Francois Furet has shown, the French revolution was dominated by a revolutionary elite as early as the summer of 1789, and its institutional form was divorced from the popular will that allowed for its emergence.[93] Like the Katipuneros' Philippines Revolution, the Jacobins also placed property qualifications for voting, and ensured that Church lands ended up in the hands of big bourgeoisie. Even worse than in the Philippine case was the use of systematic terror. Despite this, Furet did not dismiss the intellectual and political legacy of 1789. As Judt notes, Furet's central goal was to remove from the center of historical debates "the old insistence upon social categories and conflicts," and instead focus on "political and intellectual debates," reminding readers "that the Revolution was above all a radical shift in the balance of philosophical and political orders, not of economic class interests." In reimagining authority and vesting it in concepts of "the French state" and the "French people," the revolution was able to "invent modern politics."[94]

Furet and Judt were historians of the center-left (some would even contend of the right). Yet even communist historian Eric Hobsbawm acknowledges the vast ripple effects of liberal revolutions on the politics of the 20th century. The 19th-century "Age of Revolution," he explains, constituted "citizen states," with the explicit goal of representing "the people," now considered the "source of sovereignty."[95] It is these citizen-states that serve as the staging ground for the very modern politics that Judt refers to. And it is because modern politics are so tied to liberalism that the concept becomes both real and fleeting, like, as noted earlier, the air we breathe. Yet we must emphasize that it is this liberal heritage—this baseline of politics—that allows various political visions to compete within a democratically conceived polity. These visions may compliment or challenge liberalism. But they are nonetheless enabled by liberalism.

A liberal revolution inaugurated the Philippine nation-state. It did so through a promise of free and democratic self-governance. It is an ongoing promise, and its fulfillment is asymptotic yet ever-present. How Filipinos have sought to fulfill this promise for themselves is the topic of this book.

BOOK SUMMARY

THIS BOOK FOLLOWS a very rough chronology: from the 1920s until the early 1970s. It is, in effect, a short 20th century of Philippine history, and it covers a period of liberal experimentation in the wake of U.S. colonization. It begins in the 1920s, when the first batch of Filipino *pensionados* (talented Filipinos sent to America for advanced education) returned to the Philippines—then still an American colony—and began to conceive of their country-in-waiting as a liberal democracy. This book examines the events leading into independence (4 July 1946) and the immediate postwar period, when liberal elites took over their new state. The story ends in 1972, when Ferdinand Marcos declared martial law and centralized state power. Mid-century liberals, believing that their state's liberal tradition inoculated it from dictatorship, were surprised by this turn of events. Despite their incredulity, it was the end of their liberal experiment.

Several themes emerge from the narrative. Each chapter is about an intellectual who represents a key tenet of liberalism in the postcolony. These intellectuals were liberals not because they associated with a formal liberal party. As in India, liberalism was the organizing political discourse of postwar Philippines, and, as such, was not the monopoly of one organization.[96] Each chapter likewise concerns an intellectual dismissed based on a caricatured vision of liberalism. At various points, these individuals were dismissed for being pro-American "miseducators," reactionary anti-Communists, or effete hypocrites who compromised for political power.

Chapter 1 focuses on the educator Camilo Osias, the first Filipino to write a textbook for the country's emerging educational system. Through Osias, I trace how the ideas of America's leading early 20th-century liberal, John Dewey, percolated into the Philippines and merged with a domestic impulse towards a cultural canon formation that was both nationalist and internationalist. Osias represented a generation of Filipino intellectuals who were comfortable with America not because they endorsed colonialism but because they saw within it liberal potentialities for their own country. The idea of America and the ideas of its liberal intellectuals outlined a nationalism that was open-ended and experimental, not beholden to fixed notions of cultural identity. It was a democratic nationalism.

The second chapter likewise looks into an important thread within American liberalism and how it played out in America's postcolony: New Deal economics. In the 1950s, the industrialist and self-taught economist

Salvador Araneta waged a quixotic struggle against a fiscally conservative Central Bank to forward economic policy reminiscent of John Maynard Keynes and Franklin Delano Roosevelt. At stake was not just the building of an industrial economy but also a redefinition of liberal politics. In the U.S., the New Deal articulated the liberal cause with state planning and economic regulation. It was a liberalism even more conducive for the postcolony than for the metropole, since the postcolonial economy is perpetually precarious. If the U.S. in the 1930s confronted the crisis of the Great Depression, postwar Philippines confronted the perpetual crisis of third world underdevelopment. Araneta had a solution, but policy makers ignored him. The defeat of his vision for progressive macroeconomics presaged not only the collapse of the industrial state but also a revivified liberalism, attuned to class difference.

Araneta's managerial approach to economics was a liberal alternative to Communism. Filipino liberals, like their Western counterparts, were concerned about this alternative, not so much as a political philosophy as a specific political model being constructed in the Soviet Union and China. In particular, they feared the exportation of this revolution into their own country. All the intellectuals in this book were anti-Communists, but perhaps none more so than Carlos P. Romulo. Romulo was president of the United Nations General Assembly and one of the leading lights of the Asia-Africa Conference in Bandung. In chapter three, I define liberal anti-Communism and anti-totalitarianism using Romulo's vision of the "Third World." This Third World was not merely a negation of first world imperialism, but also the new colonialism of the Communist "Second World." Because of his anti-Communism, Romulo has often been caricatured as a reactionary pawn of US imperialism. I argue, however, that his anti-Communism represented the merging of third world nationalism, Asianism, liberalism, and anticolonialism.

The final chapter follows the late career of a mid-century liberal, Salvador P. Lopez, who in the late 1960s and early 1970s became the president of the University of the Philippines at the height of Maoist student unrest. When he assumed the position, commentators thought that Lopez's best days were behind him; he had been the country's leading literary critic in the 1940s, and in the 1950s and 60s, he became, like his mentor Romulo, a permanent fixture at the UN, serving as the Chairman of the Commission on Human Rights. Becoming UP President seemed like a pre-retirement post. It would, however, be his most challenging job: not only did he have to govern a university imploding from radical ferment, he also had to defend it from incursions from the Marcos dictatorship. The chapter examines how Lopez negotiated liberal principles at a time of crisis, with his ideas being challenged by both the left and the right. It was, ultimately, a futile endeavor, with Lopez becoming a liberal relic in the Philippines' own age of extremes.

This book may, thus, seem like a history of failure. And to some extent it is. Intellectually, the nativism of the Diliman Consensus deleted the outward-looking liberalism of Osias, Araneta, Romulo, and Lopez. Their greatest sin, of course, was that they learned their liberalism from American sources. As we shall see, Osias was labeled a "miseducator," someone who veiled the nation's true essence through the sophistry of pro-American internationalism. Araneta was dismissed as a crackpot, importing "foreign" ideas about pump-priming economies that were supposedly inapplicable in a third-world context. Romulo's anti-Communism, on the other hand, was simple reaction, and critics saw strings being pulled by imperial masters in Washington. As for Lopez in the early 1970s, he was horribly old-fashioned, more comfortable in the language of "Western" human rights than in peasant Maoism.

With the exception of Romulo, these intellectuals have largely been forgotten. More crucially, their political projects all ground to a halt during the ideologically charged years of the Marcos period, which pitted a dictator against a burgeoning Communist movement. The country's "age of extremes" precluded a modus vivendi.

Despite the short-term failure of the liberal experiment, I continue to write this book. I do so not simply because of a prosaic belief that liberals learn from their mistakes—a belief that is naiveté to some and humility to others. Rather, I write because liberal failures are never complete ones, because liberals never aim for complete successes. They do not propose to change the world, so one cannot blame them if they do not. Assessing a gradualist form of thought requires seeking gradual successes and the various potentialities embedded in these. It is these potentialities—their pasts and their futures—that this book seeks to unearth.

Chapter 1
Camilo Osias and the Nationalist International

We begin our story with one of the great polemics of the Diliman Consensus. In 1966, the nationalist historian Renato Constantino published his seminal "The Mis-Education of the Filipino"[1]—an essay that set a new agenda for nationalist pedagogy and became a cornerstone of the broader indigenization movement.

In the oft-quoted and oft-reprinted essay, Constantino contended that American-era education in the Philippines became a weapon of conquest, a "means of pacifying a people who were defending their newly-won freedom from an invader who had posed as an ally."[2] Because Filipinos were "trained as citizens of an American colony," they became an "uprooted race," unaware of their true identity and heritage. Reading American textbooks, they "started learning not only a new language but also a new way of life, alien to their traditions and yet a caricature of their model."[3] Although Constantino admitted that "the lives of Philippine heroes were taught," he insisted that "their nationalist teachings were glossed over," preventing the creation of a "genuinely Filipino education."[4] Constantino's reference to a "genuine" education provided the underlying logic of his essay, for "mis-education" assumed that a real national/nationalist mindset existed, with educators merely needing to peel back layers of colonial obfuscation to produce authentic Filipinos instead of "un-Filipino Filipinos."[5] Nationalist education, as such, simply became a means of returning to a more authentic Filipino subjectivity.

Absent in the polemics of the Diliman Consensus are analyses of gray areas that can only be detected through close examination of colonial-era texts. At no point does Constantino discuss the content of American-era education in detail, portraying it as a colonial monolith bereft of ambiguity. Moreover, in viewing Western thought as contaminating "true" national identity, Constantino rehearses the Diliman Consensus's aversion to the outside, neglecting that the nationalism he espouses had roots in "foreign" liberalism (see previous chapter).

Constantino's critique of "American" textbooks that allegedly obscured local realities betrays the elisions in his thinking. How "American," for instance, were these textbooks? Given the fluidity of national identity in early 20th-century Philippines, "American" versus "Filipino" was, in retrospect, a facile lens to understand changes within the educational system. Within the first decade of the American occupation, the American colonial government itself had noted the lack of textbooks suited to Filipino students and immediately rectified this problem through the adaptation of material.[6] As early as 1902, the colonial government had "recommended the preparation of textbooks possessing local color, local ideas, local descriptions, and local illustrations."[7] The nationalization of the curriculum deepened from the 1920s onward, with the basal reading material of elementary students consisting primarily of material about José Rizal and readers compiled and edited by Filipino educator, author, and politician Camilo Osias.[8] As we shall see, this material must not be regarded as a tool for "mis-education." Rather, the educational discourse of the time reflected a form of nationalism forged as an incipient Philippines sought to legitimize itself within an international system of nation-states.

Through an engagement with Osias's pedagogical work during and shortly after the American period, I contend that that era's pedagogy was anchored on a nationalism broader in its political purview than Constantino's. Osias's work was written for a nation-in-waiting; his ideas were syncretic, civic, future-oriented, experimental, and anchored on an internationalism that saw nation building as part of a broad, cosmopolitan ethics. At the peak of his career as an author, Osias was considered one of the first Filipino voices in basic education, and, eventually, as legislator, he became a prominent advocate for greater state support for education.

His ideas may be foreign in the landscape of contemporary nationalist intellectuals, but they require revisiting. Obscured by the disdain of thinkers like Constantino for "colonial mentality," the writings of Osias and other cosmopolitan educators of the early 20th century may serve as antidotes to exclusionary and inward-looking forms of nationalism. They may also provide a blueprint for new forms of deliberative public engagement that prioritizes the possibilities of democracy building over the givens of nationality.

I examine Osias's thought as composed of three overlapping lines of thought: first, the culturalist nationalism of the early 20th-century Philippine elite known as Filipinism; second, a form of late 19th-century nationalist internationalism; and, third, the open-ended pragmatic philosophy of John Dewey, one of Osias's mentors when he studied in Columbia University. These three theoretical movements propelled Osias's thought during a career that spanned six decades and defined the pedagogy of early 20th-century Philippines. The story is not just one of nationalism but also of globalization. It is a history that examines Western influence as an ideational interface and not mere contamination.

HEIR TO THE 19TH CENTURY

CAMILO OSIAS WAS a bureaucrat, politician, and author. He was born in 1889 in the small agricultural town of Balaoan, La Union province—a place "without factories or large industries" and where the "inhabitants led a simple, frugal life."[9] Osias's father, Manuel, was a farmer and a small landholder, who also served as a clerk (*escribiente*) to the justice of the peace. His mother, Gregoria Olaviano, helped sell produce and "taught her children to read, work, and pray."[10] He grew up simply, but comfortably.

Among the intellectuals of this book, Osias is the only one old enough to have had memories of the Philippine Revolution. His family provided food and shelter for anti-Spanish insurgents, and the young Camilo grew thinking revolutionaries were "good and brave."[11] As an adolescent, he organized boys his age as "insurrectos" and picked fights with the children of pro-Spanish townsfolk.[12]

Osias's admiration for the revolutionaries notwithstanding, he had the temperament of a moderate. He was never a propagandist, and, despite a passion for debating, he was not known for vicious polemics. Even at the height of his political career (he had a brief stint as Senate President in 1953), he continued to regard himself as an educator.

Osias's own education was wedged between two colonial regimes. In La Union, he was initially educated in Spanish. He then learned English after the American occupation, and moved to the United States for tertiary-level studies. A product of the *pensionado* program, which sent promising Filipino students to the United States, Osias received his teacher's diploma from Western Illinois State College in 1908 and his Bachelor of Arts degree from the Teachers College of Columbia University in 1910, where he was greatly influenced by the pedagogue and philosopher John Dewey.

Upon returning to the Philippines, Osias immediately became a schoolteacher. From 1915 to 1916 he served as superintendent of schools (the first Filipino to hold the position), and from 1921 to 1936 he served as the first president of the National University, which he oversaw during its years of rapid expansion from a small business college to a university of multiple colleges. It was at this time that he compiled, edited, and wrote *The Philippine Readers*—a seven-volume collection of reading excerpts for elementary students (see below). Along with Leandro Fernandez, the first Filipino to author a Philippine history textbook, Osias was part of the broader Filipinization of Philippine education[13]—a campaign that came in tandem with the growing independence lobby in the Philippines.

Osias flitted in and out of government service, university/intellectual life. This constant movement was the norm for a generation of intellectuals who viewed serving the state as an extension of their intellectual pursuits. While still president of NU, Osias was elected to a term in the Philippine colonial senate, and served from 1925 to 1929. From 1929 to 1935, he was Resident Commissioner of the Philippine Islands to the United States Congress. During World War II, he became the education minister of the Japanese-controlled government—part of a group of "pro-American" intellectuals who nonetheless "collaborated" with the Japanese to ensure a continuity in governance.[14]

The latter half of Osias's career was spent in the Philippine Senate, where he was elected to two terms: one from 1947 to 1953 and another from 1961 to 1967.[15] Despite being in government, Osias continued to write books and articles, primarily on education and pedagogy.

The oldest intellectual in this book, Osias is the thinker who hewed most closely to the 19th-century ilustrado tradition. He was, for instance, one of the country's most prominent masons, serving as Grand Master of the Philippine masons in 1955. Like the ilustrados, he also exhibited a secularist streak, becoming the leading defender in the legislature of the separation of Church and state.[16] More importantly, he saw his belief in liberal internationalism and human rights as stemming not just from his American education but also from Rizal's "broad" and "constructive" nationalism,[17] which placed the hero "ahead of his time in his international idealism."[18] Had Rizal been alive during his time, Osias believed, the national hero, too, would be an advocate of the United Nations and the Declaration of Human Rights since "Rizal had been a defender of fundamental human rights, individual dignity, justice and freedom."[19]

Osias was a masculine figure. In his politics and writings, Osias emphasized "vigor," and he despised effeteness, both in speech and physical bearing. He often proclaimed that his body was as muscular as his thinking. He believed in the value of manual labor, and emphasized physical activity as a key part of an education that molded active citizens. A common picture of the man finds him in a half-smirk, with a pipe extending from the side of his mouth, his gaze as steely as his jaw.

FILIPINISMO

AS AN INTELLECTUAL working in the early 20th century, Osias was part of a movement among educated elites seeking to define and mold an infant nation. The primary concern of these elites was the very notion of nationality. The early American period, as Resil Mojares has shown consistently, gave birth to multiple canonical notions of "Filipino," from the canonization of national poets to the promotion of a pantheon of national heroes.[20] Mojares writes:

> More than at any other time, it was in the first decades of the twentieth century that "Filipino nationality," the shared consciousness of *being Filipino*, was self-consciously formulated and elaborated. This seems paradoxical since this was as well the time of American colonial rule. Yet, American occupation stimulated expressions of nationality in ways symbiotic as well as oppositional. The occupation and its threat of "Anglo-Saxonization" fueled Filipino assertions of distinctness and difference. On the other hand, Filipino leaders quickly discovered there was a great

deal in U.S. colonial policies ("Filipinization," self-rule, the diffusion of "modernity") compatible with their own aspirations. Particularly after 1907 (when the all-Filipino Philippine assembly was inaugurated), the mood for constructive "nation-building"—under U.S. colonial auspices—was dominant.[21]

The early 20th century saw the rise of what Mojares identifies as "Filipinismo"/Filipinism, an ambivalent culturalist nationalism that was "congenial to leaders who invoked nationalism to distance themselves from Americans as well as deflect the radical demands of those who could not abide with U.S. rule."[22]

Osias was well aware of his place in this movement (particularly as one of its first and key exponents in the field of pedagogy) and many of his early writings in the 1920s were attempts to develop a "dynamic Filipinism." Although Mojares locates Osias within the tradition of Filipinism—comparing him to cohorts like Rizal scholar Rafael Palma and journalist/librarian Teodoro Kalaw[23]—the pedagogue does not feature prominently in Mojares's path-breaking book on late 19th-century/early 20th-century Filipino intellectuals.

Building on Mojares's work, I contend that Osias was one of the most influential proponents of Filipinism. His relevance stems not only from the caliber of his thought but also from the media he used: school textbooks. As Jurilla argues, Filipinos for most of the 20th century read primarily for the purpose of study rather than entertainment or personal edification—hence the importance of textbooks as one of the few widely circulated texts.[24] Thus, although Osias may not have been the most prominent advocate of Filipinism, he is possibly its most important popularizer.

Examining Osias in light of Filipinism is crucial to a full understanding of his political and pedagogical views. The few academic works on Osias unfortunately have refracted his ideas through the lens of American ethnic studies and, as a result, obscured his role as a domestic nation-builder (no study has hitherto tackled Osias within the purview of domestic Philippines Studies). For Roland Sintos Coloma, Osias's biography represents a "history in between" American imperialism and Filipino nationalism.[25] Unsurprisingly his work focuses primarily on Osias's life in the United States, viewing him as a liminal figure whose "resistance" to empire is evidenced by the hybridity of his subject-position. As I hope to show, however, the Filipino-American question was incidental to Osias and his primary goal as an advocate of Filipinism and Deweyan progressive education was to construct a civic and internationalist nationalism.

The theme of resistance to U.S. Empire is even more pronounced in two recently published works in *The Philippine Readers*. Revisiting his work on Osias, Coloma correctly notes that the readers were platforms for the "transmission of civic values," but inadequately concludes that they were covert critiques of empire.[26] The nationalism of *The Philippine Readers*, Coloma avers, would allow "through covert and hybrid modes" the student "to utilize the master's tools of English literacy to dismantle the master's house of empire."[27] In a similar study Malini Johar Schueller deploys James Scott's notion of a "hidden transcript" to contend that the readers, although ostensibly espousing gradualism, "contested colonial hegemony" and used "aspects of the educational apparatus to resist pacification."[28]

Questions of colonial hybridity and resistance are no doubt relevant. Nonetheless these issues remain trapped in the binary of colonizer/colonized in postcolonial theory. Its conception of "hybridity" is one constrained by the culture of the formal colonial power, while domestic nationalism becomes a way to "negotiate" the tensions of coloniality or to "resist" the "hegemony" of American Empire.[29] When applied to the Philippines, such an approach privileges America as an analytic unit and reduces the history of domestic nationalism to the narrative of those caught in between America and the Philippines.[30] The concerns, however, of early 20th-century Philippine nationalists were broader than these binaries.[31]

Situating Osias within Filipinism spares us from the tunnel vision that bedevils American ethnic studies. Indeed elite advocates of Filipinism desired independence, but this desire was largely articulated in consonance with American colonialism and hegemony (which itself ostensibly espoused Filipinization for the elite), not as a form of resistance. The emerging generation of Filipino intellectuals envisioned a future nation, which they were already constructing as mandarins of a future nation-state. There was no need for a covert nationalism, because cultural and political elites had explicitly taken on the burden of nation-building under the auspices of the colonial state (as was the general thrust of Filipinism). Osias himself argued that his pro-independence stance was "in accordance with America's promise and the universal demands of Filipinos themselves."[32]

Both Coloma and Schueller cite Osias's inclusion of selections about the lives and works of Filipino revolutionary leaders as evidence for the readers' counterhegemonic content. While possibly some students may have interpreted the texts this way, neither Coloma nor Schueller provide evidence that schoolchildren understood them as such. And while alternative readings of Osias may prove politically potent, neither do the authors provide us with a novel political discourse apart from a vague critical-theory-circa-early-1990s injunction toward "resistance." We are thus left—the theoretical and actual death of the author notwithstanding—with Osias's intentions. Understood in the context of Filipinism, Osias's references to the heroism of revolutionary thinkers like Rizal or Apolinario Mabini were not only pleas for independence, but part of a broader process of nationalist canon-formation. Along with his contemporaries like Kalaw and Palma, Osias was constructing the pantheon of Filipino national heroes.

It was in this respect that Filipinism was an externally oriented approach to the development of a local culture. Filipinism needed a nation to represent, requiring the construction of a new canon.[33] Mojares's framing of Filipinism, ignored by those espousing an American ethnic-studies approach, prioritizes the domestic demands of a decolonizing country over a politics of ethnic identity. The latter may be relevant for understanding the contemporary politics of diasporic communities in multicultural America, but the former is a better way to understand an early 20th-century Filipino thinker.

NATIONALIST INTERNATIONALISM AND EXPERIMENTAL NATIONALISM

A MORE ACCURATE understanding of Osias's thought requires a vista broader than one that focuses simply on America's domination of the Philippines. The fixation with Osias's postcoloniality has led scholars to neglect his affinities with American traditions such as American pragmatism. More importantly, the narrow focus on empire–colony relations obscures the broader cosmopolitan and internationalist ethics in his work. Osias was not just a colonial subject, reacting to the vertical pressure of American hegemony. In many ways, rather than resisting empire, his work paralleled what was happening *in* empire.

Osias was a product of late 19th-century debates—primarily Western—about the role of nationality amid major changes in geopolitics. As a political phenomenon, nationalism is driven not only by a desire to articulate a local identity relative to foreign power. The nation, which aspires for self-governance and autonomy, derives legitimacy from other nations (this is both a legal and discursive point), and thus seeks to claim a place within an international community. Paradoxically, therefore, nationalism is subtended by a form of internationalism and a concern for humanity. The "intensification" of a people's "national spirit," Osias emphasized, was "not only for the purpose of their national existence but for the purpose of laying a foundation upon which the superstructure of a new humanity will rest."[34]

While orthodox Marxism views internationalism and nationalism in opposition, the current system of international governance represented by the United Nations treats nationhood as a prerequisite for participation in the international order. Historian Mark Mazower traces this nationalist internationalism to the Italian politician Giuseppe Mazzini (1805–1872)—the leading counterpoint to Marx in discussions of internationalism.[35] According to Mazower, Mazzini's vision was simple: a world "at peace because it has been transformed into an international society of democratic nation-states."[36] From the nation, therefore, stemmed a sense of civic obligation that could be grafted unto international institutions. This form of civic nationalist internationalism would be mainstreamed by possibly Mazzini's most influential admirer: Woodrow Wilson. From the 1940s onward, American liberals working in the Wilsonian tradition blended Deweyan progressivism and Mazzinian-style internationalism in global peace movements and global political campaigns such as the lobby for a League of Nations. [37]

In the field of education the internationalism of this period was most pronounced in the Columbia Teachers College, where educators, most especially John Dewey, sought to promote values of liberal pluralism among peoples and nations. John Dewey, of course, was, along with William James and Charles Sanders Pierce, one of the key figures in a philosophical movement that would come to be known as pragmatism. As we shall see, pragmatists believed in an experimental epistemology, where ideas were not validated based on *a priori* first principles but through their ethical usefulness in specific contexts. The worldview of pragmatists was open and flexible, and it emphasized the necessity of plural ideas contesting each other in democratic praxis.[38] Many of Dewey's students in Columbia were learning this philosophy not simply as pedagogues but as citizens of decolonizing states.

The Columbia Teachers College was one of America's first truly international educational institutions, producing teachers who would define the educational policies of various countries in Latin America, Africa, and Asia.[39] One notable graduate was the Mexican pedagogue and bureaucrat Moises Saenz (1888–1941), who studied with Dewey as a doctoral student in the early 1920s. As education subsecretary, Saenz sought to use education to "blend Western method [sic] with local ways to promote the social integration of Indians and mestizos into a cosmopolitan culture."[40] Through education Saenz used outside culture to foster internal national unity.

Osias was one of the earlier graduates of the Teachers College from what is now known as the "global south," studying under Dewey roughly a decade before Saenz, albeit as an undergraduate.[41] In his memoirs Osias recalls having the privilege "of being a student of the unforgettable Professor John Dewey," who taught him philosophy and logic.[42] So high was Osias's veneration of Dewey that he saw his philosophy as one of America's greatest legacies. "Several nations," he noted, had made immense contributions to the spiritual and intellectual development of mankind:

> Greece, through Plato and Aristotle, gave her legacy of philosophy. The Hebrews gave ethics and religion. India and China gave gifts of men and philosophers like Buddha and Confucius. America evolved pragmatism because of James and Dewey.[43]

Like Saenz, Osias was dedicated to the Deweyan principle of pluralism in education, also seeking to construct a cosmopolitan nationalism through pedagogy. Any process of nationalization, he believed, should be in dialogue with the world. Upon assuming the presidency of the National University in 1921 (roughly the same time *The Philippine Readers* were first seeing print), Osias argued that the "nationalization" of education should be neither "exclusivist" nor "anti-foreign."[44] "It does not," he emphasized, "mean a discarding of subject matter and method of education which is not distinctly local."[45] Over the decades Osias emphasized that a nationalist education should be outward looking—a remarkably consistent theme in his thought that he continually returned to in his decades-long career.[46]

Writing for the *Philippine Economy Review* in 1959, he wrote affectionately about Meiji-era education in Japan. The Japanese government of the time, he noted, "sought learning from all sources."[47] From the Germans they learned vocational and technical training; from the Chinese they revisited Buddhism and Confucianism; from the French they learned how to centralize the education system; and from the Americans and British they learned new teaching methods. No doubt thinking of his own work, Osias noted that the first Japanese school reader was translated from an American one.[48]

Almost fifty years after his readers saw print, Osias remained committed to his original vision. In a 1967 speech entitled "Education: An Instrument of National Goals," he looked back on his career as an educator, returning to familiar themes like internationalism, nationalism, and civic virtue. Speaking before fellow pedagogues at the Philippine Women's University, Osias emphasized the inherent cosmopolitanism of Filipino culture, citing the various European, American, and Asian influences on Filipino identity. The Philippines, he noted, was "one country that has received the impacts of the greatest cultural streams, the best streams of civilizations in the world."[49]

Osias's internationalism dovetailed with his Filipinism. Looking and building the Filipino identity from within, he thought, would naturally lead one to see the world outside. No work better encapsulated this overarching worldview than the 1940 tome *The Filipino Way of Life: The Pluralized Philosophy*. Consistent with the logic of Filipinism, the work sought "to formulate a philosophy and adopt a way of life that serves as a guide to the citizen and the nation—a philosophy that gives cohesion to individual and collective endeavor and makes life purposeful and meaningful."[50]

Although it was a broad philosophical treatise, Osias wrote the work primarily for Filipino teachers in training. In the sense that he saw his philosophical musings as inherently tied to a system of pedagogy, Osias harkened back to a Filipino intellectual tradition shared with Rizal and folklorist Isabelo de los Reyes.[51] Like these earlier thinkers, he connected the modernity of the nation with the modernity of a progressive educational system. "The function of education," he explained, "lies close to all the springs of human action—springs which have a very direct relation to individual and national life and progress."[52]

Osias, however, did not only harken to the education ideals of Rizal and De los Reyes concerning national modernity and education. In fusing a pedagogical manual with a philosophical treatise, he also articulated the Deweyan view of pedagogy as philosophy in practice. Dewey thought that one should teach philosophy "via pedagogy"[53] because "the school is the one form of social life which is abstracted & under control—which is directly experimental."[54] Thus, "if philosophy is ever to be an experimental science, the construction of a school is its starting point."[55] As a Deweyan, Osias shared the view that a philosophy book and an educational manual were one and the same.

Osias's work brought 19th-century Philippine nationalism in conversation with 20th-century American thought. Despite having resonances with the work of earlier Filipino intellectuals, *The Filipino Way of Life* evidences a generational departure. It is a lucid, urbane, and worldly text. But it is also a distinctly Americanized text. Osias's work represented a shift from the works of older Spanish-trained intellectuals, its sparse, transparent, and structured English prose serving as a contrast to the florid and unstructured Castillan of someone like fellow Ilocano De los Reyes. Like Salvador P. Lopez's (another Ilocano) acclaimed collection of essays *Literature and Society*,[56] *The Filipino Way of Life* is a testament not only to Osias's mastery of American English but also to his command of the American essay's stylistic conventions.

Although less touted than Lopez's work, *The Filipino Way of Life* received a rapturous review from the journal *Pacific Affairs*, then the official publication of the elite Wilsonian think-tank, The Institute of Pacific Relations. While the review is an endorsement from the American policy elite, the journal's Wilsonian outlook highlighted that Osias's work was most resonant with the liberal, anti-imperialist segment of American foreign policy thinkers. Comparing Osias to Rizal and Kalaw, the reviewer Warren D. Smith proclaimed that Osias was "a distinguished representative of the Malay, or Brown subdivision of the Mongolian race."[57] Smith correctly identified the liberal democratic ethos informing the book, extolling Osias's aversion toward "the greatest curse of our time, Chauvinistic Nationalism."[58] Crucially the review also noted how Osias had been "profoundly influenced by such American philosophers and educators as William James and John Dewey."[59]

The book's debt to Dewey, James, and American pragmatic philosophy in general was not explicitly foregrounded, but a reader like Smith would have noted how it suffused various elements of the text. Consider the theme of "dynamic Filipinism" that, Coloma correctly notes, "formed the foundation of Osias's educational and political praxis."⁶⁰ Despite acknowledging the centrality of dynamic Filipinism in Osias's thought, Coloma fails to locate the concept within the intellectual traditions with which Osias was in dialogue. We have already noted the specific meaning of the term "Filipinism" in early 20th-century Philippines as the dominant form of elite nationalist canon-formation. The addition of the word "dynamic," however, introduced a pragmatist twist to the concept.

At the turn of the century (roughly the time Osias studied under Dewey), Dewey's main concern was the creation of dynamic school curricula that would complement the dynamic nature of the child.⁶¹ In particular, Dewey sought to teach the subject of history as "moving, dynamic" and "presented not as an accumulation of effects...but as a forceful, acting thing."⁶² Realizing this, the student would be able to reason in "fluid terms," adjusting his or her ethical and material aims to "the needs of the situation."⁶³ This approach to history represented the core pragmatist principle of ethics as experimental and provisional. Prior to Foucault and French poststructuralism, Dewey and other pragmatists had already argued that history establishes neither stable norms nor identities, but serves as a vast canvas for contingent ethical and political experiments. "The price of temporalization" for Dewey, as Richard Rorty explains, "is contingency."⁶⁴ This contingency demands the jettisoning of *a priori* principles in favor of plural ideas negotiated through democratic practice.⁶⁵

Taken from this perspective, "dynamic Filipinism" was a pragmatist's attempt to forge a fluid, contingent, deliberative, and inclusive national identity. This pragmatism allowed Osias to collapse various binaries like past/present and inside/outside. In the nationalist cosmology of *The Filipino Way of Life*, various pasts informed a present-in-the-making, and the inside of a nation was so intertwined with the outside such as to blur the difference.

Osias's philosophy was an examination of the progression from narrow individualism to a broad, cosmopolitan ethics. He saw human progress as an expansion or pluralization of one's ethical community, an "upward movement" from individual concerns to the recognition of the politics of "Tayo" ("we" or *datayo* in Osias's native Ilocano).⁶⁶ For Filipinos the sense of *tayo* begins with the family, where individuals first experience an externally oriented ethics. From the family, one's ethical sense should then expand to the nation and eventually to the world. Within this continuum, nationalism is a necessary "stepping stone to the development of internationalism."[67] "If we avail ourselves of the pluralizing process," Osias added, "internationalism will become a logical and natural evolution of the nationalistic idea expressive of a broad concept, as broad as humanity itself."[68] By the time he wrote *The Filipino Way of Life* he had been articulating this view for almost two decades.

In the speech delivered upon assuming the presidency of the National University, Osias explained that the "age of internationalism" was a period in which the world was "groping anxiously for a freer, happier, and more efficient existence."[69] After the Great War, the world was "war weary," necessitating the recognition of cosmopolitan values and "international ethics."[70] In noting this condition, Osias once again mirrored the discourse of Deweyan progressive educators who were influencing educational policy across the globe. After the war, Goodenow explains, progressive educators under Dewey's influence sought to educate youth to build a world free of prejudices that had led to the violence of the war.[71] In *The Filipino Way of Life* Osias revisited the link between peace and internationalism by speculating on new global systems of governance that would create international solidarity. He articulated these views after the Great War and repeated them amid the violent rise of the Third Reich. There was both optimism and urgency in his injunctions.

Although the idealistic dreams of Woodrow Wilson for an international order of states had receded amid the imminence of global catastrophe, an intellectual like Osias clung to the hope of future renewal through internationalism. He explained:

> When it is recalled that Voltaire dreamed of a "European Diet," that Kant advocated a "United States of Europe," that Tennyson had a vision of the "Parliament of Man, the Federation of the World," and that Wilson and other statesmen actually organized the "League of Nations," there is room for optimism that the day is not far distant when Jesus' idea of the fatherhood of God and the brotherhood of man will become real.
>
> The pluralized philosophy seeks to broaden regional ideas among men and nations, and to secure a human order or a world system where individuality is conserved, where republicanism shall be the political form, and where democracy is the human way of life. When these shall have become universal, we may truly say that nations of the earth have at long last been pluralized.[72]

This perspective most clearly placed Osias within the Mazzinian/Wilsonian tradition and the broader ethics of late 19th-century/early 20th-century cosmopolitanism. He had imbibed the hopes of a generation of Western internationalists. Consider, for instance, the similarities between Osias's views and Bryan Turner's succinct summary of the modernist cosmopolitanism of this period:

> In the past, writers like Giuseppe Mazzini argued that love of one's own country was perfectly compatible with commitment to a commonwealth that embraced love of humanity. Indeed, a political education in the love of *patria* moved inevitably towards a commitment to *respublica*.[73]

Turner proceeds to lament the ebbing of this discourse amid the ossification of inward-looking nationalisms. Osias would have agreed with Turner.

For Osias, nationalist navel-gazing was anathema to nation building—a view not uncommon among Filipino pedagogues of the time. Educators of the American period were no doubt enamored with American culture, but they were also worldly. They saw America's influence as part of the broader syncretism of Philippine culture. Francisco Benitez—president of the National Federation of Teachers in 1927 and Osias's roommate at Columbia—argued that America contributed values such as "tolerance in religious and political matters" to an amalgam civilization.[74] Far from lamenting the lack of an original Filipino identity, Benitez celebrated the nation's mutability. In this respect, Benitez, like Osias, was also seeking a dynamic Filipinism with open-ended discursive horizons.

Educators slightly younger than Osias and Benitez held similar views. In 1949 Benigno Aldana, a former division superintendent of schools, phrased an Osias-inflected internationalism polemically:

> Some indict the public schools with the denationalizing of the Filipino character. . . . But if this is interpreted to mean the exclusive teaching of things Philippine, then let the forum and the pulpit advocate denationalization. It would be healthy for the Filipino soul.
>
> Nationalization does not mean the exclusion of the world's masterpieces in literature and their replacement by cheap adaptations or cheaper local improvisations.[75]

Aldana added that true nationalization should involve searching for "high-quality" Philippine literature and folklore, which could be taught alongside the "world's great literary masterpieces."[76] This quote was, of course, a thinly veiled reference to Osias's textbooks.

The educator who most closely mirrored Osias's concerns was Florentino Cayco, one of Osias's collaborators and his successor as president of the National University. Having obtained a Master of Education from Columbia in 1922 (making him a likely classmate of the Mexican Saenz), Cayco was even more explicit about his admiration for Dewey and Teachers College. "Without a doubt," recalls Cayco's grandson Francisco, "the influence of Columbia University's Teachers College is evident in his thinking and philosophy."[77] "John Dewey," Cayco himself noted, was "the most outstanding philosopher of contemporary civilization."[78]

Like Osias, Cayco (1940/2007, 155) was also wary of "chauvinistic nationalism" since it exaggerated "the value of the nation even at the expense of the happiness and progress of the people."[79] Cayco, however, transcended Osias's critique of nationalism and presented it in strictly functional terms, warning against nationalism becoming "an end in itself." "Circumscribed within proper limits," he argued, "it could be made to function as a driving force for the attainment of democratic habits—sincerity instead of hatred, tolerance instead of bigotry, peace instead of war."[80]

The debates about de/nationalization occurred in an intellectual context shaped by Camilo Osias and other "progressive" educators of the time. Although Constantino did not refer to Osias and his cohorts directly, he probably had Osias's cohort of educators in mind when he argued against the education system's emphasis on internationalism.[81] Internationalism, for Constantino, was a veiled form of colonialism. He claimed that American education, secure in its sense of nation, "stresses internationalism and underplays nationalism." Thus, "[t]he emphasis on world brotherhood" and "friendship for other nations," bereft of a "firm foundation of nationalism," would result in Filipinos becoming "the willing dupes of predatory foreigners."[82] As we have seen, however, reducing pluralist internationalism to Americanism was a polemical simplification. The world of Camilo Osias and his peers was larger.

THE PHILIPPINE READERS

HAVING TRACED CONSISTENT themes of Osias's pedagogical thinking, we may now focus on what many consider to be his most significant contribution to Philippine education: the seven-volume *The Philippine Readers*, which served as basic reading material for generations of Filipinos during and immediately after the American occupation.

The Boston-based Ginn and Co. published the first three volumes (for grades 5, 6, and 7) of the readers in 1919. In 1922 it released Books 2 and 3, while Book 4 was published two years later. A final volume for the first grade was printed in 1927. The Osias Readers, as they came to be called, were consistently reprinted until 1959.[83] Filipino schoolteachers initially used the intermediate readers as supplementary materials, but the books became prescribed textbooks when six volumes became available in 1924. Naturally the textbooks sold well as a result; the colonial government of the Philippine Islands ordered so many copies that the readers accounted for 34 percent of Ginn's foreign sales and 85 percent of sales in the Philippines.[84] Parayno notes that, during the American period, "no Filipino child went through seven years of elementary education without having read the series from Grade 1 to Grade 7."[85] There is, as yet, scant research on when and why the readers went out of print, but I surmise that the books died of natural causes amid the nationalization of textbook publishing that occurred from the 1950s onward.[86]

Given their colonial provenance, it is easy to dismiss the relevance of these textbooks. Constantino himself sympathetically recalled how the anti-American Sakdal revolutionaries of the 1930s had condemned the readers for their "glorification of American culture."[87] Some years ago, writer and poet Reinerio Alba celebrated the readers for being "the first textbooks authored by a Filipino," but dismissed their content as "having hardly any relevance to the lives of young readers at the time."[88]

Alba's assessment, reflecting the broader nationalist focus on neocolonialism, fails to define relevance and merely assumes that foreign content cannot be made to dialogue with local realities. The dismissive tone, moreover, shows how quickly thinking influenced by the Diliman Consensus glosses over the nuances of a text. However, as Isabel Pefianco Martin explains, the readers were crucial to the development of a Filipino writing tradition in English because they allowed for the broadening and Filipinizing of the literary canon in the Philippines, opening the door for Filipino writers in English.[89]

Debates about nationalist relevance notwithstanding, the readers were superb books. Writing about his education in the 1920s, pioneering sociolinguist Bonifacio P. Sibayan recalled:

> *The Philippine Reader*s became a classic and were known by generations of Filipinos as Osias Readers. I have since been convinced that one reason the Osias Readers became a classic was the fact that the stories were so interesting that we read them over and over again. This cannot be said of the contents (based on so-called "word counts") of most readers that replaced them.[90]

Unencumbered by the nativist demand to Filipinize everything and to be critical of Western sources, Osias introduced the student to classics from across the globe along with local material. In Book 4, Osias juxtaposed various Filipino folktales (presumably adapted by Osias himself) with selections from sources as vast as Greek mythology, the Arabian Nights, the Bible, Rabindranath Tagore, and Benjamin Franklin.[91] He explained the logic of his selections in the introduction to the volume, claiming to have met the demand to nationalize education through "the inclusion of native folktales" and biographies of Filipino patriots. However, he eschewed content that made for "race feeling, petty sectionalism, or narrow nationalism," adding

> This is an age of internationalism, and it will not do to deny our future citizens the privilege of adjusting themselves to modern conditions. Hence much of the book is devoted to folktales and legends of people the world over, biographies of heroes of other lands, and poems and selections that inculcate ethical lessons.[92]

We have already noted the context wherein Osias used the term "age of internationalism" to signal a departure from the jingoism that led to the First World War. The trauma of the war, however, did not lead Osias to jettison nationalism. Instead, he sought to reconceive it as a bearer of international values. Looking within one's nation, one would find traces of other cultures, highlighting the inherent pluralism of national identities. More importantly, one could find in various nationalisms the seeds of a civic religion that would foster active citizenship. The key in this quest is comparison, as comparison establishes a basis for nationalist imagination.[93]

Simply because of their eclecticism, all seven volumes are comparative. It is, however, in the seventh reader that Osias explicitly challenges students to synthesize their learning through the active comparison of national traditions. The main theme of Book 7 is heroism, and in his introduction Osias tells pupils that they "will learn of great characters of all times and countries, and our own heroes."[94] The book's narratives of heroism are based on historical and mythological tales from across the globe, which Osias uses to tease out universal civic virtues.

In one chapter, Osias creatively makes students read a folktale from the Muslim trading archipelago of Sulu together with the Greek story of Theseus and the Minotaur.[95] Since both stories are about self-sacrifice for the peace of one's community, Osias uses them as tools to reflect on the relationship between sacrifice and patriotism, asking the reader to compare the dedication of a datu from Mindanao and a Greek king. In another fascinating chapter, Osias asks pupils to read a Swedish patriotic hymn (earlier readers had already introduced snippets of Swedish history) alongside the Philippine Hymn (the eventual national anthem). In the guide questions that follow, he asks the simple question: "How is this Swedish patriotic hymn like your own Philippine Hymn?"[96]

The answer to the question is no doubt obvious and superficial: both hymns celebrate the nobility of protecting one's homeland. In the other chapters, Osias makes clichéd arguments about the universality of the bravery of Filipino heroes like Bonifacio, Rizal, and Mabini (this was, after all, still a textbook for basic education). But in comparing multiple versions of dedication to one's community, Osias is able to construct nationalism as both specific and universal, inward in its affect but outward in its ethics. Within the mental tapestry of the nation lies the seed of the international.

This thinking, in effect, is the same doctrine of pluralization found in *The Filipino Way of Life*. Love of country, once pluralized, leads us to see others who have loved their own countries. And upon seeing the universal ethic embedded in loving our particular nation, we move toward greater questions of citizenship and democracy. Because they epitomize this ethic, Rizal, Bonifacio, and Mabini transcend their roles as heroes of the Philippines. They instead become exemplars for all who seek models for the cosmopolitan value of loving one's community.

Osias's emphasis on folktales from various regions of the country also reveals that, as much as he wished to pluralize the nation through internationalism, he also wished to do so through a broader conception of its internal boundaries. By calling a folktale from Sulu "our own," Osias was imagining

Muslim Mindanao as essential to the constitution of an "us," a move that once again distinguishes him from Constantino's generation of historians, who had written out Moro narratives from national history.[97]

The nation that emerges is plural, both in what it sees outside its borders and within. The readers, then, concretize for classroom usage Osias's philosophy of *datayo*. Understood within the pragmatist vision of pedagogy as philosophy in practice, the volumes become the incarnation of Osias's thought—test cases in nationalist canon-formation. That multiple pedagogues in various classrooms in the country used them ensured that Osias's experiments would be replicated in various laboratories.

CONCLUSION

CONTEMPORARY EDUCATIONAL DEBATES in the Philippines pit domestic nationalism against external forces such as globalization or regionalization. Fearing for their "own" culture, nationalists once again insist on the "nationalization" of educational content, particularly via the mandatory teaching of courses in Filipino (namely Tagalog) language and culture. These debates have brought to the surface once again the legacy of Constantino and his generation of nationalists, with their attendant needs to purge the nation of external sources of miseducation.[98] Except for rare exceptions, very little commentary mirrors the open and cosmopolitan politics of thinkers like Osias, Benitez, and Cayco. Indeed these names are rarely invoked. Like their contemporaries in Latin America, Deweyan Filipino educators have become easy targets for leftwing "anti-imperialists."[99] Perhaps the appellation "miseducators" has stuck, and the contemporary nationalist either forgets Osias and his cohorts or tiptoes around their legacy. And yet it was precisely this generation that triggered a major liberal experiment in Philippine governance.

Osias's generation of pensionado intellectuals and those influenced by them saw a mutable nation-state that they could test and reconfigure, using a vast canvas of global knowledge. This was, of course, empty rhetoric for the likes of Constantino. Internationalism was nothing but a cynical ploy to erode confidence and domestic culture, thereby paving the way for foreign capital. The contention, in effect, had been that liberal internationalism paved the way for foreign economic dominance through the creation of an intellectual climate dependent on the West. But did internationalism preclude economic nationalism? Was it not possible to use ideas from the outside to protect one's own economy?

Had Constantino bothered with nuance, he would have noted how a similar internationalism gave birth to the very economic nationalism that he thought could cure his country. This economic nationalism, as we shall see in the next chapter, also had liberal roots.

Chapter 2
Salvador Araneta and the Filipino New Deal

We now turn to a period in global liberalism when it learned to balance not only political rights but economic ones as well. In the postwar period, liberally oriented technocrats created a world not only of "growing wealth, but also more widely shared wealth."[1] They achieved this through a new liberal emphasis on economic planning.

Planning was a new liberal consensus, emerging, once again, from liberalism's nature as *modus vivendi*—from its engagement with competing intellectual tides. In the late 19th century, the emergence of socialist parties, particularly in Western Europe, put into focus the class blinders of the liberal democratic state. The solidification of a grassroots nationalism further exposed liberalism's incapacity to contain the energies of vastly new forms of politics, which it had hitherto ignored. Thus, the twin phenomena of proletarian socialism and grassroots nationalism became the two major political challenges to liberal democracy in the 20th century. On the left, there was Communism and the Soviet Union, and on the right, fascism and Nazism. The Second World War banished the latter threat, but the brewing Cold War placed the former threat at the forefront of liberal politics (see next chapter).

Liberal democracies of the early 20th century also grappled with economic catastrophe. The Great Depression of the 1930s triggered a crisis in liberal economics, and further buttressed Communism's claims of being immune to capitalism's boom-bust cycles. The depression, argues Eric Hobsbawm, destroyed free-market liberalism for half a century,[2] thus having long-term effects on how liberals viewed national economies.

Liberals needed a response to the planned economies of the right and the left. The depression highlighted this need by shattering the assumptions of 19th-century liberal economics and forging it anew. It was in this context that the liberal democracies adopted their own form of economic planning. The theoretical architecture for this period was, of course, provided by John Maynard Keynes, whose assault on the gold standard and advocacy for expansionary economic policy established the modern discipline of macroeconomics. In the United States, a form of Keynesianism would be adopted by Franklin Delano Roosevelt through the New Deal, which pump-primed the economy out of the Depression. It was the New Deal that placed economic welfare at the heart of American liberalism.[3]

The mainstreaming of Keynesianism was a blow to free-market and austerity economics. It was a time when, Mark Blyth explains, "pro-spending, anti-austerity ideas rose to prominence and pro-austerity doctrines faded into the background."[4] In Western Europe, especially within the revivified social democratic and Christian democratic parties, macroeconomic planning became fashionable, because, as Tony Judt notes, it "was quite distinctly not associated with the discredited politics of the inter-war years." More importantly, planning embodied a new faith in the state; politicians from this time "reflected a well-founded awareness, enhanced by the experience of war, that in the absence of any other agency of regulation or distribution, only the state now stood between the individual and destitution."[5]

How were these ideas about the state's role in economic welfare negotiated in the context of a newly independent state like the Philippines? If, indeed, austerity had been banished, and the period of Keynesianism brought about the growth of postwar Europe and America, why did the Philippines fail to develop? Was the alternative incomplete? Was it incompatible with the emerging "Third World?" Or was the vision inadequately translated or diffused?

These are not absurd questions, especially when one considers that similar forms of economic planning occasioned the emergence of East Asian developmental states like Japan and Korea. Moreover, Western policy makers from the period had a firm belief that their prosperity could be shared with the margins of the global system. Nils Gilman has shown, for instance, how the American "modernization" theorists of that period—though, indeed, espousing paternalistic views about the decolonizing world—also evinced a sincere desire for progressive economic planning to jumpstart Third World economies.[6] They were not rightwing imperialists but policymakers who thought countries like the Philippines could benefit from economic models like the New Deal.

This chapter examines how Keynesianism, New Deal liberalism, and economic planning were debated in the Philippines through the ideas of Salvador Araneta—an industrialist, lawyer, bureaucrat, and economist, who has been a marginal and even maligned figure in his country's economic history. Despite his present obscurity, however, Araneta's ideas were widely debated in the 1950s—a period of economic and political decolonization, a time when the Philippines was first attempting to formulate industrial policy. Araneta was a Filipino New Dealer and Keynesian. He believed in expansionary government policy, seeking government credit to finance industry and employment. In the 1950s, he quixotically promoted his ideas in a context where Keynesianism was not only new but also barely understood. These ideas put him on a collision course with the conservative Philippine Central Bank and its governor, Miguel Cuaderno (in office from 1949–1960), who advocated a policy of strict austerity. Their public arguments, played out in speeches and the Philippine press, constituted what is now called the "Great Debate" of postwar Philippine economics.[7]

It was a great debate in more than one sense. On the one hand, it was a debate that affected the long-term development of the Philippine economic policy. The domestic stakes were quite high since the issue was how best to create a modern industrial economy. On the other hand, it was also a great debate because its arguments are close to eternal, playing out even in contemporary debates about events like the Eurocrisis and the collapse of the Greek economy. The great debate was one between austerity and expansionism—the two biggest ideas in contemporary macroeconomics.[8]

Yet despite the massive rift between the economic positions of Araneta and Cuaderno, both of them operated within the largely American-influenced liberal climate of postwar Philippines. Prior to the New Deal, more austerity and lesser government intervention was considered mainstream liberalism in the U.S. It was only the events of the Great Depression and the ascendancy of Roosevelt that allowed the modern Democratic Party to equate government intervention with "liberalism."[9] Hence the Great Debate mirrored debates within American liberalism concerning the role of government in an economy. These were not debates that pitted liberalism against reaction. These were debates within the liberal tradition concerning this very tradition's future.

THE BURDENS OF THE CACIQUE LIFE

SALVADOR ZARAGOZA ARANETA was born in Manila on 31 January 1902 to Gregorio Araneta and Carmen Zaragoza y Roxas. His father was a close colleague of Trinidad Pardo de Tavera and was part of the group of ilustrados who collaborated with the American occupiers to form the pro-annexation Partido Federal.[10]

Araneta lived a life of privilege. His early years were spent in a palatial downtown Manila home, which hosted banquets for figures like then Secretary of War William Howard Taft and Philippine Governor General William Cameron Forbes.[11] The young Araneta vacationed in various summer homes and beaches with the *crème de la crème* of Philippines society.[12]

Unsurprisingly, Araneta married within his class, namely, Victoria Lopez, scion of one of Iloilo's most prestigious Chinese mestizo families.[13] Through his wife, Araneta would cultivate joint business relations with this powerful clan.[14]

In contrast to other intellectuals in this book, Araneta received a religious education—a legacy evident in many of his writings. He obtained a Bachelor of Arts from the Jesuit college Ateneo de Manila (now Ateneo de Manila University) and *licenciado en derecho* from the royal and pontifical University of Santo Tomas. From 1922 to 1923, he was a special student at Harvard, where he audited courses in Constitutional Law, Administrative Law, and Commercial Law.[15] He was primarily a lawyer, practicing with his father's firm from 1923 until 1941. During the Japanese occupation, however, he lost interest and became a businessman. It was then that he began to seriously consider economics.

Araneta's economic ideas were largely self-taught, and his writings were as much a product of his "formal education" as the "constant self studies" in economics and constitutional development combined with his experiences as a businessman and public servant.[16] His intellectual references were diverse but, in the 1950s, he often referred to John Maynard Keynes, William Beveridge, FDR, and the New Deal. In the late 1960s—after the Great Debate—he became a disciple of Louis O. Kelso, who, like him, was a lawyer-cum-economist-cum-businessman and an advocate of Keynesianism and "worker capitalism."[17] As with Keynes, Araneta's progressivism was more rooted in *noblesse oblige* and piety than in class solidarity. He was a man who believed that God expected more from people who had more.

Araneta first rose to prominence as a member of the 1934 Constitutional Convention, where he advocated for the nationalization of the retail trade.[18] During the negotiations concerning trade relations between the U.S. and the Philippines after independence, Araneta became one of the most vocal advocates of continuing preferential trade.[19]

By the 1950s, he was in and out of various government positions. In September 1950, President Elpidio Quirino appointed him Secretary of Economic Coordination, prompting optimism in the media that the president had selected someone who was willing to "put money to work."[20] The following year, he resigned from the Quirino administration because of a tiff with the president over the issue of exporting sugar to Japan.[21] After Ramon Magsaysay became president in 1953, Araneta returned to government as Secretary of Agriculture, but resigned the following year, largely because of growing tensions with labor groups and fiscal conservatives in the administration.[22] Magsaysay then appointed him to a part-time position in the National Economic Council (NEC),[23] which he also left in 1956 after perceiving that his policy recommendations had become marginalized.[24] Despite his time in government, Araneta was primarily a businessman and industrialist. His businesses included manufacturing animal feeds; wheat flour milling; production of electric motors, transformers, and electric floor polishers; solvent extraction of soybean; and biochemical research and medicine production.[25] He also had major ties to the powerful sugar lobby—a business interest he was open about. He was a member of the board of trustees of the Philippine Sugar Association and at one point served as the director of the Lopez Sugar Central.[26]

In today's parlance, Araneta would probably be described as an active member of "civil society." He was a citizen whose professional life intersected neatly with his political wealth. He used his wealth to found FEATI (Far East Air Transport Inc.) University, serving as its first president. He was also a founding member of the National Economic Protection Association (NEPA), founded in 1934, and considered to be the oldest NGO in the Philippines. During the period of martial law, Araneta, a critic of the Marcos dictatorship, was exiled in San Francisco and, eventually, Vancouver.

Araneta was tall, fair-skinned, and handsome—the platonic image of the Spanish-mestizo elite—and spoke Spanish to his children and was fondly called "Don Badong" by those around him.[27] He described himself as a proud man, sure of himself and his ideas, quick to take offense.[28] It was this personality trait that kept him away from long stints in the government, where he exhibited an insubordinate streak.

Araneta was prophetic, defending expansionary economic policy at a time when austerity was mainstream. This intellectual backdrop made Araneta an outlier. His daughter, Lina Araneta Santiago, recalls that even some of his closest friends snickered at his ideas since "they were new or sounded as ridiculous as Don Quixote battling the windmill." Carlos P. Romulo thought Araneta's ideas were "revolutionary," appearing at first to be "unorthodox and as heresies," but eventually "were found to be sound and constructive."[29]

Romulo may have been too optimistic. No work has revisited Araneta's ideas, and the few scholars who discuss him dismiss his ideas because he was a member of the oligarchic, landowning "cacique" class. Historian Nick Cullather refers to him as a "Scion of a Negros sugar dynasty" and passed off his land reform advocacy as a means for "landowners to diversify, and to assure cacique control of the rapidly growing industrial sector."[30] Similarly, in an account largely drawn from Cuaderno's memoirs, Amando Doronila called Araneta a member of the "agriculture-based elite," whose recruitment into the Magsaysay cabinet evidenced "powerful economic interests" entering "the highest levels of government."[31] Paul Hutchcroft does not directly criticize Araneta, but he, too, reduced the Great Debate into "an intra-elite rift" that "pitted Central Bank Governor Cuaderno and his allies against leading members of the sugar bloc."[32]

Araneta's reputation is not aided by the fact that his *bête noir*, the Central Bank's Miguel Cuaderno, has been favorably represented in recent historical work. In the first systematic study of Cuaderno's term at the Central Bank, Yusuke Takagi portrays him as an effective technocrat, successfully navigating economic decolonization and the forging of state institutions. He notes that, under Cuaderno, the Bank took "charge of the country's development policy," and "fended off remaining American colonial interests and then resisted pressure from Filipino agro-export industries."[33] Similarly, the relative immunity of Cuaderno's Central Bank to the corruption of cacique politics led Patricio Abinales and Donna Amoroso to describe it as "an island of state strength" that "fought a rear-guard action to limit attempts by rent-seekers and others to eliminate import controls."[34] Thus, Cuaderno emerges as the disinterested technocrat defending state strength, while his foes (and Araneta was the biggest) become agents of the state's weakness.

It is indeed true that Cuaderno was a professional and that he was relatively above factional interests (although I have previously written of one incident where Cuaderno engaged in rent-seeking).[35] For this reason, he rightly deserves the praise of writers like Takagi and Abinales and Amoroso. But the political question is separate from the economic one. To put it bluntly, Cuaderno may have been relatively clean, but was he correct? Were his economic policies sound?

Instead of examining actual policies and their effects on economic indicators, recent accounts have parked economic analysis of the Great Debate in favor of investigating the class interests that informed its actors. In accounts like Hutchcroft's and Cullather's, the actual content of intra-elite debates barely matter, because elites are homogenized, represented as forwarding amorphous class interests. I hope to show, however, that the nuances within intra-elite debates have had immense effects on the development of the Philippine economy—effects that, naturally, extend beyond the elite.

The Great Debate concerned monetary and fiscal policy, and assessing it requires an examination of macroeconomic strategy and its effects, not a simple identification of corrupt rent-seekers. For the history of macroeconomic policy—from America's New Deal to Japan's developmental state—proves that, though corruption and rent-seeking may be enabled by an interventionist state, this grim reality does not obviate the benefits of extending credit. Attending to macroeconomic history allows us to revisit the Great Debate using data that illustrate the effects of policy. In this respect, I contend that Araneta was far more trenchant than his adversaries. More than a rent-seeker, he was an economic visionary, proclaiming the virtues of a Filipino New Deal that could have been but never was.

ECONOMIC PLANNING AND ECONOMIC LITERACY IN THE 1950S

THE PHILIPPINE ECONOMY in the 1950s was in the process of decolonization, and America was perennially in the backdrop. In 1946, the United States made postwar rehabilitation aid contingent on the signing of the infamous Bell Trade Act. The act was a "comprehensive trade agreement that limited Philippine exports to the United States, denied the Philippines tariff and currency autonomy and granted special economic privileges to American investors and traders."[36] And though this agreement was modified in 1955 under the Laurel-Langley agreement, the new treaty maintained parity rights for American businessmen in the Philippines, who remained entitled to 100 percent ownership of businesses and investments in the Philippines. According to Steve Dale MacIsaac, the effects of these policies were massive trade deficits. In the immediate aftermath of the Bell Trade Act, for example, the demand for rehabilitation and consumer goods was high, but there was little to produce either for local consumption or for export. This situation resulted in a "bonanza for importers, ninety percent of whom were American."[37] This trade deficit continued throughout the 1950s, such that, by the end of the decade, export earnings amounted to less than 10 per cent of the country's income.[38] These exports, moreover, remained almost entirely agricultural.

The unreliability of census data at the time prevented economists from having concrete statistics on unemployment.[39] However, it was clear that, in the 1950s, manufacturing employed very little of the labor force,[40] and that rural productivity was in decline.[41] To say, therefore, that the Philippines was undergoing a period similar to the Great Depression would be an exaggeration. However, the lack of domestic productivity and the perennial balance of payments crisis prompted people like Araneta to look towards the New Deal for inspiration.

Amid economic decolonization, the emerging mandarin class of the Philippine state viewed financial independence as an expression of nationalism and modernity—rhetoric that would take concrete form through the foundation of the Central Bank in 1949.[42] The Central Bank evidenced the greater power of the Philippine state over the economy. Apart from the Central Bank, the National Economic Council (NEC) was founded in 1936 as another possible locus for economic planning. In quarrels with the Central Bank, the NEC could be used as a bully pulpit to articulate alternative views—a favorite strategy of Araneta's. But its diffuse membership, consisting of members of Congress and presidential appointees, "subjected it to congressional interference and correspondingly encouraged its isolation from the executive."[43]

Despite the weakness of institutions like the NEC and the Philippine government's tendency for "paper development plans,"[44] however, the 1950s were a relative high point for economic debates within the bureaucracy. As Teresa Tadem argues, "the dramatic increase" of the government's powers "due to its implementation of import and exchange controls" allowed for the entry of a technocracy whose education afforded them social and political capital.[45] This was the reason why a technocratic argument like Araneta's and Cuaderno's could be considered "great." It was a time when the bureaucracy still mattered.

At the same time, the polemical intensity of the debate was a function of that same bureaucracy's lack of training. Unlike the cooler macroeconomic debates between today's officials, where the marshaling of statistics and the use of complex models create a patina of detached civility, the Great Debate was conducted by truculent autodidacts. In the 1950s, the economics profession in the Philippines was in its infancy. "Until the mid-1960s," de Dios and Fabella explain, "economics in the Philippines had barely extricated itself from management and finance." At the University of the Philippines, for instance, academics teaching economics were merely merged with those teaching business administration.[46] At Araneta's alma mater, the Ateneo de Manila, an economics department was established in 1953, but with only one faculty member.[47] As a result of the profession's weakness, de Dios and Fabella continue, "the distinct relevance of economics as a discipline" to the public was unclear, and "lawyers, businessmen, journalists, and other sorts of what Keynes called 'practical men'" presumed "themselves equally qualified to give advice on and to make economic policy."[48] This observation is applicable to both Araneta and Cuaderno, both lawyers, who learned economics on the job.[49]

PUTTING MONEY TO WORK

THE GREAT DEBATE began early, during Araneta's first stint in the Quirino government, when he started to critique the deflationary policies of the Central Bank. When Araneta was in the Magsaysay administration, it played out within the government, in institutions like the newly created Committee on Employment and Production.[50] At this time, Araneta was criticizing the

Central Bank internally and also in op-eds written for *The Manila Times*. As noted earlier, however, Araneta left the Magsaysay administration, embittered by the rejection of his ideas. When Magsaysay died in a plane crash in 1957, it gave Araneta and his allies hope that they could once again gain traction in the new government of Carlos Garcia.

These hopes were short-lived, as Cuaderno once again consolidated his influence. Takagi provides a pithy summary of the chronology and resolution of the Great Debate between Cuaderno and Araneta:

> Under the Quirino administration they fought each other over deficit financing, resulting in the resignation of Araneta. The inauguration of the Magsaysay administration led to the rise of Araneta and he drafted laws aimed at allowing deficit financing and eliminating exchange controls. Cuaderno, however, had never lost the confidence of the president. When Magsaysay reconsidered the impact of inflation, Cuaderno remained governor of the Central Bank, while Araneta left the government again. Cuaderno succeeded in consolidating an advantageous position in the subsequent Garcia administration and in maintaining the foreign exchange control policy despite the recurring hostility from the strong pressure group and the opposition party.[51]

The Great Debate, therefore, had an obvious loser: Araneta. His ideas remained dreams, while Cuaderno's became reality.

At all phases of the Great Debate, Araneta advanced three interrelated arguments. First, he favored targeted spending to boost both agricultural and industrial production. Second, he called for a devaluation of the peso. Finally, he advocated full employment. We shall briefly summarize these proposals in turn and proceed to assess them in light of economic theory and the arguments of the Great Debate.

The idea of state financing is simple enough. As early as 1952, Araneta had called for a "New Deal for the Philippines," calling for a "bold program of wise spending to attend immediately to essential needs, to put together manpower and undeveloped natural resources." It was not wanton spending, as the Philippine New Deal would prioritize agricultural production and the creation of a stronger industrial base. In particular, Araneta wanted credit for land resettlement, the construction of roads in undeveloped areas, the establishment of heavy industry, and the immediate parceling of landed estates.[52] Liberal credit was necessary, and he always reminded his readers and politicians that deficit spending would boost economic activity and reduce unemployment. He decried attempts by Congress and the Central Bank to balance the budget, noting that postwar America had never balanced its budget, even during the more conservative Truman years. "So long as more money would be circulated against assets, the Central Bank should not be afraid to increase the money supply which could only be used for productive purposes," he argued in 1955.[53]

Araneta's second advocacy, that of a devalued peso, was premised on a concern that the Philippines was becoming import-dependent, both with capital and consumer goods. In the 1950s, the peso was favorably pegged to the U.S. dollar at a rate of two pesos to one dollar, making it cheap for Filipinos to import from the United States. To limit imports, the Central Bank was meant to control the amount of dollars importers could access to buy foreign goods, denying foreign exchange to non-essential imports.

The limiting of dollars to importers was a form of import control, but it is distinct from exchange control. At the outset, it is best to clarify the definition of "controls" from that period, as there were two types of controls, which, ironically and confusingly, produced opposing results. The first form of control was the currency peg of two pesos to one dollar, which made imports cheaper and exports dearer, thus increasing the incentive to import. The other form of control involved the limiting of the dollar supply that importers could access, thus decreasing their capacity to import. Put simply, the first form of control benefited importers, while the second control disadvantaged them.[54] Both "controls" existed at the same time.

Araneta was consistent in seeking to aid exporters, and he was candid enough to concede that this position was self-serving.[55] His form of economic protectionism began with monetary policy: he supported limiting dollars for imports and depreciating the peso—controlling the dollar supplies but de-controlling the exchange rate.[56] He believed, however, that limiting dollar allocations was unwieldy, especially in the hands of Miguel Cuaderno. And he criticized the Central Bank for its unstrategic allocation of dollars, believing that dollar allocations should have been reserved for industrialists, who would need to import raw materials and machinery. He decried that the bank had denied dollars to companies like steel mills, even as it allocated some of those reserves to tobacco.[57] To truly boost exports, Araneta contended, the government needed to reduce their prices through a devalued peso, which would allow Philippine products to compete in the world market at a time when export commodities were getting cheaper. Moreover, since the U.S. would start increasing its duties on Philippine products through the removal of preferential tariffs in 1956, the Philippines needed to make its products cheaper in the American market.[58]

This system would be fairer to exporters, and would incentivize them to produce. The government, Araneta explained, insisted on overvaluing the peso, resulting in "commandeering the dollars earned by our producer exporters at the official rate." As a result, they were getting paid two pesos for every dollar earned, when they would receive more if the peso were cheaper. "This amounts," he concluded, "to a conceal [sic] tax on our exports, and therefore on our production and our laborers."[59] Thus, his concern for domestic production was tied to a concern for labor.

Araneta's third advocacy of full employment was his most important one. For Araneta, economics was a tool for social justice, and, in this regard, national progress was better judged through employment rather than through simple production. National production, he argued, was "only a measuring tool to determine if the national output is adequate to provide for the needs of the people, but it should not be the main objective." For "modern economists," "the first essential requirement of an economy" is the provision of employment to all.[60] This was an economic, civic, and religious belief for Araneta—an integral part of his vision of a Christian Democracy in the Philippines, which he derived from a Catholic, Jesuit education that he valued. Employment was essential to human dignity.

Once again, the key ingredient for employment was credit. Like the New Dealers, Araneta believed that unemployment would be solved through government support. The state, he proposed, "should be willing to give work to all unemployed willing to work." Policymakers needed to "decide how much money the Government can afford to invest in the solution of unemployment for increased production." He called on them to allocate money and to "stretch that sum to cover as many laborers as possible."[61]

As we shall see, an employment policy was necessary at the time, since the Central Bank's deflationary policies created great unemployment in the 1950s. During Araneta's time, however, he did not have longitudinal data on unemployment, and he defensively noted that a "lack of adequate figures on the present unemployment situation" should not prevent the government from creating jobs. Only through creating jobs, he explained, would it be obvious how unproductive the economy had been. "For what good is the hay when the horse is dead?"⁶²

Once again, the goal of his full employment advocacy was increasing production. It was a position consistent with his broader thinking, since the three prongs of Araneta's economic policy were geared towards a single goal: industrialization. In this regard, one of Araneta's main allies was the nationalist senator Claro M. Recto, whose ideas Araneta saw as being "[f]ull of patriotism, boldness, realism and yet imaginative."⁶³ Like Recto, Araneta argued that the U.S. opposed Philippine industrialization to ensure its continued dominance in the Philippine market.⁶⁴ The artificially expensive peso encouraged Filipino businesses to import from America, making it dependent on American industry, while the lack of credit for heavy industry ensured that the Philippines would remain an agricultural economy. In the language of Recto (which would eventually be adopted and radicalized in the 1970s by the Maoist Communist Party), Araneta criticized "the preservation of American semi-colonialism in the Philippines, forgetful that the Philippines can never become a strong ally of the United States under it present pauperism and economic dependence."⁶⁵

Araneta's belief in industrialization was not simply a product of inward-looking nationalism. During this period, he evinced an awareness of developments in the science of economic planning, particularly in Europe and the United States. Like Camilo Osias (his neighbor during the Japanese occupation),⁶⁶ he situated the Philippines within a global community of nations. He too insisted that the belief in a "brotherhood of man"—reflecting a common "duty towards humanity"— was not inimical to "nationalistic defenses."⁶⁷ Rather, it required participation in a global modernity that allowed individuals and states to "make possible in practice the actual exercise of that equal opportunity which is the core of true democracy."⁶⁸ If Western nations could become modern, industrial states, why couldn't the Philippines? Araneta contended that industrial economies could not "be the sole patrimony of elite nations," and that "[a]gricultural economies must become the rare exception rather than the rule." "In time," he believed, there would "no longer" be "uncivilized countries, nor undeveloped countries."⁶⁹

Like Osias again, comparison was key to Araneta's nationalist internationalism. He asked: was it possible to "learn from the experiences of other countries—the failure of the first Labor Government in England after the First World War, and the social revolution resulting from the policies of Franklin Delano Roosevelt?" "And to what extent," he added, "can we attribute the miracle of economic development of Europe after the Second World War, with a production rate surpassing that of the United States in recent years?"[70]

By the 1960s, Araneta was referencing not only Western Europe but also the emergent developmental state in Japan. In a 1960 speech in Araneta University, he celebrated the progress of Japanese industrialization, resulting from liberal credit directed at specific industries. Unlike Japan, he explained, Filipinos did not spend enough of their postwar American aid to set up industries. This underutilization of credit resulted in feeble industries, like the textile industry, and, ultimately, reduced working shifts.[71] He made similar points in 1961 in a speech to the Manila Rotary Club, titled "Can We Approximate the Rate of Economic Growth of Japan?" He concluded, once more, that better monetary policy and the express protection of local production could set the Philippines on a course similar to its neighbor's.[72]

INFLATION RHETORIC AND A FALSE ECONOMIC POPULISM

ARANETA'S CHIEF INTERLOCUTOR, Miguel Cuaderno, ultimately had one reply to his proposals: inflation. Given recent experiences of massive price increases resulting from mismanagement of the Philippine National Bank in the 1920s[73] and the overprinting of currency during the Japanese occupation, it was easy for politicians and the public to agree with Cuaderno. More importantly, the election cycle primes politicians to fear rising prices, given the unrest and subsequent criticism caused by inflation. This dynamic explains why, for instance, Araneta could partially sway presidents early in their terms, only to be defeated by Cuaderno later on. The resonance of inflation rhetoric was, ultimately, the reason why presidents from Quirino to Garcia would shun Araneta's ideas.

Cuaderno's arguments feature the hallmarks of anti-Keynesian austerity rhetoric: the disdain for deficit financing, sensitivity to the size of the money supply, and the notion of "responsible spending"—a simplistic metaphor, equating the economy to a household that requires miserly discipline. With Cuaderno, however, this rhetoric was given a Third World twist: Government financing was a luxury of the developed world, and poor countries needed austerity. A reply to Araneta from 1958 best summarizes Cuaderno's macroeconomic approach. In it, he argued that:

> An underdeveloped country such as ours lacks the capacity necessary to develop the economy. Aside from the meager foreign capital entering the country and the limited pool of voluntary savings, its program of economic development can only be financed with revenues raised from taxation and by expansion of bank credit. The fund which can be raised from taxation however is inadequate, considering the country's state of underdevelopment and popular aversion to tax legislation. Furthermore, because underdeveloped countries have definite shortages of resources, it is inconceivable that a rate higher than 9 per cent of the national income in any of such countries could be saved for the acceleration of economic development. It is not unusual therefore to find the government resorting to deficit financing and credit expansion in order to hasten the pace of economic development. Needless to say, this method is highly inflationary.[74]

Araneta was, thus, perpetually warding off concerns of inflation and also the erosion of the "strong peso." Cuaderno argued that not only would the proposed spending drive up the cost of products, the devaluation of the peso would also increase the costs of imports, creating further inflationary pressures.[75] Like contemporary neoliberal and conservative economists, those opposed to Keynesianism styled themselves as responsible managers, whose advocacy of austerity and "sound" monetary policy kept at bay irresponsible spenders. As Frank Golay noted at the time, "Advocates of conservative economic policies, by identifying themselves as proponents of the 'sound peso,' introduced a shibboleth which severely circumscribed the debate."[76] This position was, of course, as Power and Sicat note, "biased against both agriculture and exports," and it had a negative impact on the country's foreign reserves.[77] A boost in the production of rice and corn through devaluation would have saved foreign exchange, as it would have required less importation of basic food commodities. Similarly, increasing the production of agricultural exports like sugar and coconuts would have earned the country more foreign exchange.[78]

Araneta continually made arguments about the need to support agriculture and industry, but was perennially dogged by his associations with "the sugar bloc." Moreover, arguing for "weakness" was a counterintuitive position, especially since the advocates of austerity projected notions of national pride onto the strength of the currency. It was a rhetorical disadvantage that prompted a defensive tone in almost all Araneta's speeches and writings. One can understand the difficulty in arguing a Kenyesian position by examining the career of Keynes himself, who struggled to defend depreciation in the UK—a struggle that Araneta was aware of.[79]

Keynes introduced his ideas gradually to chip away at the orthodoxy of austerity. In 1923, his main villain was the gold standard and the straitjacket it imposed on the money supply. Although he discussed the tradeoffs between inflation and deflation,[80] it was only in the early 1930s that he assaulted the conventional wisdom of strong currencies. As late as 1931, Keynes was still arguing that import controls would suffice to sustain British production and exports.[81] It was not until 1936, with the publication of his seminal *The General Theory of Employment, Interest and Money*, that Keynes presented a systematic defense of devaluation. In his early commentary on the British economy, he claimed that monetary authorities only needed to control the amount of imports, but did not have to depreciate a currency to ensure cheaper and more competitive exports. This was the position of Miguel Cuaderno—a supporter of import controls and tariffs, but an opponent of devaluation.

Despite initially tiptoeing around devaluation, however, it was clear that Keynes had room for a limited defense of inflation. His thoughts on inflation, as with monetary policy in general, were not absolute, but involved the careful calculation of tradeoffs. In 1923, Keynes argued that inflation is disadvantageous to investors (since the value of their investments decline), while deflation is bad for labor and employment, because it leads enterprises to reduce production in anticipation of declines in future profit.[82] Both, therefore, had their advantages and disadvantages, with deflation being more dangerous. According to Keynes,

> inflation is unjust and deflation is inexpedient. Of the two perhaps deflation is, if we rule out exaggerated inflations such as that of Germany, the worse; because it is worse in an impoverished world, to provoke unemployment than to disappoint the *rentier*.[83]

Keynes also saw inflation as an indirect method of taxation for cash-strapped governments.[84] Governments could print money and risk a certain level of inflation, which would result in a simple trade off: the state would have more funds to finance itself, but consumers would pay more for goods in the market. Too much inflation would naturally freeze consumption, but this should not prevent governments from occasionally using it as a policy tool.[85] "Just as a toll can be levied on the use of roads or a turnover tax on business transactions," Keynes argued, "so also on the use of money." He added that "[t]he higher the toll and the tax, the less traffic on the roads, and the less business transacted. So also the less money carried. But some traffic is so indispensible [sic], some business so profitable, some money payments so convenient, that only a very high levy will stop completely all traffic, all payments."[86]

Weighing the possible effects of inflationary policy was a task for economic managers, not something left to chance. It was thus context-specific and therefore "the subject of *deliberate decision* (emphasis in original)."[87] Like that era's liberalism as a whole, Keynesian economics eschewed dogma in favor of specific solutions to specific problems. This flexible approach, however, was unheard of in the Central Bank of the Philippines, where austerity made common sense. The inflexibility stemmed not only from Cuaderno's personality, but also from the same attribute that made the Central Bank institutionally stable: its bureaucratic consistency. Unlike the NEC, which was rendered ineffective by a fickle system of presidential and congressional appointments, the Central Bank had a stable monetary board, with Cuaderno as its head. Thus, what insulated the Central Bank from political bickering was also what caused it to become unresponsive to changing circumstances. And this problem was attenuated by the NEC's inability to serve as an alternative locus of economic policy.[88]

Without an alternative, it was easy, given electoral pressures and the prevailing common sense, to pass off economic populism as sound policy. As we can glean from Keynes's own gradual challenging of austerity, forwarding expansionary monetary policy forces one to argue from a counterintuitive position. Is it not obviously a bad thing for the prices of commodities to climb? Is it not obviously better for one's money to cost more? Isn't it obvious that cash-strapped economies should spend "responsibly?"[89] Because these positions are simpler to argue in public and because of recent experiences of massive inflation, economic populism in the 1950s took the form of defending the citizenry against the horrors of higher prices.

Cuaderno relished his capacity to tap into this populism, and engaged in economic fearmongering. "Unsound currency," he claimed in a speech to the Philippine Junior Chamber of Commerce in July 1957, "makes people suffer. Peace and order is seriously impaired when the country's currency becomes worthless. It is vital, therefore, that the integrity of the currency be kept inviolate."⁹⁰ Speaking to students at the University of the East in 1958 in an event called "Austerity Day," he spoke of inflation in a Manichean, moralistic tone:

> I need not discuss here the undesirable results that inflation brings about, such as the deterioration of the standard of living because of the rapid rise in prices, the redistribution of income and wealth in society which is prejudicial to the majority of people who depend on salaries and wages and other fixed income, and the distortion in the allocation and utilization of the nation's resources used in production. Inflation is an economic evil (emphasis mine) which not only retards economic progress but also multiplies its basic problems.⁹¹

This was a far cry from Keynes's approach, which refused to fixate on eternal "economic evils."

Cuaderno evinced an equally populist, even nativist, tone regarding Keynesianism, dismissing it as a Western trend inapplicable to the conditions of developing countries. In 1960, he told the University of the Philippines Economics Club that "the Keynesian prescription of deficit spending has from time to time been uncritically suggested by some of our own economic thinkers, in the naïve belief that it would accelerate economic development." It was, however, inapplicable to the Philippines since "in a country like the United States during a depressed period when labor is unemployed, there also exists in the economy a substantial amount of unused planned facilities," unlike in a country like the Philippines. Thus, the "rise of effective demand stimulated by Government deficit spending reacts immediately on the reservoir of unemployed or idle resources which are harnessed back to production without too much delay." And because of the quick expansion of production, "an inflationary increase in the domestic level brought about by the injection of additional purchasing power via government deficit spending is avoided."⁹² Ultimately, the New Deal was judged based on its effects on inflation. It was Cuaderno's trademark rhetorical move: a long-winded diatribe, followed by the simple conclusion that the policy would cause inflation.

In retrospect, Cuaderno's arguments were incredibly facile. For one, the New Deal *was* inflationary, and it was precisely the expectation of inflation that incentivized consumers to spend their way out of the Depression.

"Without actual inflation and actual declines in real interest rates" writes economic historian Christina Romer about the New Deal, "the recovery stimulated by a change in expectation would almost surely have been short-lived."[93] Moreover, the history of the New Deal itself shows that deflationary economics stalled the progress of the New Deal. When Secretary of the Treasury Henry Morgenthau persuaded Roosevelt to balance the budget in 1937 for fear of inflation, it produced a second downturn in the economy, which would eventually be called the "Roosevelt depression."[94] Finally, nothing in Keynesian policy proscribes government financing intended to immediately boost productive capacity. In fact, Araneta's plans precisely included the mobilization of resources to promote production, particularly in the agricultural sector. Moreover, as Keynes himself noted, inflation can serve as a form of taxation that allows government to invest in productive capacity.

Finally, and most importantly, the threats of overblown inflation and great deficits were ruses. Even then, Golay had already noted that "Philippine domestic prices have declined through much of the postwar period."[95] The UN statistics office reported a net deflation in the first 8 years of Cuaderno's term (1949–1957).[96] "The downtrend in Philippine costs and prices," argued Golay, "strongly challenges an explanation of Philippine external disequilibrium in terms of high levels of domestic investment generating inflationary increases in income."[97] Golay also explained that "deficit financing by the government has been modest" and were often matched by foreign exchange receipts, meaning "the cumulative deficit has been small when compared with the relevant economic aggregates."[98] Furthermore, the inflation produced by devaluation would not have had a tremendous effect on the poorest of the poor. In 1971, Power and Sicat critiqued the policies of the 1950s, arguing that "the rural masses consume very little of imported or import-dependent products where the price increases will be concentrated."[99] As for the urban worker, inflation would, indeed, have affected them more in the short run, but a devalued currency would have provided "incentives for increased domestic supply" of essential goods in the long run.[100] Put simply, there was plenty of room for less austerity.

Where Araneta failed was in his inability to articulate a systematic defense of moderate inflation, and, conversely, a critique of deflation. He accepted the terms of Cuaderno's argument, conceding the inherent evil of rising prices. It resulted in feeble arguments about mitigating the inflationary effects of his proposals.

At no point does Araneta explain how inflation can be a legitimate and effective macroeconomic option given certain circumstances. In 1952, he argued: "I do not intend to underrate the problem of inflation brought about by a program of increased spending. But the problem can be controlled. The science of economics, what with the experience obtained in two world wars, has progressed sufficiently to make the forces of inflation manageable and tolerable."[101] In 1958, he promised that any inflation would simply be temporary and that the building of productive capacity would ultimately be deflationary. Replying to Cuaderno in the *Philippine Economy Review*, he claimed that inflation "cannot be counteracted with measures to restrict credit" and that it "can only be overcome by increasing our capacity to produce."[102] In 1965, Araneta wrote his most systematic essay on inflation, but still returned to the contention of achieving deflation in the long term, claiming that "money expended for development, whatever its source, is inflationary only while the development has not reached the production stage." Once the production "of needed commodities and especially of capital goods" occurs, however, "the project becomes deflationary."[103]

The assumption of Araneta's response and also in Cuaderno's critique of the New Deal is premised on the theory now labeled "capacity utilization," which says that economies can expand without an increase in inflation if labor and capital are underutilized. The boost in production, according to the theory, increases the amount of available goods, which reduces prices by increasing supply. As we saw in the case of the New Deal, however, the utilization of productive capacities still led to inflation. Recent analysis, moreover, has proven that capacity utilization, while making logical sense, cannot be proven empirically.[104] Instead of fixating on utilization, Araneta should have attempted to complete his Keynesian view of the economy. But he was too constrained by a rhetorical and electoral domain dominated by the ideology of austerity. Even Araneta had to pay obeisance to this ideology, despite not obviously believing in it. In 1958, in an obvious attempt to ingratiate himself on President Garcia who had made austerity a cornerstone of his economic policy, Araneta said: "I am wholeheartedly for austerity as proposed by President Garcia." If the country wanted to "reach the promised land of plenty," it had "to cross the desert of austerity."[105]

In accepting the mitigation of inflation as a long-term goal, Araneta defanged his own arguments. At no point does he mention the threats of continually reduced prices: the increase in the cost of debt, the reduced incentive to produce, and, most importantly, a reduction in the amount of money firms had for wages. For someone who also advocated full employment, this was a crucial error. As we shall see below, unemployment in the Philippines was such that the economy actually necessitated inflation in the 1950s.

Araneta's economic bag of tricks was lacking. But this was not wholly his fault. At the time, Keynesian theory had yet to adopt the full arsenal of theories that allow for the defense of inflationary monetary policy. For instance, it was only in 1958 that William Phillips wrote an influential article in *Economica* where he observed that high inflation correlates with low unemployment—what we now know as the Phillips curve.[106] And it was not until the years following the publication of his article that central banks began controlling unemployment through inflation.[107]

THE VINDICATION: PHILLIPS IN THE PHILIPPINES

IN HIS 1984 address to the Philippine Economic Society, former Minister of Economic Planning and then Director-General of the National Economic and Development Authority Gerardo P. Sicat reflected on the failed industrial policy of postwar Philippines. "I attach to foreign exchange policy—the act of delayed adjustments in the value of the peso—the most serious economic policy error of our independence," he declared.[108] Monetary policy under the Central Bank in the 1950s was "autocratik [sic]" and failed to take advantage of trading opportunities by pegging the peso "sentimentally to its prewar parity with the U.S. dollar."[109] Thus, industrialization was supported by an overpriced peso, which made firms dependent on imported raw materials. Sicat also argued that when "foreign exchange resources became scarce because the trade system was largely consuming foreign exchange and not producing it (witness the persistent balance of payments deficits), these industries became very vulnerable." As imported raw materials became too expensive or got cut off, the "industries floundered and many failed to survive harsher times."[110]

Similarly, economic historians Vicente B. Valdepeñas and Germelino Bautista argue that "the Filipino manufacturers of the 1950s did not raise too much capital nor did they introduce or innovate any technical progress." Since the peso was stable relative to the dollar, "they borrowed foreign technology, imported raw materials and capital goods mainly from the United States, and produced imitations of American consumer goods."[111]

More recently, Cayetano Paderanga has compiled data on the postwar macroeconomic history of the Philippines, providing figures for indicators like GDP growth, unemployment, investment rate, inflation, etc. It establishes, quite convincingly, the consistency of the Phillips Curve in the Philippines from the 1950s until 2012 (even during the period of so-called "stagflation" in the 1970s, which saw both inflation and low growth in the developed world).[112] The stability of the curve in the Philippine economic history is also supported by data from Furuoka, Munir, and Harvey, which shows "a long-run negative causal relationship between inflation and unemployment rate in the Philippines."[113]

In his most telling graph, Paderanga compares the levels of inflation of three different periods in Philippine history: 1956–1970, 1970–1985, and 1985–2012 (see figure 1). The graph, he notes, "indicates the varying levels of what may have been deemed as acceptable levels of inflation by our policy makers."[114] The graph moves from a period of extremely low inflation, to a period of high inflation during much of the sweep of the Marcos period, and, finally, stable inflation from 1985 onwards. Now that we can see the full sweep of postwar macroeconomic history, the Cuaderno era and its aftermath looks like a period of austerity fundamentalism.

Austerity's implications on growth were palpable. From 1951 to 1955, the average GDP growth rate was 8.078. And from 1956 to 1960, that rate dropped to 4.8, which would only see a partial recovery in the 1970s.[115] "It is very clear," Paderanga concludes, that immediate postwar Philippines was so "bent on maintaining a particular exchange rate," that "it was willing to sacrifice growth."[116]

The conclusions of these economists were exactly those of Salvador Araneta in the 1950s. He complained about the scarcity of foreign reserves caused by a dependence on imports, lamented the autocratic nature of currency policy that hampered the growth of an export industry, and decried the inability of deflationary policy to create jobs. Unfortunately for Araneta, he had neither access to the longitudinal data nor the economic sophistication to develop a predictive economic model.

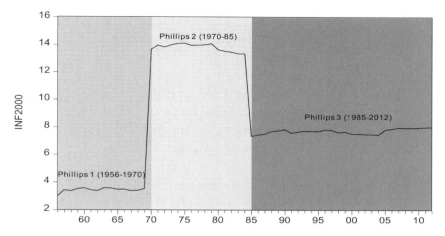

FIGURE 1: Comparative inflation rates with year 2000 as baseline
SOURCE: Paderanga, "The Macroeconomic Dimensions of Philippine Development," 21.

Ironically, it was Ferdinand Marcos—the man responsible for Araneta's exile—who implemented Araneta's vision. It was, for instance, during the Marcos years that the government departed from Cuaderno's policies and became comfortable with a complete floating of the peso (the government was forced to partially devalue in the 1960s because of the currency peg's strain on foreign exchange reserves), leading to the cultivation of an industrial base that was no longer dependent on American imports.

Without discounting the corruption and the brutality of the regime, Caroline Hau has persuasively argued that the first years of the Marcos period represented a genuine attempt at export-oriented industrialization. In the early years of martial law, the country was posting positive economic growth despite a global recession in developing countries and there were "solid gains in the export of low-wage manufactures." This growth, however, was stymied by plunging global commodity prices and increased protectionism in the United States and other developed countries in the late 1970s. These were factors outside the control of domestic policy makers.[117]

Hau shows that developmentalism in the Philippines was not doomed to fail. "To write the history of the Marcos era as if the future crises that beset the Philippines could be foreseen misses out on the contingent confluence of timing, environment, policy choices and contestations, and popular mobilization in shaping the events that spelled its demise," she explains.[118]

There was, indeed, hope for a renewed industrial movement in the 1970s. And nobody understood this better than Salvador Araneta. Marcos may have been his political enemy, and the exiled Araneta was naturally very critical of the dictatorship. But he knew when to give credit. In a 1975 interview, Araneta acknowledged the early successes of the Marcos administration in boosting exports through devaluing the peso.[119] He added that Marcos was not afraid to antagonize American businessmen who used to sell their products cheaply because of the overpriced peso. He explained:

> Marcos is now implementing many of the economic theories I had advocated. He does not have a Cuaderno around him. He doesn't care about the advice of the Americans and to that extent he is being praised by the people. In this matter, he has guts.[120]

His ultimate assessment of Marcos is even-handed and fair. But it also hints at an interesting counterfactual:

> While Marcos has done many good things, such as the green revolution, irrigation, all of those things *could have been done* (emphasis mine) by President Magsaysay, for example, and others with a bold financing program. I had one but it was opposed by Governor Cuaderno and the American embassy. One good thing that Marcos is doing right now is his socioeconomic policies. But that does not justify his continuance in power as a dictator.[121]

What would, indeed, have happened if the Philippines had not waited for a dictator to implement bold financing strategies? What if developmentalism had taken root before the global crises of the 1970s, which, as Hau correctly notes, crippled Marcos's economic project? Counterfactual history is a controversial and unreliable method. But it is tempting, especially for the nationalist, to imagine a better version of one's society. This counterfactual hope is evident even in the dry detachment of Paderanga's statistics, Sicat's frustration, and Araneta's bitterness.

CONCLUSION

TO UNDERSTAND HOW unpopular or incomprehensible Araneta's ideas would be even today, one merely has to tune in to Philippine news on television or radio. On the evening report, the price of the peso serves as an indicator of economic health. When the price of the currency drops, it is bad news. Similarly inflation—*pagtaas ng presyo ng bilihin*—is reported as another indicator of economic decline. Even the Left, from the social democrats to aboveground groups of the Communist Party, rail against the rising costs of goods, without the nuance of the unemployment rate and the state of debtors. This simplification is, of course, inevitable, as neither media reportage nor agitprop speeches can examine the vagaries of economic trade-offs. The inadequacies of reportage and protest language, however, speak to a larger issue: that of a limited economic imagination that circumscribes the terms of debate.

Like the broader liberal method, the science of Keynesian macroeconomics involves trade-offs and the negotiation of grey areas. Perhaps nobody understands that governance is not a zero-sum game better than economic managers do; they know, for instance, that growth usually comes with inflation. It is because of this disposition that they seek compromise and balance—essential traits of the liberal. The liberal politician, like the macroeconomic manager, asks: What is the marginal benefit? What is the net effect of a policy? These questions may be difficult to comprehend in a world that looks for fundamental evils and roots causes. Yet they are the dull but necessary questions of the pencil-pushing liberal.

Araneta's intellectual bravery lay in his stubborn upholding of ideas that are difficult to understand and that had not gained sufficient traction in the Philippines. Though Keynesian economics had mainstreamed in the 1950s through the Bretton Woods institutions, these ideas remained alien to Filipino policymakers—which gives us insight into the problem of postwar development in the Philippines. If the Philippines did not partake of the global growth of the postwar period, is it partly or largely because it inoculated itself from the very ideas that informed this growth? The era of the Keynesian consensus, a period that had supposedly banished austerity, did not take root in the country.

In the immediate postwar period, prior to the neoliberal turn of the Bretton Woods institutions, this Keynesianism was ripe for globalization. At the time, the IMF supported the ideas of Araneta, allowing Cuaderno to dismiss his interlocutor as espousing "foreign ideas." That IMF was not the caricatured IMF of the present—an institution associated with austerity and inflation-fighting. Neoimperialism thus becomes an inadequate lens to make sense of the failed Philippine industrial state—even though Araneta himself was fond of simply blaming "the Americans." It is true that American import interests preferred an expensive peso, which would, in turn, benefit them. But it is equally true that the "Western" Bretton Woods institutions were promoting a notion of economic modernity that privileged autonomous, industrial, and planned economies. There was no homogeneous imperialism, but a global contestation of ideas in which the Philippines took part. And it is through this intellectual exchange that we must revisit the economic trajectory of the country.

As we examine the competition of ideas, we are able to transcend the common view of Philippine underdevelopment, namely that of corrupt, rent-seeking caciques rigging the political system in their favor. State and regulatory capture are, of course, real phenomena, and they have had deleterious effects on the Philippine state.[122] Still, these are not necessarily death sentences for a decolonizing nation. Even corrupt states are not immune to potent ideas, which can then be concretized into policy.

Araneta saw the growth of managed economies, and proposed these as models, based on a set of theories that defined postwar liberalism. Economic planning revived liberal democracy in the West by allowing it to address simmering class tensions. It conjoined late nineteenth-century socialism with liberalism, thus creating forms of socialism congenial to liberal democratic politics: social democracy and Christian democracy. These movements believed that a more equitable society could be forged without overthrowing the state: all you needed was planning. In this way, planning not only averted economic catastrophe but also reoriented the trajectory of electoral politics in Europe. Marxian theory, despite its trenchant critique of capital, was articulated during the era of the gold standard, and thus has little to say about fiscal and monetary policy. The managed but democratic economy was the terrain of Keynesian managers; it was the terrain of liberals.

But this new form of liberal economics did not take root in the Philippines, despite Araneta's own advocacy for Christian democracy and concerted attempts by university intellectuals from his alma mater to build a Filipino social democracy in the 1970s and 1980s. The consistent failure of economic planning ensured that fundamental critiques of "the system" remained the norm for leftwing activists from 1950s onward, detracting from liberalism's message of moderation. The greatest failure of mid-century Philippine liberalism, as such, was its inability to propose solutions to manage class differences.

Hence, the grammar of the Philippine Left has remained predominantly Marxist. The boldness of Marxist theory, especially when it came to the colonial question, turned it into the default discourse of anticolonial progressives. Liberals, especially those who wanted to speak of economic and political decolonization, had to stare Marxism in the face. In the next two chapters, we examine how Philippine liberalism negotiated with its most formidable Enlightenment cousin.

Senator Osias delivers a fiery privilege speech on controversies in Philippine history (26 August 1966). *Source: Manila Times Photo Archive, Rizal Library, Ateneo de Manila University (ADMU).*

Gallery

Carlos P. Romulo watches Camilo Osias deliver speech (n.d.).
Source: Manila Times Photo Archive, ADMU.

Covers of the revised editions of Books 3 and 5 of Osias's *The Philippine Readers* published in 1932.
Photo c/o Dhea Santos and Filomeno V. Aguilar, Jr.

Illustration for "Why the Crow is Black" labeled as a Filipino folktale from Mindanao taken from Book 6 of Osias's *The Philippine Readers*.
Photo c/o Dhea Santos and Filomeno V. Aguilar, Jr.

Agriculture Secretary Salvador Araneta, criticizing Central Bank monetary policies and arguing for "selective devaluation" (23 July 1954).
Source: Manila Times Photo Archive, Rizal Library, ADMU.

Araneta with family at FEATI (Far East Air Transport, Incorporated) (n.d.).
Source: Manila Times Photo Archive, Rizal Library, ADMU.

Areneta is sworn in as a member of the National Economic Council by President Ramon Magsaysay (18 August 1955).
Source: Manila Times Photo Archive, Rizal Library, ADMU.

Carlos P. Romulo and Jawaharlal Nehru at the latter's residence during the Delhi Conference in Indonesia (18 January 1949).
Source: Manila Times Photo Archive, Rizal Library, ADMU.

P Lopez and Romulo—a "Thirty-year Romance" (n.d.).
Source: Manila Times Photo Archive, Rizal Library, ADMU.

SP speaks to students, teachers, and staff in front of the administration building, Quezon Hall, during the Diliman Commune (7 February 1971).
Source: Manila Times Photo Archive, Rizal Library, ADMU.

SP meets with students in his Quezon Hall office. To his right is Dean of Student Affairs, Armando J. Malay.
Source: Manila Times Photo Archive, Rizal Library, ADMU.

President Marcos inducts SP as UP president. Behind them from left: Romulo, Imelda Marcos and Onofre D. Corpus. *Source: Manila Times Photo Archive, Rizal Library, ADMU.*

President Ferdinand Marcos meets with SP (n.d.).
Source: Manila Times Photo Archive, Rizal Library, ADMU.

Chapter 3
Carlos P. Romulo and the Anti-Communist Third World

For many, Third Worldism was simply an opposition to Western colonialism. Hardly surprising. Most of the countries that gathered at the 1955 Asia-Africa Conference in Bandung, Indonesia, were former colonies of the West; many of the leading lights of that event, from Indonesia's Sukarno to Egypt's Gamal Abdul Nasser, were prominent critics of Western colonialism and neocolonialism.[1] However, it is inadequate to focus only on the anti-Western rhetoric of Third Worldism, for the concept involved the charting of a road independent of two systems: Western imperialism and Soviet Communism. Despite this, contemporary historiography largely ignores Third Worldism's challenge to the Communist "Second World"—a tendency pronounced in both general 20th-century histories and contemporary revaluations of Bandung. "The Bandung philosophy," writes the conservative 20th-century historian Paul Johnson, "was for the new nations to create their own industrial bases as fast as possible, making themselves independent of 'imperialism,'" which, for Johnson, is a negation of the West.[2] The progressive historian of Marxism David Priestland acknowledges that the Bandung participants saw themselves as independent of the Western

First World and the Communist Second World, but ultimately concludes that "[t]he conference agreed on the need to escape economic dependence on the First World."[3]

In a volume examining the legacies of Bandung, Christopher J. Lee writes that the Bandung participants based their solidarity on a "shared history of Western aggression."[4] In a chapter from the same volume, Michael Adas views Bandung's Afro-Asia solidarity as an "assault" on the West's civilizing mission.[5] Elsewhere, Lee notes that the "historical importance of Bandung is that it points to the inter-connected world created by western imperialism and anti-colonial resistance."[6] In these studies, the Second World, if mentioned at all, is a mere afterthought. It is thus unsurprising for Roland Burke to observe that in Bandung historiography, "few studies devote much attention to those aspects of the conference outside the categories of colonialism, the politics of Afro-Asian solidarity, and the evolution of non-aligned movement [sic]."[7]

While anti-Western interpretations of Bandung are not entirely incorrect, they are also incomplete, revealing how contemporary postcolonial theory may create a tunnel vision that places Third Worldism in a binary relationship with Western colonialism, thus deleting once again liberalism's role in decolonization.[8] In contrast to these one-sided studies, Pang Yang Huei posits a "fractured" approach to the history of Bandung, emphasizing that the success of the conference lay in preventing both the United States and Russia "from creating monolithic blocs."[9] From this perspective, the conference curbed the power of both systems by creating independent geopolitical solidarities. The political threads competing in Bandung were multifaceted; thus, the conference cannot be reduced to singular narratives, such as its being an assault on the West.

Certainly the critique of Western imperialism was more refined in Bandung as this had been—and still is—the primary locus of postcolonial nationalism. However, I hope to show that anti-Communism, the "other Bandung," was an incipient and radical discourse that cannot be ignored, especially if one wants to capture the textured Third Worldism that began to emerge in the conference. Third Worldism's twin negation of the First World and the Second World was not mere rhetoric. The Third World was in many ways the first of the many "third ways" of the 20th century, much like the European Social Democracy that Araneta admired, which was both anti-fascist and anti-Soviet. There is, as such, a need to grapple with a hitherto unacknowledged ideological current that informed the rhetoric of the Third Worldism: anti-Communism (which I define, narrowly, as opposition to Leninist Bolshevism).[10] Given the McCarthyite brush that has tainted criticisms of Communism, it is difficult to confront the latent and, at times, explicit anti-Communism of the Bandung Conference and Third Worldism. To excavate the anti-Communist genealogy of Third Worldism, however, does not necessarily entail playing fire with reactionary politics. On the contrary, beyond providing a fuller historical account, this allows progressive scholars to examine the antitotalitarian potentialities embedded in Third Worldism.

A richer understanding of Third Worldism requires an unpacking of its anti-Communist underside. To this extent, I examine the writings of the diplomat and public intellectual Carlos P. Romulo, a leading figure in the Bandung Conference and vocal exponent of Third Worldism. While the fulcrum of my analysis is Bandung, I also attend to the ideas that radiated into global intellectual debates in its wake. Romulo, both before and after Bandung, wrote eloquently against Western colonialism and Soviet Communism, and for this he was duly acknowledged as a leading voice of the Third World. Through Romulo, we will be able to see how Filipino liberalism was articulated outside the country, as it sought to forge solidarities with other postcolonies. Indeed, as I have continually emphasized, internationalism is not the exclusive domain of Marxists.

I contend that Romulo should be understood as an Asian equivalent of pre-McCarthyite critics of Communism, locating him within a global intellectual history of liberal anti-Communism. I posit what may seem like an oxymoron for contemporary readers: that Romulo represented a progressive anti-Communism, which, while condemning Leninist strategy and ideology, did not reject certain principles of socialism such as economic planning. More important, this anti-Communism spurned the witch hunts and repressive policies of McCarthyism, criticizing the latter for merely replicating the terror tactics of Communists.

Concomitantly, I contend that Romulo's anti-Communism forms part of an Asianist worldview. It was an approach to postcolonial politics that saw in Asian solidarity a way to transcend the aggressive international posturing of international Communism and the more established Western imperialism. For Romulo, Asianism was a mutable project, able to absorb foreign principles such as liberalism while remaining grounded in the concerns of largely postcolonial societies.

I seek to examine Romulo's thoughts as constitutive of a normative vision for the Third World. This vision remains important today despite the collapse of the Cold War's tripartite division of the world. Many states of the contemporary Global South remain caught between reactionary imperial formations from above (the IMF, the WTO, etc.) and repressive revolutionary movements from below. Romulo's own country is threatened by both neoliberal policy[11] and a Maoist Communist movement that has not only refused to repudiate Stalinism[12] but has also committed atrocious acts of violence against its own members and other leftists.[13]

In many respects, this chapter complements the work of Augusto Espiritu, who has previously argued that "Romulo's ostensibly nationalist, anticolonial, and antiracist views, and his simultaneous hostility to communism and enthusiasm for the free market—which has proved more enduring than socialist visions of the Third World—need to be seriously reread and reexamined, both for their pitfalls as well as for the critical perspectives they raise."[14] Despite his sympathy for Romulo, however, Espiritu dismisses the diplomat's anti-Communism as part of a "transcript that American empire" had "written for him."[15] In what follows, I hope to show that Romulo's anti-Communism was more than an imperial script. I propose to interpret it instead as an integral element of a coherent, liberal worldview that opposed various forms of domination. Rather than simply being a form of Americanism, Romulo's anti-Communism reflected a deeply rooted Asianist perspective, critical of foreign intervention in Asian affairs.

LIBERAL ANTI-COMMUNISM

A PROGRESSIVE ANTI-COMMUNISM was invigorated amid increasing evidence of atrocities committed by the Soviet Union and, to a lesser extent, Red China. This thinking emanated from Western—mostly European—intellectuals, beginning in the late 1930s and early 1940s, but it radiated outward and shaped mid-20th century global debates.[16] Romulo articulated an anti-totalitarian opposition to Communism that mirrored these debates. A brief intellectual history of postwar liberal anti-Communism during and after Bandung thus helps set his opposition to Communism in context.

Non-fascist opposition to Communism arose almost directly after the Bolshevik revolution of 1917.[17] Unlike the McCarthyism of the United States in the 1950s, this opposition began with leftists. As early as 1920, for example, Leon Blum, chair of the Section Française de l'Internationale Ouvrière

(SFIO, or French Section of the Workers' International), opposed participation in Lenin's Communist International. Blum argued that Bolshevism was the "first time in the history of socialism" that terrorism was "not merely a final recourse, not an extreme measure of public safety to be imposed on bourgeois resistance, not as a vital necessity for the revolution, but as a means of government."[18] For Blum, it was the Communists' "emphasis on dictatorial terror" that distinguished them from socialists.[19]

The common defense of Communism—the one most constantly forwarded by Trotskyites—is premised on the claim that Stalin betrayed the noble vision of Lenin.[20] However, Blum's argument reveals that the violence of the USSR can be traced to its foundation. Prisons for political prisoners arrested by an unaccountable secret police (Lenin's Cheka, which would eventually become the NKVD) were the brainchild of Lenin. Under Lenin, the Cheka would administer the various gulags that would become emblematic of the USSR's systematic terror. In the early 1920s, socialists in the USSR relaunched a prison aid organization called the Political Red Cross. Prior to 1917, the organization had publicized and lobbied against the imprisonment of socialists under the Czar. With Lenin's regime imprisoning the same socialists under similar conditions, the organization was resurrected and became integral in publicizing the crimes of the Leninist regime.[21] Thus, the socialists sidelined by Lenin may be considered progenitors of non-fascist anti-Communism.

Lenin designed the totalitarian system of governance that Communist Parties the world over would inherit, and much of liberal anti-Communism has been a reaction to the all-encompassing dogma of the Leninist vanguard party—a party that seeks to be the vehicle of History and ultimate representative of the proletariat. The critiques of systems such as Lenin's would eventually fall under the blanket term "antitotalitarian thought." The characteristic of totalitarianism, as the Polish philosopher Leszek Kolakowski notes, can be found in "such formulas as Lenin's: people may be executed for views that may 'objectively serve the interests of the bourgeoisie.'"[22] Under this system, there is neither law nor a set criminal code, only what the Party deems objectively errant at a given moment. The Leninist Party's ability to determine counterrevolutionary guilt, based on the whims of its central authority, was the basis of the arbitrary justice system that informed the show trials of Stalin. Noting this inherent violence of Leninism and its inextricable connection to Stalinism, George Orwell remarked in 1939:

> It is probably a good thing for Lenin's reputation that he died so early. . . . The essential act is the rejection of democracy—that is, of the underlying values of democracy; once you have decided upon that Stalin—or something *like* [emphasis in original] Stalin—is already on the way.[23]

Despite objections from leftists such as Blum and Orwell, the Bolshevik revolution would, until the 1940s, be treated as a victory not only of the Communists but also of the majority of leftists from various tendencies. After 1917, Eric Hobsbawm (1996, 74) explains, "Bolshevism absorbed all other social-revolutionary traditions, or pushed them to the margins of radical movements." The rise of fascism in Europe, moreover, created an enemy that allowed different leftists to unite either as Communists or as fellow travelers. During the Spanish Civil War and the Second World War, Communism became intimately associated with the anti-fascist cause, thus allowing Communists and fellow travelers to dismiss anti-Communists as fascists.[24]

By the late 1930s, however, evidence of the show trials and purges, in which high-ranking opponents of Stalin were publicly forced to confess to bogus crimes against the revolution, had already leaked into the Western European press. In 1937, for instance, pro-Soviet French intellectuals were already on the defensive, arguing for the necessity of the "Inquisition" that was occurring in the USSR.[25] A turning point for anti-Communism occurred in 1940, when the Hungarian ex-Communist journalist Arthur Koestler published the novel *Darkness at Noon*, which dramatized the imprisonment, torture, confession, and execution of Bolshevik leaders through its main character, Comrade Rubashov—an amalgam of revolution-era Bolshevik leaders purged by Stalin.[26] Together with Orwell, Koestler would become one of the leading anti-Communist voices on the British Left (Koestler settled in the United Kingdom after the Second World War).

The thread uniting intellectuals such as Koestler and Orwell (along with other prominent liberal and socialist anti-Communists of the time such as Ignazio Silone, Raymond Aron, and Albert Camus) was their condemnation of the authoritarianism of both the far Left and the far Right. This was a distinctly postwar perspective, produced by these intellectuals' engagement with two extremes that defined the century's first decades. Koestler and Orwell, for instance, were as committed to resisting Generalissimo Franco's fascism as Stalin's Communism (Koestler served jail time in Spain, while Orwell fought with antifascist Trotskyites).

Anti-Communists such as Orwell and Koestler expanded their critiques of totalitarianism to denounce the repressiveness of all forms of imperialism. As Christopher Hitchens notes, Orwell's journalism from Paris immediately after the war, which criticized Charles de Gaulle's extension of Vichy-era colonial policies in Indochina, stressed "what might be termed the 'Third World' dimension of the struggle against fascism."[27] At roughly the same time, Koestler, according to biographer Michael Scammell, was writing political essays, consistently examining "the way the Soviet system had evolved from a radical experiment in socialist revolution into a classic case of reactionary imperialism."[28] The categorization of the Soviet Union as imperialist would become a crucial debate in Bandung.

Despite the onset of the Cold War and the concomitant mainstreaming of McCarthyite anti-Communism, many intellectuals held the torch for liberal anti-Communism in Europe. The philosopher Bertrand Russell, who many times expressed sympathy for socialism and Marxism, nonetheless grew critical of Communism's illiberalism as the Cold War deepened, bringing him closer to the likes of Koestler and Orwell in the immediate postwar years.[29] In France, Albert Camus's isolation from mainstream French intellectual life (which ultimately led to a break with his good friend Jean-Paul Sartre) was occasioned by his growing disillusionment with Communist revolutionary rhetoric. From 1945 until the late 1950s, he published philosophical essays condemning rhetoric that justified revolutionary violence in favor of a political Utopia.[30] Viewed from the perspective of European Cold War-era intellectuals, therefore, anti-Communism takes on a new intellectual depth beyond simply the witch hunts in the United States.

The globalization of an initially European liberal anti-Communism occurred through the Congress for Cultural Freedom (CCF), established in 1950 as a cultural front to resist Soviet propaganda. Older European intellectuals such as England's Bertrand Russell, Italy's Benedetto Croce, and John Dewey gave the organization its gravitas, but its intellectual direction came primarily from young anti-Communists such as Koestler, Aron, Sidney Hook, and Silone.[31] In particular it would be Hook who would conjoin Deweyan pragmatism with liberal anti-Communism.

The CCF formally operated in 35 countries and sponsored cultural publications established to rally intellectuals, mostly on the Left, against Communism.[32] The CCF's Office for Asian Affairs was run out of New Delhi, with Bombay newspaper editor Prabhakar Padhye serving as its Secretary.[33]

As Secretary, Padhye marketed and distributed CCF publications such as Stephen Spender's literary and political review *Encounter*[34] and set up regional conferences.[35] One such conference was held in Rangoon in 1955, with over 35 participants from various countries in South, Southeast, and East Asia.[36]

In the Philippines, Padhye recruited the journalist and fictionist F. Sionil Jose, who in June 1960 attended the CCF's 10th anniversary in Berlin along with Raul Manglapus[37]—a diplomat who had accompanied Romulo to Bandung five years earlier.[38] Like the European anti-Communists of the CCF, Jose is an intellectual who has remained sympathetic to socialism and class politics while condemning the practices of Communist Parties.

With money from the CCF, Jose established the literary and political quarterly *Solidarity*, to which Romulo contributed articles. With the same money, he also set up the publishing house Solidaridad. The first book issued by the new publishing house was Romulo's *Identity and Change: Towards a National Definition* in 1965.[39] In 1970, Solidaridad published Romulo's *The Asian Mystique: A Clarification of Asia's New Image*. (These books, as I discuss below, are key texts in which Romulo discusses his nuanced approach to Communism.)[40] At around the same time, in 1964, the entrepreneurial Jose also opened Solidaridad Bookstore in the Ermita district of Manila. Romulo was the guest of honor at the bookstore's opening.[41]

There is no evidence that Romulo, like Jose and his subordinate Manglapus, ever became a member of the CCF. However, the closeness of Romulo to these figures and to endeavors financed by the CCF reveals that Romulo occupied an intellectual space similar to that of the Congress.

ROMULO, THE UN, AND THE THIRD FORCE

CARLOS PEÑA ROMULO is the most prominent diplomat in Philippine history. At the height of his political career, his aplomb was greater than that of some of the presidents he served. As noted by Gregorio Brillantes, a doyen of Philippine journalism and literature, Romulo did "more to enhance the country's image abroad than any other Filipino in his time."[42]

"CPR" was born in 1899 to a landowning family in Camiling, Tarlac province. Unlike Osias, he was too young to have memories of the Philippine revolution. But, like Osias, he, too, viewed himself as an heir to the nationalism of the 19th century. In a self-promoting memoir, he narrated that he was born only nine days after the anti-Spanish revolutionaries declared victory and proclaimed an independent republic, deliberately constructing an analogy between his birth and that of the nation.[43] Like his country, moreover, he was initially anti-American. His first political memories were that of his father sneaking trips home while fighting American soldiers in the hills of Tarlac. He claimed to have despised the "blue-eyed foreign devils" whom his father fought "with a child's helpless hatred."[44]

But he changed his mind after befriending an American sergeant who made him believe that Americans wanted peace, prosperity and happiness for Filipinos. Similarly, his father, having been convinced of America's good intentions, became the first man in Camiling to study English and served as a mayor and governor under the American colonial regime.[45] "With such a beginning," explains Resil Mojares, "everything in his life"—from his exploits during the Second World War to his time at the United Nations—"would unfold with a clear and sure logic."[46]

Educated at the University of the Philippines and Columbia University, Romulo began his career as a journalist and publisher. During the Second World War, he served in the U.S. Army as General Douglas MacArthur's press officer, delivering lectures in the United States about the Pacific War. Under MacArthur, Romulo rose to the rank of colonel in 1942 and brigadier-general in 1944.[47] It was, however, after the war, as the Philippine chief diplomat to the United Nations, that Romulo became a prominent figure in global politics. From 1949 to 1950 he was president of the United Nations General Assembly, and he would remain a fixture in the United Nations until his retirement in 1984.[48] With the exception of a brief stint as president of the University of the Philippines from 1962 to 1968, Romulo devoted his postwar professional life to the foreign service, serving as Secretary of Foreign Affairs for Presidents Elipidio Quirino (1950–52), Diosdado Macapagal (1963–64), and Ferdinand Marcos (1968–84).[49]

The best description of Romulo comes from Singapore's former Prime Minister Lee Kuan Yew:

> His [Marcos'] foreign minister, Carlos Romulo, was a small man of about five feet some 20 years my senior, with a ready wit and a self-deprecating manner about his size and other limitations. Romulo had a good sense of humour, an eloquent tongue and a sharp pen, and was an excellent dinner companion because he was a wonderful raconteur, with a vast repertoire of anecdotes.[50]

Viewed from the perspective of the unrelentingly nationalist Philippine Left,[51] Romulo is an inconsequential figure, a pro-American glitch in the broader narrative of the Philippine nation. Very few left-wing intellectuals, especially those from the University of the Philippines, recall Romulo as a prominent Third Worldist. Commenting on his tenure as UP president, Jose Maria Sison, the founding chairman of the Maoist Communist Party of the Philippines, and his wife, Juliet de Lima, dismiss Romulo as a "chief agent of cultural agencies of the US government."[52] Francisco Nemenzo, a prominent Marxist professor during Romulo's term as university president (who would himself become UP president in the 1990s), claims that campus nationalists were barely cognizant of Romulo's role in Bandung and ignored his claims of being an anticolonial intellectual. Nemenzo adds that progressives at the university viewed Romulo as a subpar intellectual who was more adept at sweet-talking the intelligentsia than producing relevant scholarly work.[53] Reinforcing Romulo's reputation as a pseudo-intellectual was the widespread belief that most of his writings had been penned by ghostwriters, whose egos the diplomat stroked as enticement to work for him.[54] The Romulo that emerges is at best a dilettante opportunist, and at worst an embodiment of reaction.

Perhaps the outright dismissal of Romulo stems from the evolving and contradiction-ridden nature of his politics. Filipino leftists ignore Romulo not only because of his anti-Communism, but also because he was never as categorical about his geopolitical positions as the more prominent nationalists of the left-wing canon. The Maoist Communist Party and other leftists influenced by it, Patricio Abinales notes, derived their categorical anti-Americanism from the nationalist and anti-American senator Claro M. Recto—Romulo's political *bête noire*.[55] As a result, the Philippine Left remembers Romulo as an opportunist and American lapdog, ignoring the various nuances in his positions that made him indeterminable and difficult to place within neat binaries such as anti-American/anti-Filipino, nationalist/American lapdog, or revolutionary/reactionary.

I hope to show that it is precisely the evolving nature of Romulo's thought that makes him crucial to an understanding of a concept such as the Third World, which is in itself a nuanced, contradiction-ridden, and evolving category. Romulo may not have been the most prominent delegate at Bandung based on historical accounts; other leaders such as Sukarno are certainly better remembered. Nonetheless, Romulo represents a crucial strand in the plural narratives present at the conference. To reiterate Pang's point, Bandung is best understood as containing a plurality of postcolonial positions, contradicting, intersecting, and mutually reinforcing.

A revisiting of Romulo's legacy requires a different vista, a perspective broader than that of the domestic politics of postwar Philippines. In doing this, I neither seek to exonerate Romulo of his various dalliances with reaction nor do I aim to reconstruct him as a hero. Many times, he was, indeed, hopelessly pro-American, as when he allowed research that would benefit the U.S. Army in Vietnam to be conducted at the UP.[56] He was also a periodic liar, self-promoter and plagiarist,[57] who perennially walked the tightrope between sweet-tongued diplomat and outright huckster. Most scathingly, Romulo's lifelong commitment to liberalism was severely compromised when he became a loyal minister of the dictator Ferdinand Marcos.

Nevertheless, Romulo was a genuine voice of the Third World and one of the most articulate exponents of the concept. Even his staunchest critic, freelance journalist Pio R. Andrade, concedes that Romulo "spoke against imperialism and colonialism, and he championed the rights of colonial nations to independence."[58] He also noted that Romulo received "well-deserved international kudos for his winning battle for the inclusion of "independence" in the UN Charter."[59]

That the Filipino diplomat was a close U.S. ally is a given. But in his UN career he made efforts to continually signal his affinity for former colonies. In votes where the main protagonists were the United States and Russia, Romulo naturally sided with the Americans. However, in votes that pitted "small nations" (a term Romulo used for the pre-Bandung Third World) against powerful ones, Romulo took the side of the former. In discussions about the wording of the UN Charter, for instance, the Big Powers wanted the Charter to state that non-self-governing nations should aspire only toward self-governance. Romulo led the delegates who wanted to insert the word "independence." Big powers such as England, France, and Russia opposed Romulo and his allies, while the United States abstained from the vote. The Philippine proposal eventually won.[60]

In the case of the partition of Palestine to create the state of Israel, Romulo opposed the proposal, claiming that it was "repugnant to the valid nationalist aspirations of the people of Palestine."[61] This was obviously a position contrary to the United States'. Manila, having been threatened with a withdrawal of aid, eventually ordered Romulo to support the formation of Israel. Romulo saw the actions of the United States as arm twisting, and until his death he maintained his views concerning the dangers of partition.[62]

Finally, Romulo contradicted the United States on the issue of veto power in the UN. According to Romulo, the leitmotif of his 38 years in the UN was the struggle to revise the UN Charter and to limit the veto power of the five permanent members of the UN Security Council. For his entire UN career, he was at loggerheads with the United States on the issue of the veto.[63] Even during his time as Marcos's foreign minister, Romulo argued for a review of the charter to prevent the abuse of the veto. All these proposals were shot down by the United States.[64]

Crucially, even the United States did not view Romulo as its lapdog. A declassified CIA document from 1949 notes that "[a]lthough the Philippines generally supports U.S. policy in the UN, there has been some deviation largely owing to Romulo's championship of dependent peoples of Asia, for whom he has become a leading spokesperson."[65] It was Romulo who began to craft an explicitly anticolonial foreign policy for the Philippines. Before Romulo, the document adds, "Philippine policy toward colonial peoples has [sic] been limited to expressions of sympathy for national aspirations." With Romulo at the helm of foreign policy, however, the Philippine delegation to the New Delhi conference on Indonesia in January 1949 played a leading role in pushing the UN to support Indonesian independence.[66]

Robert Trumbull of the *New York Times* observed that the New Delhi conference—the first time Asian countries "had come together on a matter of common concern"—was a landmark moment that sent a message concerning Asia's desire to "play a stronger role in international affairs."[67] This manifested in a call for a permanent pan-Asian organization—a Romulo proposal, which drew massive applause from the audience.[68] Jawaharlal Nehru and Romulo, for Trumbull (1949, E5), were "two of the strongest figures" in the conference. A few days after the end of the proceedings, the two leaders delivered interviews that were "in contrast to the deliberately moderate tone of the conference itself."[69] Summarizing their statements, Trumbull noted that Nehru and Romulo "warned the West" that Asia's peoples had "definite objectives" and were "determined to obtain these by concerted effort if necessary."[70] One objective was economic independence: for Asian countries to cease being mere suppliers of raw materials to Western countries.

New Delhi foreshadowed Bandung. Even before he was elected president of the UN General Assembly, Romulo was already a prominent pan-Asianist who styled himself as a representative of formerly colonized peoples. In this regard, he was capable of criticizing his erstwhile superpower ally. In May 1949, for instance, Romulo and Chinese UN delegate Dr. Lee Wei-kuo condemned the United States for halting the delivery of Japanese reparations to wartime opponents (the United States was seeking to prioritize Japan's economic recovery).[71] Romulo declared that he was "flabbergasted" by the decision and blamed the United States for paving the way for Japanese revanchism—the primary victim of which would be Asia.[72]

Romulo's anti-Communist credentials allowed him to criticize U.S. foreign policy without fear of being branded a Communist sympathizer. On 2 March 1950, for example, he sent a personal and confidential letter to U.S. Secretary of State Dean Acheson condemning the United States' decision to recognize Emperor Bao Dai's government in Vietnam; he viewed Bao Dai as a puppet of French colonialism. In supporting Bao Dai simply because he was an anti-Communist, Romulo wrote, the United States "may have unwittingly espoused even the demonstrated iniquity of colonial imperialism."[73] The decision, moreover, gave Communists "the enormous advantage of plausible and logical insistence on anti-Communism being pro-imperialism," reinforcing the notion that only Communists were anti-imperialists.[74] Consistent with his self-aggrandizing style, Romulo, who viewed himself as a mediator between Asians and the West, declared that U.S. policy in Vietnam would lead to "the virtual isolation of American policy from the sentiment of Asian countries."[75] Most surprisingly, Romulo explained that Ho Chi Minh was a potentially independent Communist who "could make all sorts of trouble for Stalin."[76] In the meeting with Acheson that followed, Romulo told the Secretary that Ho Chi Minh was a patriot who would refuse to simply become a tool of Mao or Stalin.[77] He advised Acheson to negotiate with Ho Chi Minh and suggested that France and the United States assure the Communist leader that Vietnam would gain independence.[78]

Romulo believed he spoke from a position of authority, because he claimed to know Ho Chi Minh personally. In a likely fabricated account, the diplomat said he met Ho Chi Minh in 1948 after a UN meeting in Paris (various accounts, however, state the Vietnamese revolutionary was in Vietnam in 1948, having last been in Paris in September 1946). Hearing that Ho Chi Minh was in the city, Romulo claims, he sought out the Vietnamese leader. They met in a "small bistro in a by-way in Paris" and spoke about Philippine history, with Ho Chi Minh discoursing fondly about General Emilio Aguinaldo's struggle against Spanish and American colonizers.[79] Romulo considered the Vietnamese leader a "true patriot" who was forced to seek assistance from the USSR only because the United States refused to support his anticolonial cause.[80] This story may be apocryphal, or Romulo (or his wife, Beth Day, who edited the book after his death) may have confused the date. Nonetheless, Romulo's praise for Ho Chi Minh reveals his sympathy for national liberation movements, despite their affiliation with Communism.

Romulo's letter and subsequent meeting with Acheson revealed his prescience. He knew that Vietnam would not support a puppet regime. Moreover, the engagement with Acheson exhibited Romulo's nuanced anti-Communism. For Romulo, anti-Communism was not to be viewed as an automatic endorsement of imperialism. To resist Communism, one had to acknowledge its appeal to anticolonial nationalism—a perspective Romulo gained through his advocacy for Asian independence. This perspective was not inconsistent with what Romulo had already said in public. The previous year, he had explained his vision for an anti-imperialist *and* anti-Communist Asia.

The person credited with coining the term "Third World" in its contemporary geopolitical sense is the French demographer Alfred Sauvy, who in 1952 compared former colonies to the "third estate" (the people) of the French Revolution.[81] In a 1949 speech at the University of Chicago, however, Romulo had already used the term "third force" to describe Asia—"the most dynamic region in the world," which was "interposed between the two great powers."[82] A little over a week before he was elected president of the General Assembly, Romulo had published a version of this Chicago speech in *The New York Times*. As in his conversation with Acheson, Romulo conceded that Communism appealed to colonized peoples, particularly in Indochina, where "the Communist party was identified with the nationalist struggle, first against the Japanese and later against the French."[83] For Romulo, "the methods and principles of communism have an appeal" for peoples who, by virtue of their colonial history, "may be led to believe that they have nothing to lose from aligning themselves with communism, which generously promises plenty for all and loudly professes its irreconcilable antagonism to the colonial system."[84] It was in this context that Romulo would put forward liberalism and human rights as battle cries for colonized peoples.

A few years before the conference, Romulo had already outlined the Asianist version of anti-Communism that he would take to Bandung. Speaking at Johns Hopkins University in 1952, he declared that the threat of Communism was more pronounced in Southeast Asia, because the region was in "a position of vital strategic importance to the whole free world."[85] Citing Lenin, who believed that "the road to Europe lies through Peiping and Calcutta," Romulo argued that "Southeast Asia is the last remaining roadblock to Soviet hegemony in the whole of Asia."[86] Foreshadowing the anti-imperial language of Bandung, he added, "The struggle against Communism and Soviet imperialism may well be won or lost in Southeast Asia."[87] Romulo's comments may sound exaggerated today, but it is important to recall that he made them in the context of the Korean War—a war he believed evidenced Soviet-Chinese aggression.

Romulo was right about his assessment of the Korean conflict. The most recent scholarship based on recently opened Soviet archives proves that Stalin, with Mao's support, encouraged Kim Il-Sung's invasion of South Korea in a reckless attempt to drag the United States into a protracted Asian conflict.[88] Romulo was thus justified in going to Bandung with deep suspicions about the Chinese delegation. Indeed, Communism could threaten the stability of Asia, and Romulo would make this point eloquently during the conference.

THE ANTI-COMMUNIST BANDUNG

THE PHILIPPINES PARTICIPATED in Bandung because of Romulo's view that the event would transcend the narrow anti-Western perspective that many had already associated with it even before its commencement. Even within the Philippines, President Ramon Magsaysay—a staunch U.S. ally—was initially hesitant to send a delegation. It was, however, Romulo who convinced the pro-American president that the Philippines had a place in the conference.[89]

In his oft-cited book *The Meaning of Bandung*, Romulo sets out to correct the popular perception that Bandung was simply a challenge to Western power.[90] He begins by decrying how the U.S. press prejudged the conference, noting the popular belief shortly before its commencement that it would degenerate "into an anti-Western political demonstration."[91] In response, Romulo's goal was to outline Bandung's "unpublicized nuances" in order that "its historical import and flavor may be better appreciated."[92] He emphasized that the countries in the conference were not homogeneously anti-Western, and that they reflected "different shades of political persuasion."[93] Early on, Romulo was critical of the simple East vs. West binary that subtended interpretations of Bandung.

The tendency to homogenize the Bandung narrative as anti-Western was not only the myopia of the pre-conference Western press. This narrow-minded interpretation is replicated in current Bandung historiography. For example, according to Burke, the focus on the anti-Western aspects of the conference has led scholars to ignore Bandung's contribution to human rights discourse.[94] He contends that studies easily assume that the anti-colonial ethos of the conference translated into a critical attitude toward "Western" human rights. Burke demonstrates, however, that human rights discourse was essential to the vocabulary of Bandung, and that the latter's debates mirrored those in the United Nations over the Universal Declaration of Human Rights (UDHR).[95] Of more importance for this article, Burke posits that criticism of the Soviet and Chinese governments, forwarded by conference delegates such as Romulo and Sri Lankan Prime Minister Sir John Kotelawala, "raised arguments with important consequences for human rights and democracy."[96] Simply stated, anti-Communism and human rights were intimately linked in the minds of some "Third World" strategists as early as 1949. In this regard, the Asia-Afro debates concerning Communist imperialism and totalitarianism foreshadowed intellectual shifts in Europe. As Tony Judt notes in the case of Western Europe, human rights discourse did not enter mainstream international discourse until the late 1980s, amid the discrediting of Communist totalitarianism.[97]

In the conference, the anti-Communism of many of the delegates was immediately palpable. Initially, Chinese delegate Zhou Enlai forfeited his right to deliver an opening speech. "But as the addresses proceeded, and when some countries went out of their way to express their attitude to Communism," recalls Kotelawala in his memoirs, "Chou En-lai rose and said that he reserved his right to deliver an address of his own."[98] C.P. Fitzgerald, an Australian historian watching the proceedings, noticed a conciliatory Zhou, who claimed he was not in Bandung to promote Communist ideology. For Fitzgerald, Zhou's speech represented a "marked change of attitude, if not policy" on the part of the Chinese premier.[99] Kotelawala, on the other hand, claimed that Zhou's comments were "satisfactory," "but what was more satisfactory" was that Zhou "should have been forced to make them."[100]

Zhou was placed on the defensive because of the pervasive anti-Communist sentiment at Bandung—a sentiment immediately perceptible to the Philippine press, though neglected in accounts from neutralist countries such as India.[101] The leading weekly news magazine *Philippines Free Press* began its report on the first two days of the conference as follows:

> Outright anti-communist speeches were delivered at the opening of the Afro-Asian conference in Bandung, Indonesia, by Iraq's Foreign Minister Fadhil Jamali, Pakistan's Prime Minister Mohammed Ali, the Philippines' Carlos Romulo, and Thailand's Foreign Minister Prince Wan Waithayakon. It was clear from the speeches the conference would not develop into a communist propaganda vehicle. For example, Ambassador Romulo, while criticizing Western colonialism past and present, warned that communist imperialism is today a great danger to the new nations in Asia and Africa.[102]

The report added that Zhou was "surprisingly mild in his speech Tuesday."[103]

The *Free Press* also declared that Romulo found the conference "more than reassuring," because many countries shared the sentiments of the Philippines against "communist domination."[104] It added that Zhou, surprised by the turn of events, was "forced to sit back and listen to unsparing attacks against communism."[105] It is in this context of hostility to Communism that we should situate Romulo's famous quip that Zhou "had taken a leaf from Dale Carnegie's tome on *How to Win Friends and Influence People*."[106]

The opening speeches, however, would not be the last time Bandung delegates attacked Communism. In September 1955, writing for the local Philippine press, Romulo recalled that one of the most dramatic parts of the conference was the "fight over communism and colonialism."[107] Serious debate went into the definition of colonialism to be placed in Bandung's final communiqué. The communiqué is a pathbreaking document, which, beyond articulating the "Bandung spirit" of Asia-Afro solidarity, also allowed for a radical redefinition of colonialism. It condemned "colonialism in all its manifestations" and affirmed that "alien subjugation, domination and exploitation constitutes a denial of human rights."[108] In his newspaper account (a clearer and more detailed account of the colonialism debate than *The Meaning of Bandung*), Romulo reported how the conference arrived at this definition.

The debate began when Iraqi Foreign Minister Muhamad Fadhil Jamali "opened up the heavy artillery against Soviet imperialism."[109] However, "Powerful forces" (Zhou and the neutralist Nehru)[110] wanted to block any reinterpretation of colonialism. For them, there was "only one form of colonialism—Western—[and that] [n]othing else counted."[111] The Philippine delegation and the majority of the conference participants supported Jamali. Romulo narrates:

> We took the position that the conference must condemn all colonialism, both overt and potential. *We were opposed to every form of domination, subjugation, or the exploitation of peoples* [emphasis mine]. Everyone present knew we referred to communism.
>
> Powerful support came from Ceylon's Prime Minister, Sir John Kotelawala, who with the caliber of a world leader could set aside restricted regional loyalties for a greater cause. Turkey's Deputy Prime Minister Fatin Rustu Zorlu also was a real fighter for democracy and so we were able to show the conference—meaning representatives of half of mankind—that we spoke for the security and interests of all. And all finally rallied to stand with us—condemning not only Western colonialism but colonialism "in its various forms."[112]

Perhaps no statement better encapsulates Romulo's vision for a Third World that served as a dual negation of both the First and Second Worlds. It is a vision that, like those of the liberal anti-Communists discussed earlier, condemned all forms of domination and totalitarianism. Naturally, Romulo was delighted that his views received much support in the conference, particularly from Kotelawala, who until then was a known neutralist like Nehru.[113] In his speech, the prime minister asked the delegates to consider the Soviet satellites in Eastern Europe.[114] "Are not these colonies as much as any of the colonial territories of Africa or Asia?" he asked. If the conference was united against colonialism, he added, "should it not be our duty to declare our opposition to Soviet colonialism as much as to Western imperialism?"[115] Kotelawala thus affirmed Asia and Africa's solidarity with the occupied peoples of countries such as Poland and Czechoslovakia.[116] Hearing Kotelawala's remarks, Nehru and Zhou took umbrage,[117] and the two issued a statement extolling the values of neutralism.[118] Nehru followed this up with a speech, which Romulo immediately refuted.[119]

Romulo's response to Nehru is one of the most eloquent speeches of his career. First, he argued that the expansionist nature of global Communism was "not a charge made by non-Communist countries" but "the explicit declaration of international communism."[120] Moreover, he noted that Communist Parties did not respect elections and merely used these for propaganda purposes.[121] And, echoing Blum's comments on Leninist terror from 1919 (see above), he explained that Communism's "schism with socialism is based upon the fact that Communists see violence as the sole means of achieving social reform."[122] He then reminded the audience of the 1950 Chinese attack on South Korea, which was condemned by 50 countries at the UN.[123] Quoting statements from Chinese officials about the need to encourage and organize armed rebellions in other Asian countries, he argued that China had violated the non-aggression principles of the UN.[124] Peaceful coexistence with China, he believed, was impossible. In concluding the speech, he declared, "What we fear now is the new empire of communism on which we know the sun never rises. May your country India, Sir, never be caught by the encircling gloom."[125] Once again, Romulo was prescient. Exactly five years after Bandung, after China had seized Indian border territory, Nehru called China's methods "coercive" and labeled the Communists in India "a destructive opposition factor."[126]

Writing 30 years after Bandung in his memoirs—long after he and Nehru had become good friends—Romulo recalled the debate in Bandung:

> I warned Nehru in my debate with him that there would be an aggression against India from the North. He didn't believe me. He said that I was wrong. That the Chinese were not aggressors and that we should speak of peace, brotherhood, neighborliness, and not make any statement about aggression. Yet, within four years, China attacked India's borders.
>
> Several years after that when I was invited to New Delhi by Nehru for a lecture series and I went to call on him, he was already ailing. As I entered his bedroom he said:
>
> "General Romulo, how right you were at Bandung! And how wrong was I."[127]

Despite their eventual rapprochement, however, Romulo and Nehru in Bandung represented two differing perspectives on the ossifying Cold War. For much of the 1930s and 1940s, the Indian leader was an ardent student of Marxism. Even when he became critical of official Communism in the

1950s, criticizing the religious dogmatism of Soviet leaders, he was never an outright anti-Communist and continued to admire certain facets of Soviet socialism such as public education and health care.[128] Like Romulo, however, Nehru held a position that was at the crossroads of multiple ideologies, reflecting a syncretic and flexible political worldview. For Orest Martyshin, the three pillars of Nehru's worldview were Western liberalism, ideas of national liberation, and Marxism.[129] With the exception of Nehru's more sympathetic approach to Marxism, therefore, Romulo and Nehru already had much common ground, even when they were each other's interlocutors.

THE AFTERGLOW OF BANDUNG

UPON RETURNING FROM Bandung, Romulo wrote of anti-Communism as a source of solidarity among many Afro-Asian nations. Summarizing the sentiments of the anti-Communists in the conference, he said:

> We are anti-communist because we know communism endangers our liberties. That our position happens to be that of the United States or of most countries of the West, is only because the ideals of freedom as enshrined in the Magna Carta of England, the Declaration of Independence of the United States, and the Declaration of the Rights of Man by France, are universal.[130]

Once again, Romulo posited the intimate relationship between human rights discourse, anticolonialism, and anti-Communism. His argument was not a Western position but an Asianist one.

In the wake of the Bandung Conference, Romulo continued to articulate his views on the intimate connection between anti-Communism, anti-colonialism, and human rights. And the CCF-funded Solidaridad Publishing House continued to make these writings available to a wide audience. Romulo's dedication to human rights, anti-Communism, and anti-imperialism stemmed from a liberal commitment to freedom. He was a quintessential mid-century liberal, who, because of his liberalism, condemned colonialism. Like Camilo Osias, this liberalism was cultivated through a life immersed in the West. Like Camilo Osias, he believed colonialism contradicted Western liberalism's core tenets.

It was in this regard that Romulo was both an advocate of Western liberal principles and an antagonist of Western colonialism. In *Identity and Change* (1965), Romulo explains:

Colonialism was a contradiction of moral principles in politics; in terms of the 20th century, colonialism was some kind of saurian moment remnant of the [sic] political evolution—a monster that failed to develop with other sub-species of the Western liberal tradition.[131]

If Romulo loved the West, it was not only because he trusted Western democratic governments but also because he believed in the ideals that emanated from the West's political history. These ideals, however, are not exclusive to any country, and Romulo could thus view his liberalism as an integral facet of his Asian identity.

In *The Asian Mystique* (1970), Romulo says that democracy, which he construed in its liberal sense, is not "a national property."[132] It is a concept that can "yield to the necessities of a particular social context" and can therefore be truly Asian. "Asians," he explained, "deplore the readiness of America to claim as pro-American any of their leaders who affirm the democratic way of life." Any Asian duplication of "Western life," as such, would inevitably "be a forgery."[133] In the CCF-funded *Solidarity*, he notes that, like Jose Rizal and other Filipino nationalists of the 19th century, Filipinos need to be "cognizant of our social, political, and economic situation but without any timidity to study, confront, analyze and integrate into national intelligence the best values and aspects of other civilizations."[134]

Romulo saw the future of Asian politics as open-ended, flexible, and provisional. Democracy would allow Asians to build their own unique political systems, which was not the case with Communism. In contrast, "totalitarian communism does not accept any deviation" and its adherents must be "in complete conformity with the official doctrine."[135] Indeed, *pace* the earlier reference to Kolakowski, Communism establishes objective class enemies who are lesser beings according to its tenets.[136] Moreover, as the case of Eastern Europe proves, Communist governance is inflexible, hence the crushing of the 1968 Prague Spring. Unlike the strictures of Communism, Romulo argues, the "liberal imagination" is premised on "the principles of tolerance of differences."[137]

For Romulo, then, it was no surprise that many former colonies at Bandung would be anti-Communist. After all, who better to understand the trappings of a new form of colonialism than those previously colonized? Romulo believed "It is foolish to think that, after fighting the Dutch, the British, the French colonial regimes, Asians will now accept willingly

Communist totalitarianism."[138] Anti-Communism in Asia, then, was not so much pro-Western apologia as a properly Asianist and postcolonial position. It is not—contrary to Espiritu's claim—an imperial script aped by U.S. allies such as Romulo.

The dovetailing of anti-Communism with pan-Asianism is not without precedent. As Pankaj Mishra notes, Japanese intellectuals in the 1930s often saw the Soviet Union and the United States as "Western" threats to China.[139] This critique of Communism—part of the rhetorical arsenal of Chinese and Indian nationalists as well as pan-Islamists—was part of a broader pan-Asian polemic against Western modernity.[140] Romulo, a secularist,[141] did not appropriate many of the spiritual underpinnings of this position (the first chapter of *The Meaning of Bandung* is titled "The Spiritual Offensive," but it barely talks about religion or spirituality). Moreover, though a great admirer of Gandhi as a peaceful anticolonialist, Romulo was not disposed to extolling the values of spirituality over liberalism.[142] Nonetheless, it is important to emphasize that his vision of the Third World as a dual negation of Western colonialism and Soviet Communism has clear Asianist antecedents.

Since the twin bases of Romulo's anti-Communism were liberalism and Asianism, it is unsurprising that he had a strong aversion to anti-Communism's illiberal, American offshoot: McCarthyism. Like colonialism, McCarthyism betrayed the liberal principles Romulo held dear. For McCarthyites, he observed, "everything progressive, because it proposed change, was tagged as Communist subversion."[143] Romulo worried that applied to international relations, McCarthyism would become a tool for neocolonialism. Speaking once more as an anticolonial Asianist, Romulo explained, "The communist danger became an excuse for intervention; the politics of fear became the politics of the West." He added that McCarthyites did not understand Asian nationalism. Under the spell of this false philosophy, the West "failed to be discriminating," and what they did not understand "tended to be propagandized as Communistic."[144]

Even later in his life, Romulo would brag about recognizing McCarthyism as a misguided, temporary fad.[145] Reflecting on his career in the United Nations, he recalls his admiration for UN Secretary General Trygve Lie, who was attacked by the Russians for allegedly being a U.S. lapdog and by McCarthy for allegedly being a Soviet lapdog.[146] "Apparently the American public never appreciated the irony of an international servant who was simultaneously being vilified by Russia and the shameless Senator McCarthy," he quipped.[147] Like the Third World, Lie was caught between First World America and Second World Russia. And like imperialists, Senator Joseph McCarthy did not understand the nuances of provisional alliances that emerged in international affairs.

Romulo's liberal opposition to McCarthyism was strengthened by his international work, and he brought this attitude back to the Philippines. When Romulo assumed the presidency of UP, one of his first acts was to take a strong stand against on-campus McCarthyism, seeking to end the witch hunts against student activists that had occurred during his predecessor's term.[148]

Romulo's refusal to crack down on student radicalism surprised many. The university's Board of Regents had nominated him to serve as president believing that he would combat campus activism and Communism.[149] And yet, even Nemenzo—a staunch critic of Romulo—cannot recall a single crackdown on student radicals.[150] Benjamin Muego Chair of the UP Student Council in the academic year 1984–85, likewise recalls a very permissive president. Muego, who was a champion debater like Romulo in his youth, developed a close fraternal relationship with the university president—a relationship that did not sour even when Muego became involved in radical politics.[151]

In 1966, Muego became a charter member of Senator Lorenzo Tañada's Movement for the Advancement of Nationalism—a broad nationalist coalition that included Sison and his fellow Communist militants (Muego himself was not a member of the Communist Party). And in July 1967, Muego, along with Sison, De Lima, and 13 others went to Communist China upon the invitation of the All China Youth Federation. As a member of MAN (an organization critical of Romulo) and a close ally of Sison's Kabataang Makabayan, Muego became a prominent student activist. Despite this, he remained close to Romulo, something Muego finds striking in retrospect:

> Given his [Romulo's] background (if indeed he was an agent of US imperialism) and given the degree of supervision he had over us, he could have very easily said, "I want you to ease up, because it's hurting my fundraising in the US." He didn't. And he knew what we were doing; the papers would carry our pictures with slogans, and burning effigies and flags.[152]

Whenever Muego saw Romulo, the diplomat would simply give him a "fatherly slap on the back" and joke "make sure you're behaving, okay?" And that was the end of it. In retrospect, Muego is surprised at how much anti-Americanism Romulo tolerated on campus given the amount of fund-raising he was doing in the United States.[153]

Romulo, adept at the art of persuasion, did not need to repress. Muego, like Nemenzo, claims Romulo "co-opted" many progressive intellectuals—most of whom, he confirms, became ghostwriters for the university president. Unlike Nemenzo, however, Muego ascribes this co-optation to more than opportunism. He claims that intellectuals were attracted to Romulo's genuine liberal humanism and his vision of creating a national university.[154] For example, he explains that Romulo's main speechwriter, Petronilo Bn. Daroy, who eventually became a close ally of Sison and the Communist Party, was "enamored" with Romulo because both men were true liberals. Similarly, Muego claims that nationalist intellectuals such as the historian and public intellectual Cesar Majul wrote speeches for Romulo not simply for career advancement, but because they saw in the president someone who valued intellectual work.[155]

Through Romulo, and even more so through Salvador P. Lopez (see next chapter), we see how liberalism, through its permissiveness, paved the way for the emergence of radical politics. One can hardly imagine, for instance, the blossoming of the radical nationalism that would inform the anti-Marcos movement without reference to the University of the Philippines. And had liberals such as Romulo and his protégé and closest associate Lopez not led this university, nationalist dissent on campus would likely have been repressed. Romulo may have betrayed his liberal principles when he worked for Ferdinand Marcos, but Marcos's downfall—one triggered by the work of nationalist militants—was already prefigured by the intellectual climate he helped nourish.[156] Even Romulo's morally bankrupt decision to support Marcos, however, must be understood in the broader context of his commitments as an internationalist and Asianist.

BUILDING THE THIRD WORLD THROUGH A DICTATOR

THE TRAGEDY OF Romulo's career lay in his struggle to operationalize his vision for the Third World while the divisions of the Cold War intensified. As the tensions between the United States and the USSR deepened, it became more difficult to maintain a third way; states had to choose. On the part of the United States, its position of "preserving freedom" in postwar global politics metamorphosed into a paranoid policy of anti-Communist containment, which led it to support violent rightwing regimes such as the apartheid regime in South Africa, the Pinochet regime in Chile (at the expense of the democratically elected Allende), and Diem in Vietnam. Conversely, the Soviet strategy of financing national liberation movements (even as it crushed nationalist dissent in places such as Poland and Hungary) led many to champion the Communist cause. Fidel Castro's Cuba, for instance, which initially attempted to curry favor from both the United States and the Soviet Union, quickly became a beneficiary of Khrushchev's largesse and thus the Soviet Union's ally—a replication of a decision made earlier by Ho Chi Minh's Vietnamese revolution.

Even Nehru's, Sukarno's, Josip Broz Tito's, and Kwame Nkrumah's Non-Aligned Movement (NAM), founded in 1961 in the afterglow of Bandung, could not stay neutral for long. The movement fractured over the position of Castro's Cuba to support the Soviet invasion of Afghanistan. It was for this reason that Romulo, although sympathetic to Nehru and Sukarno, was always critical of the NAM.[157]

How did Romulo navigate the increasing divisions of the Cold War? As a bureaucrat, he could only do so much. Within the divisions of the Cold War, the Marcos regime in the Philippines quickly became one of the United States' most prominent client regimes and a bedrock for containment in Southeast Asia.[158] As someone who tied his fortunes to those of the state, Romulo had to operationalize his ideas under the ambit of a U.S.-backed dictator. The endeavor was ultimately quixotic.

When asked why he thought Romulo supported Marcos even after the declaration of martial law in 1972, Muego speculated it was because Romulo refused to leave the public limelight.[159] Phrased differently, Romulo did not want to end his career as a diplomat. Speaking to the journalist Brillantes in 1984, a dying Romulo explained that he was primarily nonpartisan. "My main preoccupation," he said, "has been foreign relations and not domestic partisan politics. It is with that overriding concern that I have served all the Presidents, from President Quezon to President Marcos."[160] This does not exonerate Romulo. As a member of Marcos's cabinet, he would have been aware of the widespread repression during the dictatorship, especially after the declaration of martial law in 1972. He surely would have known of the persecution of student activists at the university he once led.

It is, thus, unsurprising that Romulo's break with his former protégé and successor as UP President, Lopez, was a result of the former's collaboration with the dictator. In 1980 Lopez called Romulo's life a "tragedy," claiming that Marcos's chief diplomat had turned his back on the principles he stood for, namely, "human rights," "democracy," and "press freedom."[161]

Despite the inadequacy of his defense of simply being a bureaucrat, Romulo's statements nonetheless provide us with a glimpse into his thinking. His priority, above all, was the formation of the Third World. From the beginning of his diplomatic career, Romulo sought to construct a foreign policy grounded on the concerns of Asia and other decolonizing states. He took offense whenever someone cast doubt on his credentials as an Asianist. His famous debate with Nehru in Bandung, for example, was triggered when Nehru questioned the credibility of Asian leaders supporting the U.S.-backed Southeast Asian Treaty Organization (SEATO, founded in Manila in 1954). According to Romulo, Nehru's comments "got me," which led to his extended rebuttal of the Indian leader.[162] Romulo's reputation as "America's boy" was obviously a sensitive spot for him. And in his career after Bandung, he would attempt to distance himself from this image. More importantly, after Bandung he would continue his career as an advocate of the Third World. A post in the Marcos government allowed for this.

In the second of his two posthumously published memoirs, he recalled that Marcos was a "receptive and able ally" in his goal of forwarding an independent Philippine foreign policy. "We agreed that it was time for our former colony to distance itself from the towering shadow of its old patron, the United States."[163] In the 1970s, the Philippines opened diplomatic relations with China and the Soviet Union, "independent of the US position."[164] Romulo, in fact, claimed that Richard Nixon credited him with the idea of opening diplomatic relations between China and the United States in 1972.[165] Though at no point did he retract his criticisms of Communism, Romulo began to espouse a more pragmatic approach to relations with Communist countries.

The shift to a more independent foreign policy reflected Romulo's changing views in the late 1960s and early 1970s. At the time, he no longer believed that Asian nations could be divided between a non-aligned bloc and those, like the Philippines, that supported the United States. In a speech following the conferment of an honorary degree from the University of the East, an unusually humble Romulo reflected on the changes in Philippine foreign policy since Bandung:

In recalling the events of the 1950's, especially with reference to Bandung, I consider it one of the little ironies of our time—and I did not foresee it then when I clashed with Jawaharlal Nehru in the Bandung Conference—that the positions of India and the Philippines would somewhat change, one moving slightly to the other's position. But this would be a story of the 1960's after India was to suffer, as she did, the trauma of military aggression by Communist China, and the Philippines was to begin to realize the full implications of her one-sided policy.[166]

He concluded that both India and the Philippines would likely "move nearer to each other, and to the rest of Asia, moving in the same direction."[167]

What did Romulo's shift in orientation mean in terms of concrete policy? Beyond opening ties with new states, it meant turning the United Nations into a venue for Asian and Third World solidarity. During a trip to India in 1969, Romulo drew attention to India and the Philippines' joint support of policy recommendations from the United Nations Conference on Trade and Development (UNCTAD).[168] At the time, UNCTAD was led by Raul Prebisch, one of the leftwing pioneers of dependency theory in economics, which called for the economic independence of peripheral countries in a world economic system.[169] In India, Romulo rehearsed the ideas of left-wing Third Worldists, echoing UNCTAD's critique of unfair tariff policies that protected First World markets from Third World goods.[170] He also congratulated the Indian government for nationalizing its banks in a bid for economic self-sufficiency.[171]

Moreover, as Marcos's foreign minister, Romulo participated in the formation of the ASEAN, which he viewed as "an Asian Third World grouping."[172] One of ASEAN's primary goals was ensuring "freedom from interference in the internal affairs of the countries of the area by outside Powers."[173] Of course, ASEAN then was spearheaded by brutal domestic dictators such as Marcos and Suharto. But for Romulo, ASEAN was a concretization of his Asianist worldview. As a diplomat wedded to the nation-state, he saw developing world solidarity through the narrow lens of state-to-state relations. His notion of protecting states from external threats allowed him to justify dictatorial threats from within. Ironically, it was Romulo's dedication to Third Worldism that made him a servant to a U.S.-backed dictatorship. Close to his death, he wrote a final justification for his support of Marcos: "If only he would be judged by his conduct of foreign relations, Marcos would go down in history as an excellent leader of the Filipino people.¹⁷⁴" It was almost a plea for forgiveness.

Romulo eventually resigned from the Marcos administration in 1983. The assassination that year of oppositionist Benigno "Ninoy" Aquino triggered a political and economic crisis—one that would lead to the dictator's ouster. The crisis gave Romulo an excuse to leave. After his final appearance at the UN in 1983, an ailing Romulo said he was "heartsick." Speaking from a hospital bed in the United States, the 85-year-old admitted defeat: "For the first time in 37 years, I appeared before the United Nations with my head bowed in shame. . . . It was hard for me to explain. . . . I have done my best building up Philippine prestige abroad. That prestige has been destroyed."¹⁷⁵

That same year, Lopez once again mused about his former mentor whom he claimed to "know better than anyone else." By this time, Lopez had started to regard Romulo "more in sorrow than in anger" and started reflecting on the latter's appetite for power and attention: "When a man says, and says it proudly, that he has served all presidents of the Philippines from Quezon to Marcos, one must ask: Is that supposed to be a cause for pride?" Not so, Lopez added, "because what does that say of him? That he has no principles of his own? That he has been all things to all men?" Carlos P. Romulo, he concluded, was "the quintessential man of opportunity—not necessarily in the derogatory sense, but in the sense that when an occasion presents itself, it has to be grabbed; he feels he has to take it."¹⁷⁶

CONCLUSION

The broad, democratic Left shies away from anti-Communism by virtue of the position's intimate association with reaction. Anti-anti-Communism—the equation of all criticisms of Leninism with fascism¹⁷⁷—has prevented a progressive reinterpretation of the phenomenon, thus allowing the terms of the discourse to be dictated by the modern-day heirs of McCarthy on the Right. Indeed, anti-Communism has a dark history, particularly in Southeast Asia.¹⁷⁸ But, as with most ideological constellations, anti-Communism does not come in one strain. As I outlined earlier, opposition to Leninism began on the Left. A committed socialist like Blum, for instance, believed Bolsheviks had betrayed their socialist cause.

Romulo was not a man of the Left. Nonetheless, his views mirrored those of liberal and socialist anti-Communists—views that the statesman articulated in the language of Asian solidarity. That he was an anti-Communist is not as scandalous as a contemporary progressive might assume. Removed from the paranoia and propaganda of the Cold War, elements of Romulo's anti-Communism would not be controversial in the context of the contemporary democratic Left. In the Philippines, for instance, progressive scholars publishing in progressive journals have replicated his criticisms of Communism's inflexibility and its disdain for democratic structures such as free elections.[179]

Romulo's oeuvre, however, goes beyond merely proving that anti-Communism can transcend its fascist associations. In this chapter, I hope to have shown that liberal anti-Communism was essential to the birth of Third Worldism and the solidarities it produced. It is, thus, his unique synthesis of liberal antitotalitarianism and Asianism that makes Romulo an important figure in global intellectual history.

That Romulo betrayed his ideals when he became a servant of the Marcos dictatorship does not negate the relevance of his ideas. It did mean, however, that his reputation as a liberal would forever be questioned. Romulo would be unable to carry the mantle of liberalism into the charged years of the 1970s. This task would fall into the hands of his former employee, ghostwriter, and protégé, Salvador P. Lopez.

Chapter 4
Salvador P. Lopez and the Space of Liberty

In 1965, the Marxist literary critic Petronilo Bn. Daroy proclaimed the decline of Philippine liberalism. "The most influential persuasion in the national culture now," he explained, "is not liberal but Leftist and this is now being expressed by politicians, students, the working classes. In short, by individuals other than the members of the liberal intelligentsia."[1] The situation was surprising for Daroy, for he knew how closely liberalism and nationalism were linked in the immediate postwar period. Citing the economic nationalism of esteemed Senator Claro M. Recto, he explained that the Filipino intellectual once used liberalism to "defend unorthodox ideas" even "when it was politically dangerous."[2]

But something happened starting in the 1950s. As the Filipino liberal became "more abstract in his defense of freedom, he was increasingly forced to abandon his criticalness to the status quo." His intellectual skills were "readily submitted to the rigid terms of Cold War politics."[3] Thus, "the Filipino liberal intellectual today is bourgeois, and the national bourgeoisie is anti-intellectual."[4]

The crisis of liberalism merely exposed what liberalism always was: elitist. Even in its heyday, Daroy avers, it was never "egalitarian or socialistic."

With hindsight, it was clear to him that liberalism's energy was merely "directed at the achieved canons of Filipino writers and artists, and only timidly impinged upon political and social issues."[5]

Daroy's essay is polemical and short on exposition. Reading between the lines, however, one may guess that he was bemoaning liberalism's perceived detachment from emerging socialist movements in the countryside. As we noted in the introduction, the Huk Rebellion polarized the intellectual, ilustrado class. Some sided with the Huks and viewed them as heir of the "unfinished revolution," while others, mostly liberals like Carlos P. Romulo, rejected Communist-inspired violence. Though their anti-Communism was grounded on anti-authoritarian liberalism and not McCarthyism, it nevertheless alienated them from class-based politics.

In Chapter 2, we saw how liberalism failed to create any form of welfare society that would have shielded it from more radical, socialist politics from below. Salvador Araneta had a roadmap to create a more equal country, but liberalism never absorbed his progressive ideas. Daroy, therefore, had a point: liberalism had done nothing to address the country's poverty, and a "Left" was necessary to revitalize intellectual discourse.

Yet Daroy's Manichean view of liberal versus leftist is belied by his own biography. As he was writing his critique of liberals, Daroy was working as the primary ghostwriter for the most prominent of the anti-Communist liberals he publicly derided: Carlos P. Romulo.[6] In doing this, he was not simply being an intellectual mercenary. Romulo hired Daroy because he was dazzled by the young critic's grasp of liberal literature and philosophy. Because of their discussions on liberalism, the two forged a genuine intellectual connection.[7] Daroy was on very good terms with the university's top liberals and would even stay on to also write speeches for Romulo's successor as UP President, Salvador P. Lopez.[8] The young critic believed that Lopez was "our first critical intelligence to have demanded that literature be committed, and to insist that art keeps commerce with life."[9]

Daroy's life was squarely situated in the liberal institutions of the University of the Philippines; he was employed by its presidents and he wrote for its publications. His own radicalization occurred within the auspices of this liberal space—a trajectory similar to many of his generation's leading Marxists. Like Daroy, Jose Maria Sison, the founding chairman of the Communist Party of the Philippines, studied at UP's English Department, where his Marxist consciousness "grew on the democratic kernel of liberal philosophy."¹⁰ Moreover, in his early activist years in the late 1950s, Sison was surrounded by liberals, who preferred Arthur Koestler and Milovan Djilas to Marx. One of his first advocacies was to fight for academic freedom amid incursions from government McCarthyites, working under the Committee on Un-Filipino Activities (CUFA).[11]

The critique of liberalism was birthed within it. This should be unsurprising, as liberalism yearns to correct itself and the society it operates in. It opens up new political possibilities, which can eclipse it in the short-run, without foreclosing its return in a different form. Because it reinvents itself, it has no terminus, no concrete goal like the withering of the state or the purification of the *volk*. Liberalism, as such, is not simply a political platform but also a political method.

As modus vivendi, liberalism concerns itself with creating and recreating democratic space—the very space that constitutes its possibility to begin with. This chapter explores this space of democratic liberty. It asks how this space is created, seeks its limits, and locates what sustains it. It does so through examining the late career of Salvador P. Lopez, who, as noted, was Romulo's successor and UP President. As UP president, "SP," as he was known to friends and admirers, became the leader of a liberal laboratory. The secular state university is an analogue for liberal society, and liberal education, as its name implies, is the pedagogic articulation of the liberal method.

SP's years as UP president from 1969 to 1975 were some of the most turbulent years in 20th-century Philippine history. It encompassed the founding of the Maoist Communist Party of the Philippines (CPP) in 1968, which led to the events of 1970's "first quarter storm"—a series of protests that became the high-water mark of the student movement against the dictatorship of Ferdinand Marcos.

The Maoists benefited from the surge of revolutionary energy after the Sino-Soviet split of 1969. Anti-Communists could no longer pass Marxism off as a tired creed of a sclerotic and authoritarian Soviet Union, since Maoism was the new language of youth rebellion. In response, Marcos magnified this "threat" to bolster his own form of authoritarian project, declaring martial law in 1972 and perpetuating himself in power.[12] This solidification of state "fascism" only reinforced the *raison d'être* of Maoism as an ideology that resisted "fascism." If Eric Hobsbawm described the 20th century as an "age of extremes," which pitted Communism on the left and fascism on the right,[13] the 1970s saw the century's tensions distilled for the Philippines.

Trying times for any liberal. Even more so for one who had two clashing constituencies. As UP President, SP led a key state institution, which made him directly accountable to the dictatorship. But the same position made him the steward of the very activists Marcos's martial law tried to "discipline." Unlike his predecessor Romulo, SP could not afford to simply distance himself from the student activists. Police brutality had forced him to categorically defend civil liberties, even as he sought to placate authoritarian power.

Confronting the student radicalism of the late 1960s/early 1970s (the radicalism of the global "68 generation") placed SP in a similar position to the Western liberals of his generation—a generation whose youthful political energies were expended in two World Wars and not domestic protest. Some of these liberals regarded the youthful militancy of the period with distaste. Raymond Aron, the leading French liberal of the time, famously dismissed the 1968 protests and general strike in France as a "psychodrama."[14] In Marcos-era Philippines, however, SP saw in the emergent "New Left" a brand new nationalism and a social involvement that tackled issues of political freedom and class inequality. He could respect these ideals. As a liberal, however, he distanced himself from the excesses of the ascendant Maoism.

In examining the period in SP's life as UP President, we are able to reflect on liberalism under siege. Liberalism at this point no longer held the prestige it did in decades past, but it remained open and capacious in the hands of relics who continued to practice it. As a mediating philosophy, liberalism has no permanent enemies or allies. Its bureaucratic, managerial ethos thus becomes a form of risk-taking in times of crisis. For pitting extremes against each other is a dangerous and risky endeavor, and it involves the risk of hypocrisy. If liberalism has any radicalism, it is its willingness to sacrifice its purity.

Unlike previous chapters, this final one is largely propelled by narrative, and my preferred method is biography rather than exegesis. For it is only in the life and actions of the liberal that we see liberalism as a method and as ethics.

AGAINST DILETTANTISM

SALVADOR PONCE LOPEZ was born on 27 May 1911 in Currimao, Ilocos Norte. Unlike the other intellectuals in this book, he was educated locally, obtaining a Bachelor's degree in Philosophy in 1931 and a Master of Arts in

English Literature in 1933. Despite this, his education remained Anglophile. His high school English teachers in Manila and Laoag were American. At the University of the Philippines, he took Elizabethan, Romantic, and Victorian literature under the famed Australian critic Tom Inglis Moore.[15] And he learned American literature under a young Carlos P. Romulo, who had just returned from Columbia.[16]

Upon completing his studies, SP initially wanted to pursue a career in teaching. After reading his work in the *Philippine Collegian*, however, Romulo, then editor of the *Philippines Herald*, hired SP as a columnist and eventually an editor.[17] The relationship with Romulo would last for decades, as SP would follow his mentor from journalism to the diplomatic community and, eventually, back to the academe. It would become, as SP said in the 1980s, "a 30-year romance."[18]

In 1940, SP won the Commonwealth Literary prize for his collection of essays *Literature and Society*, where he advocated for literature that interprets "the experience of the working class in a world that has been rendered doubly dynamic by its struggles."[19] The book established his place as one of the country's pre-eminent literary critics, whose relevance continues to be discussed by present-day Filipino critics.[20]

After the war—which saw him as a captain in the Philippine army, a POW, and eventually a guerrilla officer—SP became a diplomat, serving in multiple capacities as ambassador, representative to the United Nations, and foreign secretary. In his diplomatic work, he became a key advocate of human rights from the Third World, serving as the Chairman of the Commission on Human Rights. According to historian Roland Burke, in 1965, John Humphrey, the primary drafter of the Universal Declaration of Human Rights, described SP as "the best ever Chairman of the Commission of Human Rights ahead of such eminent figures as Charles Malik and Eleanor Roosevelt."[21]

SP saw himself as "ambidextrous," maintaining a "two-pronged interest" in both "the social sciences and the humanities."[22] Yet despite his interest in diplomacy and current events, he was grounded in the classics. His three favorite books were Plato's *Dialogues*, Francis Bacon's *Essays*, and the collected poems of John Keats.[23]

SP's career mirrored that of the similarly "ambidextrous" Romulo: after decades of working as a diplomat, he returned to the Philippines in 1969 to replace the latter as President of UP. He was, in many ways, Romulo's ideal replacement: he was a seasoned diplomat, capable of balancing interests and playing sides off each other with finesse. He was also a man known for pursuing multiple intellectual pursuits, from literature to law to global politics—an intellectual worthy of leading the country's premier educational institution.

In other ways, however, he was Romulo's opposite. While Romulo was known for his sense of humor, friends described SP as serious and reserved. His second wife, Adelaida, recalls him as having an "executive" bearing, formal and perennially obsessed with protocol.[24] For his close friend, novelist F. Sionil Jose, SP's obsession with protocol made him a "stuffed shirt."[25] Moreover, while the voluble Romulo was known to regale students and friends with stories about himself, SP evinced an inward-looking humility. "He was modest to the point of being self-deprecatory, and his assessment of the worth of his contemporaries extended to his own valuation of himself and his works," recalls Daroy. "To the end, SP Lopez never realized the actual worth or importance of his writings."[26]

The quintessential image of SP as UP President is that of a broad shouldered, bald man, in an office polo barong, speaking before a crowd of rallying students. It is an apt image, for it depicts his resolve amid a political storm.

SP'S MID-CENTURY LIBERALISM

TO UNDERSTAND THE liberal script that SP adhered to in the 1970s, we need to return to his philosophical origins. Whenever he explained his politics in philosophical terms, he did so with reference to his very early liberal writings, constantly affirming that he was "the same old liberal" who wrote *Literature and Society*. The default script of his politics was formed in the 1930s, during the time he wrote the essays for his classic tome. Therefore, although his admirers on the left remember him for what he did in the 1970s, he remained a figure of an earlier era. SP was not only a political intermediary, negotiating the tensions between a dictatorship and a budding radical movement. He was also a generational intermediary, introducing the liberalism of his generation to a generation of radicalized youth. It was the liberalism of Osias, Araneta, and Romulo.

Literature and Society, an impressionistic series of essays covering multiple topics is often misread, its liberal thesis easily neglected. Ricaredo Demetillo, for example, argues that SP's "ontological foundation is that of the proletarian school derived from Marx."[27] Marxist critic E. San Juan Jr., on the other hand, lumps SP with Teodoro Agoncillo and Renato Constantino (the godfathers of the Diliman Consensus), and claims that he was part of a movement to "challenge U.S. hegemonic authority" amid a "global crisis of capitalism" and "intense peasant dissidence."[28]

But as Rafael Acuña argues, "Lopez's intellectual influence do [sic] not lie primarily with Marx, but with several intellectuals ranging from Marx to Arnold to Nietzsche, and more important, to American leftists who advocated proletarian literature that did not narrowly disallow creativity nor singularly insist on propaganda."[29] Indeed, as SP himself explained, the heroes of his generation at the time he wrote *Literature and Society* "were people like John Steinbeck (*The Grapes of Wrath*), André Malraux (*Man's Fate*), and Hemingway (*For Whom the Bell Tolls*)."[30]

While Acuña's analysis best accounts for the textured and, indeed, contradictory aspects of SP's work, it still does not place SP within the broader development of 20th-century Philippine nationalism. Resil Mojares locates him within the same strain of civic nationalism as Camilo Osias. Like Osias, SP too was a nationalist internationalist who, Mojares explains, "warned against chauvinism and conservatism." And, despite SP and his cohort's "dalliance with Marxism," they remained "quite comfortable in their relationship with the state."[31] His presidency of the state's premier educational institution was simply a manifestation of his erstwhile political disposition: critical yet comfortable with state power.

SP's intellectual heritage as an heir to the long Philippine liberal tradition is clear. His first major work, for instance, was a Master's dissertation on the ideas of the grandfather of Philippine civic liberalism, T.H. Pardo de Tavera,[32] and Pardo's influence on SP's view of Philippine history is palpable. In the introduction, we saw how Pardo was the first to view Philippine history as a movement from Spanish-era conservatism to a rekindling of liberal hope during the American period. It is the same view that SP adopts in *Literature and Society* when he claims that his generation was the first to be "reared in the shadow of American democracy," thereby having no experience of Spanish "misrule" and "oppression." When his cohort was "old enough to understand, the great principles of individual freedom, constitutional rights and democratic government had become household words."[33]

But SP's understanding of liberty is not premised simply on the creation of a legal system that guarantees basic protections, what Michael Sandel refers to as the "procedural" version of American liberalism. In contrast to procedural thinking, Sandel offers a republican version of liberty that begins with Aristotle and percolates into the Jeffersonian agrarian tradition. In this tradition, "liberty is understood as a consequence of self-government," and citizens are free because "they are members of a political community that controls its own fate," participants "in the decisions that govern its affairs." In this active vision of liberty, "we are free only insofar as we exercise our capacity to deliberate about the common good, and participate in the public life of a free city or a republic."[34]

SP understood his country's independence in these terms, arguing that how or when the Philippines would be legally independent was less important than the ongoing, civic project of "keeping that independence once achieved."[35] Like Sandel's civic republicanism, his vision also had an Aristotelian basis. His defense of socially relevant literature did not stem from Marxism, but from the Aristotelian belief that "man is a 'political animal,' whatever else he may be."[36] Incorrectly, Demetillo criticized this quote as reducing human beings to doing politics, while neglecting their affective dimensions.[37] Yet this critique ignores that the Aristotelian definition of "political" was broad, since the philosopher famously believed that ethics is merely a subdivision of politics. Politics defines ethics insofar as it is the act of engaged living within a polis. SP's work was therefore an injunction to exchange the pieties of metaphysics for the realities of politics.

Artistic production cannot be divorced from this ethics because "artistic freedom" is "not a thing apart but a mere outgrowth of political liberty in general."[38] In other words, SP was not a literary dictator, who ordered writers to be politically relevant. He was a critic who argued that no artist can escape the inherently political nature of creation; they are part of an ongoing process of exercising political freedom, of constituting the space of liberty.

This is, of course, an ambiguous process and requires not only the articulation of political positions but also their mediation. Any democratic space, artistic or intellectual, requires the renewal of its political liberty as new conflicts emerge. The civic version of liberty always entails conflict, and it is in these conflicts that we see liberalism as modus vivendi. SP's time at UP allowed him to continually reconstitute the university as a space of ongoing liberty. When he could no longer do this, he burnt his bridges.

THE PROBLEMS OF THE WORLD FOR THE PROBLEMS OF THE COUNTRY

WHEN SP BECAME President of UP, he was returning from an illustrious diplomatic career, and the new job may have seemed like a demotion. For much of the late 1960s, he had occupied himself with helping craft the human rights architecture of the United Nations. In particular, he successfully led a group of Third World diplomats who argued for the right of citizens from any state to petition the UN Commission on Human Rights concerning human rights violations in their countries.[39] By 1968, he was concurrently UN Representative and Ambassador to Washington. If he were to return to the Philippines, he probably expected to resume his old post as Secretary of Foreign Affairs. Yet his fate, as always, would be determined by Carlos P. Romulo. In 1983, SP narrated:

> General Romulo had previously come to Washington twice to talk me into succeeding him at the UP. "But why," I asked the General, "should I give up the two highest positions in our diplomatic service, to serve in a hot spot like the UP?" As UP President, Romulo was no longer able to enter his office. The rebellious students barred his way. So since he couldn't persuade me, he requested President Marcos to call me on the phone, and practically order me to come home. Of course, CPR at the time had another thing in mind. He wanted to preempt me at Padre Faura [the location of the Department of Foreign Affairs], because (Narciso) Ramos was on his way out, and I was being groomed to succeed Ramos. And CPR had nowhere else to go from UP except Foreign Affairs! How cunning! What a perfectly typical Romulo operation! He got me to go to Diliman so that he could go to Padre Faura. Perfect! Well, if CPR thought he had put me where he was sure I would utterly fail, in the face of a violent student revolution, I proved him wrong.[40]

At a testimonial dinner for his investiture as UP President in 1969 (almost a year after taking his oath of office), SP told the same story more diplomatically. "When I accepted the position of President of the UP in December last year," he told guests, "my fellow ambassadors in The U.N. and in Washington said that I should have my head examined." Seeing how much student unrest there had been in the university, he thought his colleagues might have been right and he was almost "willing to believe that General Romulo, my distinguished predecessor, had deceived me when he assured me in New York last November that being President of the UP was the best job he ever had, better than being Ambassador or Sec of Foreign Affairs, two positions which both of us have held."[41] But SP was a nationalist, and returning to the Philippines was inevitable.

This return was the theme of his inaugural speech. In the UN, SP confronted issues like "the liquidation of colonialism, the economic development of backward nations, war and peace." These issues, however, were remote compared to those faced by a UP administrator, who had to deal with "the raw material of the nation's life." Upon taking his oath, he noted that he "agreed to exchange the problems of the world for the problems of campus." "Time will tell," he concluded, "whether this will have been, for the nation at least, a fair or advantageous exchange."[42]

The "raw material of the nation's life" was something SP wished to experience daily. Because he had been away from the university since 1941, his immediate task was keeping abreast of student and faculty life. In his first address to the faculty, he told them of his aim to "bridge the gulf of time by intensive study and discussion of the mission, facilities and resources of the University." "I shall be most persevering," he added, "and I must ask all of you, who are all my seniors, to be patient with me." He decided to be the first UP President to live on campus to expose himself to "all the winds that blow on campus."[43]

SP also returned to the classroom, which was not commonly done by previous presidents. In his first semester, he taught a seminar on the United Nations for three hours every Saturday, absenting himself only once in the semester. In his second semester, he taught another class on the United Nations, but added a new class "devoted to some of the principal fields of modern literature, world literature."[44] After 30 years away from teaching, he wanted to be "as close as possible" "to what the main business of the University really is, mainly teaching." "The University," he noted, "is a place of learning and teaching and therefore the President of the University must know something about the business of learning and teaching."[45]

The everyday life of the university, however, was not something SP would find in the classroom, but in the student militancy outside it. Less than a week after taking his oath, "[a] group of students, some members of the faculty, and of the non-academic personnel" came to him with a list of 77 demands, claiming that they would go on strike if their demands were not met.[46]

The situation on campus was near boiling point, forcing SP to forego a trip to the United States in which he planned to bid farewell to his old office staff.[47] Though he quibbled with specific demands, he accepted the main principles behind them, which he summarized into three general ideas:

> The first is that the University needs to diffuse its benefits so that true equality is achieved and that it should share its burden of government and decision-making with elements that constitute it: the students, the faculty, and the non-academic personnel. The second is that the University must strive to make itself more relevant to the needs of the national society. The third is that the nation—the government and the people—must accept the obligations of higher education in the country, that is, that the University must enjoy greater autonomy and must be supported by the people in order to give it more independence of criterion in accepting and using aid from external sources and in its exchange programs.[48]

Student radicals were cynical about SP's willingness to negotiate. After his first meeting with the student council, three Maoist-aligned student councilors, (including the council chairman Fernando Barican) wrote a letter to the editor of UP's student paper, *The Philippine Collegian*, claiming that they "were greatly disappointed" by SP's statements during their luncheon. "President Lopez," they explained, "told the Council members and the *Collegian* staffers present that he would first study 'slowly' the demands of the students because he does not know anything about the university." They also disagreed with his "old fashioned concept of the true mission of a university," when he claimed that his administration would concentrate on "academic excellence and scholarship," while "leaving out the equally significant task of encouraging student leadership and activism."[49]

SP, however, was more open than the student council assumed. On 4 February, *The Collegian* reported that, after the student council distilled their demands into 18 key issues, SP granted most of them and "pledged to follow up on the rest."[50] For most of February 1969, SP issued a flurry of executive orders, mostly promoting on-campus democracy. His first executive order as president gave greater autonomy to student organizations, allowing them to manage their own funds, and rescinding "all existing orders effecting suspension or withdrawal of recognition to student organizations."[51] He also opened official records for consultation by the University of the Philippines constituency,[52] prohibited any form of reprisal against rallying students,[53] established freedom parks in all campuses,[54] and formed a preparatory committee for a re-organization of the university that would enable more transparency and representation.[55]

If Romulo maintained a hands-off policy towards student activism, SP seemed more inclined to enable it. The new president obviously admired the students who had protested before him. Instead of causing disillusionment, the crises made him "fall in love with the University." At the tail end of his first year, SP would claim:

> Today, nine or ten student demonstrations later—plus one case in the Supreme Court—I am able to affirm that being UP President may not be the best, most pleasant or comfortable job I have ever had, but it is certainly the most difficult, the most challenging, the most demanding job I have ever had. In a very real sense, therefore, it is also the most satisfying.[56]

What was it about student activism that appealed to SP? It was not the allure of Communist anti-imperialism and class struggle, since he was not a fellow traveler. In the United Nations, he had continued Romulo's critique of the "new imperialism" of the Communist bloc (see previous chapter), charting, according to Burke, a "skillful course that combined anti-Soviet and anticolonial elements."[57]

SP valued both the individual rights promoted by the "free world" and the economic and social rights associated with Communism. "But, where a choice must be made as regards importance and priority," he believed that Filipinos "should not hesitate to stand on the side of individual rights and the freedom of mind."[58] With these freedoms, he added, "it is possible for a people eventually to win also the rewards of social security and economic abundance." However, when "economic and social security is made possible only through a system of dictatorial regimentation, the respect for individual liberties cannot subsequently be accorded by the state without risking the collapse of the system itself."[59] Dictatorship, for any ends, was its own poison. Thus, though not as passionate an anti-Communist as Romulo, SP knew his side in the Cold War.

Still, as UP President, he saw beyond (or perhaps deliberately ignored) the incipient Maoism on campus. His capacious liberalism also wanted these alternatives articulated within the open space he was seeking to build. In the activists, he saw a studentry deeply involved in national life and was glad that students responded to a social role outside campus.

It was not a position he always held. In the 1950s, he thought universities had "no other function than the improvement of the mind." By 1969, however, he was "prepared to admit that" he had made "too narrow a claim for the University in modern times." The university, he now believed, was not just a place for professional training and intellectual training, but one with a duty to "train men and women who will become useful members of society and leaders in the movement for national growth and development." The University of the Philippines had "the first responsibility to make itself relevant at all times to the principal concerns of the nation."[60] And if the ideas of national relevance needed testing, the university would serve "as laboratory for the rapid transformation of society so that the freedom and happiness of our people may be effectively enhanced. This commitment, SP believed, was UP's "solemn contract with the Filipino nation."[61] In explicitly foregrounding an analogous relation between polity and university, SP would place a high burden on himself. He was not meant to simply educate young men and women—he was now tasked to create for them a democratic space.

SP regarded the student demonstrations from this beneficent vista. He admired the students not so much for their ideological commitment as for their activism that evidenced "a growing sense of responsibility of the youth and their insistence that, instead of merely being passively integrated into a condition of society they did not create, they should have a voice in the shaping of social realities."[62] SP was willing to listen and he admired the students' active articulation of liberty.

THE FIRST QUARTER STORM

SP'S LOYALTY TO free speech and expression would be on full on display during the events now known as the "First Quarter Storm" of 1970. The year opened with SP being picketed by students who had hitherto admired his liberal policies. On 7 January, the University Student Council, the Arts and Sciences Council, and members of the Maoist Samahang Demokratiko ng Kabataan (SDK or Union of Democratic Youth) protested outside his office in Quezon Hall. They criticized him, first, for allegedly not signing a faculty statement against police brutality; second, for praising ground rules on student mobilizations in the City of Manila that purportedly favored the police; third, for issuing guidelines on mobilizations that made participation in rallies voluntary;[63] and fourth, for issuing a circular that required students to inform the Dean of Student Affairs before undertaking protest actions.⁶⁴ Once again, the students were insisting that the sympathetic SP be completely on their side.

SP's problems within the university, however, would be overrun by events outside campus, and he would once again find a way to stand by his students. On 26 January, protestors mobilized outside the Philippine legislature as Marcos delivered his state of the nation address. The country was plunging into a deeper crisis, and, as veteran journalist Nick Joaquin remembers: "No weatherman could have predicted the storm's advent, and yet it was inevitable."⁶⁵ Debt and inflation triggered an economic crisis, anti-American sentiment intensified as the Marcos government supported U.S. bases and the war in Vietnam, and the increasing militarization of the country caused an opposition senator to warn of the emergence of a "garrison state."⁶⁶ When Marcos gave his address, these tensions were heightened by rumors that the president would rig a constitutional convention in 1971, allowing him to run for a third term.

The main student groups in the rally were the moderate National Union of Students of the Philippines (NUSP) and the Maoist fronts Kabataang Makabayan (Nationalist Youth) and SDK. The NUSP was composed mostly of students from elite Catholic schools like the Jesuit Ateneo de Manila University, while many of the radicals were from UP. The highpoint of the mobilization occurred when Marcos stepped out of the Congress building where the protesters displayed "a cardboard coffin representing the death of democracy at the hands of the goonstabulary in the last elections; a cardboard crocodile, painted green, symbolizing congressmen greedy for allowance; a paper effigy of Marcos."⁶⁷ As Marcos walked out, the protestors set the effigy on fire and shoved the coffin towards him. The police, according to journalist Jose F. Lacaba, reacted violently and "gave chase to anything that moved, clubbed anyone who resisted, and hauled off those they caught up with."⁶⁸ After the initial scuffle, a two-hour battle between the police and the activists ensued, with policemen mercilessly clubbing protestors, most especially, members of the KM.⁶⁹ By the end of the day, Lacaba had found over thirty bloodied activists in the nearest hospital.⁷⁰

The day after the protest, SP was conferred an honorary degree by Centro Escolar University. In his acceptance speech, he described the events as a "grave portent for the future of our nation." He then presided over a faculty meeting on 28 January, and they resolved to "take a definite stand by adopting a resolution" that denounced "police brutalities committed against the students who demonstrated in front of Congress on January 26."[71] They also agreed that faculty would be free to join rallies and that they would contribute at least one percent of their month's salary to the establishment of a Legal Defense Fund for students. Most significantly, they resolved to stage a peaceful rally on the next day in front of the presidential palace.[72]

When they held the rally, SP led a delegation of 16 faculty and 4 students for a consultation with Marcos that lasted more than two hours.[73] There are differing accounts of what happened during the consultation. SP complained that press reports had "distorted" the meeting, depicting an "angry President berating the faculty of his Alma Mater for daring to present him with a Declaration on a matter of national concern."[74] Indeed, press coverage had been unsympathetic. Journalist and fictionist Kerima Polotan, writing for the *Philippines Free Press*, reported that SP was "roundly scolded by Mr. Marcos in the Palace." SP, she argued, used the faculty march as a way to "throw a smokescreen over his own not-so-little troubles at the U.P.," which included the continued protests against the administration and complaints about a raise in his pay (something he claimed occurred without his intervention). The protest in the presidential palace was nothing more than political theater, a way for him to get "snapped doing something momentous, his broad face turned symbolically somewhere, that mouth open, his large hands spread." This development was unsurprising for Polotan, since SP had "been taught all the tricks of success by a master, the great CPR [Carlos P. Romulo] himself, whose ashtrays he probably fetched in his *Herald* and UN days."[75] Like his mentor, SP was a hypocritical diplomat, and Polotan portrayed the meeting with Marcos cynically:

> He [SP] was against whoever had just turned his back, and was for whoever faced him at the moment, and when he walked into Mr. Marcos who asked, first, if the resolution was the best the U.P., known for its proficiency in English, could muster ("This reads like a student resolution!"); second, if in condemning police brutality, Lopez had all the facts?; and third, in "holding the Administration responsible for the pattern of repression and violation of rights," wasn't Lopez making "a general gunshot accusation"?
>
> If Lopez had been sincerely convinced about the justice of his cause, he would have stayed firm, wouldn't he, now, but having patently espoused the students' cause out of convenience, Lopez, again out of convenience, began to backtrack. He apologized to Marcos for wording the resolution and said

it was not possible to "include all the specific issues"; moreover, it was not a resolution of accusation, Lopez now said, but a "declaration of concern."[76]

Polotan was echoing the sentiment of many radical students who wanted SP to categorically take their side. Quoting one of the student leaders, she claimed that SP was like a Pontius Pilate who had washed his hands of student concerns once he was in front of Marcos. There was, for Polotan, nothing at stake for him since he was "a man who had worked all his life" and who looked "forward only to retirement and a regular paycheck in the sunset of his life."[77]

In SP's account, there is no mention of an apology or backtracking. Instead, he recalled Dean Cesar Majul defending the faculty position by quoting "Rizal's statement that when a house is in disorder, the master of the house can be held responsible and therefore accountable."[78] He also claimed that he defended the editors of UP's official paper, *The Philippine Collegian*, against accusations of fomenting subversion after it published a manifesto of the newly-formed Maoist Communist Party.[79] "Far from being a meeting between an angry and intolerant President and a group of tongue-tied and intimidated professors," he explained, "the meeting was a full, frank and cordial exchange of ideas and opinions."[80] Marcos, in turn, did not mention SP in his diary entry about the meeting. In his account, most of the conversation occurred between him and the deans.[81] Marcos told his interlocutors that he was "disappointed" with his alma mater and countered that UP had become "the spawning ground of communism and that the manifesto was full of ambiguous generalities that had a familiar ring to them."[82] There is no mention of an apology from SP.[83]

Regardless of which account we accept, however, the faculty protest was a turning point in UP's politics, presaging the solidarity between liberal professors and leftwing students during a time of upheaval. Such was clear to SP:

> Although the sentiment in favor of holding the faculty demonstration was both spontaneous and enthusiastic, there has been no lack of criticism since then from those who seem to feel that the professors, by taking to the streets had betrayed the academe. I feel exactly the contrary. For the first time in its history, the U.P. is developing the sense of being a single, indivisible community of scholars composed of professors and students who are

involved in each other as well as together in the problems of the society and the nation. The U.P. will never be the same after the faculty march of January 29, 1970.[84]

The statement was portentous.

The biggest student protest of SP's tenure was the fabled "Diliman Commune," from 1 to 9 February 1972. Jeepney drivers were then protesting the rising cost fuel, and they were joined by students (led by the SDK), who barricaded the UP campus, disrupting classes and shutting down many university operations. On the first day, a mathematics professor, with a reputation for being anti-activist, shot into the crowd, after protestors pelted his car with Molotov cocktails. He hit a student, Pastor Medina, who died four days after. The shooting gave fifty students an excuse to storm into SP's office and shout invectives at him. More crucially, it also prompted police authorities to enter the university.[85]

When the police tried to enter again on 2 February, it was SP himself who attempted to arrange their withdrawal, asking the Chief of the Quezon City Police to let university administrators conduct negotiations themselves. The Chief refused, gave SP five minutes to go back to the student line, and broke through the protestors. Hundreds of students retreated to the College of Arts and Sciences, which they barricaded with chairs, tables, benches, bulletin boards, etc.[86] On 3 February, a community meeting gathered by SP decided to continue the commune in opposition to the campus incursions. But before the meeting could finish, the police entered university grounds again.[87]

Remembering the events ten years after, SP recalls that he phoned Marcos the following day, "to warn that a repetition of the police invasion of the university could result in the loss of many lives and the destruction of the university." He "asked that the police be kept out of campus" and that he "be given time to bring about the removal of barricades by peaceful means." Marcos replied that he would give those orders provided that SP dismantle the barricades as soon as possible. He would hold SP accountable for any on-campus violence.[88]

The events on 4–9 February were comparatively peaceful, consisting of teach-ins and a few tense moments, when students feared further incursions.[89] But it was difficult for SP, who had promised Marcos to end the commune quickly. SP describes the events better than I can:

> During that whole week, I maintained close contact with the student leaders. The fact that I lived on campus, at the Executive House, proved to be a great advantage. I was a member of the beleaguered community of students and professors. I was on their side of the barricades. We sent the militants food as they kept vigil at their posts and I visited them at night. But they demurred when I asked them to dismantle the barricades at a stipulated time.
>
> Time was fast running out on me. On the night of February eight I slipped out of the dampus [sic] and took a room at the Sulo Hotel nearby. Then I dispatched an urgent letter to the student leaders in which I said: "Tomorrow is the deadline set by the authorities to bring down the barricades. If the barricades are still standing by daybreak, the police will break through in full force. Since I am not prepared to accept responsibility for the bloodshed and destruction that could ensure, I will resign as President of the University this night, if you ignore my demand."
>
> At one hour past midnight the word came: the barricades would be removed at daybreak.[90]

A catastrophe was averted, thanks to SP's Solomonic effort.

THE SAME LIBERAL

THE DILIMAN COMMUNE again proved that SP would do his best to protect his students. But this still did not mean they thought he was on their side. In fact, it did not seem like he was on anyone's side. His allegiances were shifting, and his politics seemed vague to a generation accustomed to certainty. There was a simple reason why many students, faculty, and critical reporters could not place SP: he was a mid-century liberal. He was not of the era of ideological certainty.

"It seems I am [a] problem," he explained in a speech to one of the university fraternities, "because I cannot be categorized." The kinder critics, he added, claimed that he was "too much of a diplomat to be truly involved and genuinely committed," while others simply called him "an equivocator and an opportunist."[91] SP understood well the contradictory perceptions of his constituencies, noting:

> The evidence of my words and actions—past as well as contemporary—only adds to the confusion. I am supposed to be an old "Romulo boy", and yet

in one year I have taken the University on the road to autonomy, especially student autonomy, that would have been inconceivable in the time of my predecessor. I am supposed to be a part of the Establishment (TUTA NI MARCOS! [Puppy of Marcos]), yet I led a faculty march to Malacañang that could hardly have pleased its distinguished occupant. I am supposed to be a little more than an old-fashioned, perhaps obsolescent liberal, yet I have appointed a number of radical progressives, left-wing intellectuals to faculty who would never have made it under my predecessors. I am supposed, by some, to be a smooth diplomat disdaining trouble, and yet I have just been slapped down by the Supreme Court for transferring a dean who had lost the confidence of a substantial portion of his faculty and students. I am alleged, by others, to be indifferent if not hostile to the student movement, and yet as some of your own members know, I was abroad in the streets, during the nights of Jan. 26 and 30, to help our students who were hurt or taken to jail.[92]

The explanation for the confusion was simple. "I am an old fashioned liberal," he declared. He belonged, he added, "to the intellectual left, and even more precisely, to the non-violent left." He was someone who believed that society must "change rapidly and radically, in order to establish a more just, more abundant, more humane system of political, economic and social relations among its members"—a change that would, naturally, be effected peacefully. He did not believe in violence, but recognized its existence, "sadly, as a fact of life." "The author of *Literature and Society*," he explained, had "never been able to outgrow his early faith in reason and the efficacy of intelligence."[93]

For SP, the best definition of a liberal was "one who runs away as soon as the fighting begins."[94] "If I had stayed in the diplomatic service of the Republic, I would have had no difficulty remaining a liberal—and without having to run away when the fighting begins," he explained. But the circumstances in the University of the Philippines were difficult for a liberal, because there could "be no running away." SP knew there was "no place to hide." And even if there were, he concluded, "I would not take it."[95]

SP did not mind if his indeterminacy annoyed his constituents. He reveled in his liberalism and the flexibility it gave him as a thinker and administrator. In private, he was exasperated by student radicals. By December of 1971, a number of occurrences led to what SP saw as a "defusing" of campus radicalism. Red China had sided with the American "imperialists" in the

India-Pakistan war, Nixon had visited Beijing, and the Philippine Supreme Court had upheld Marcos's decision to withhold the writ of habeas corpus (the first step towards his eventual imposition of martial law). Dean of Student Affairs Armando J. Malay remarked that this had caused SP to gloat. "That's why we liberals are all right," he told Malay. "We can adjust easily to any situation. The Maoists are out in the cold."[96]

But SP's room for adjustment would not last very long. The liberal's instinct may be to balance interests, and it may take time for him to take on categorical stances. Once the stakes become clear, however, his resolve settles, and he returns to first principles. From being a mediator, he becomes a defender of freedoms. When the space of liberty is being crushed, mediation becomes impossible. A liberal may, indeed, run away from fighting, but he cannot run forever. The Marcos regime would increasingly reveal itself to be the very antithesis of the liberalism that SP advocated, and the 1970s would bring this into stark focus.

UP UNDER MARTIAL LAW

ON 23 SEPTEMBER 1972, Ferdinand Marcos issued Proclamation 1081, placing the entire country under martial law. The government immediately arrested thousands of Marcos critics, from politicians, business leaders, peasant and labor organizers, opposition politicians, and student activists. It also shut down universities, and it banned groups like the KM and the SDK. Student radicals were caught unawares, forcing many of them—even those who were unprepared—to flee to the countryside, joining clandestine cells of the Communist Party. In UP, as many as 3,000 students failed to attend their classes once these had resumed later in the year.[97]

On 28 September, SP was summoned to the presidential palace for a one-on-one meeting with Marcos. When he asked Marcos what he intended to do with UP, the dictator "replied that the military had advised him to close six universities indefinitely." SP "did not have to inquire whether the U.P. was one of the six."[98] The two met a second time on 16 October, and Marcos indicated that he was in favor of reopening classes at UP. "If you think you can handle the situation, "he told SP, "I am prepared to order the opening of all units of the University, it being understood that you will assume responsibility therefor."[99]

Classes reopened on 19 October.[100] The agreement with Marcos, however, required that SP strictly implement the terms of martial rule on campus, from the suspension of campus organizations (including the student government), the proscribing of group meeting and assemblies that were not "purely academic in nature," the banning of "campus newspapers, the writing of graffiti," to "the distribution of manifestos" that violate existing laws, as well as Proclamation 1081.[101]

SP also had to pay lip service to Marcos's efforts at building a "New Society." In the commencement exercises of May 1973, he pointed to the "radical change" that transformed the University of the Philippines from a haven of activism "into a tranquil grove of academe." "Instead of marching in the streets," he explained, "the students have queued up to enter the library, theatre, gym or swimming pool."[102] But this situation did not mean that universities had "subsided into a state of total paralysis since martial law." Rather:

> they are humming with more activity than before, though this is the more meaningful activity of the mind and the more salutary activity of the body. We are, in effect, returning to the simple, traditional wisdom embodied in the ancient motto: mens sana in corpore sano.[103]

The required sycophancy was evident enough. But the speech also hinted at a subtle critique of Marcos, which would only become stronger as martial law continued. Towards the end of the speech, he warned that emergency curbs on democracy could not continue indefinitely:

> We are running a race with catastrophe. For it is far easier to lose freedom without bloodshed than to regain freedom without bloodshed. One should never assume that a people willing to sacrifice freedom and democracy for the sake of necessary reforms are prepared to bear the sacrifice indefinitely. Quiescence is not necessarily synonymous with tranquility, nor acquiescence with affirmation. The crucial problem, therefore, is to determine the precise point at which the sacrifice ceases to be supportable and grievances become explosive—the point, in other words, at which the restitution of civil liberties and the restoration of representative government become imperative.[104]

This same form of doublespeak is evident in many of SP's other speeches from the time. His dilemma was that of ameliorating the effects of dictatorship, while holding on to the position that would allow him to do so. Former student activist and UP professor Roberto E. Reyes summarizes how activist students saw SP's predicament:

> It was not the case that the UP administration, now under a tamed Salvador P. Lopez, was out to eliminate student organizations and activism outright. "SP" Lopez knew better than that. He knew in his heart that if stopping the activities of young people was next to impossible, what more in the case of UP students with their tradition of rebellion?
>
> They were incorrigibly political and outspoken. Besides, I was not convinced that Lopez, who sincerely took the cudgels for the students during the Diliman Commune, had completely decamped to Marcos. To me, he was too much of a democrat to act as the campus fascist. Besides, Lopez loved UP too much.[105]

In retrospect, SP acknowledged how slow he was to see the extent of political deterioration under martial law. He was initially optimistic about the capacity of Philippine democratic institutions to withstand challenges from a dictator. In 1976, he asked "why, having so candidly noted the danger signs in the nation's political firmament, I nevertheless tended to minimize them, and instead pretend to harbor an exaggerated optimism that I had no intention to feel." "I have a feeling," he said, "that my optimistic assessment of the enduring quality of Philippine democracy may have been strongly influenced by the prevailing mood of the time."[106] He noted how Marcos's formal commitment to liberalism assuaged his concerns about the eroding "strength of Philippine democracy."[107] It was a liberal hope that would prove naïve.

In the interim, SP worked towards the incremental re-democratization of the university. Without a student council, there was no organization to articulate student concerns. Worse, Jaime Galvez Tan, the Communist-backed student council president (who concomitantly served as student representative in the Board of Regents) had gone into hiding to avoid arrest. With assurances from SP and his dean at the College of Medicine, however, Tan resurfaced and continued serving as regent. Thus, despite the absence of a student council, the Office of the Student Regent functioned as an aggregator of student interests in the first half of 1973. When Tan organized a student rally to protest a tuition fee increase in June, however, the administration abolished his position.[108]

As for student media, SP's administration could not prevent the permanent shutting down of DZUP, the university's official AM radio station. The station was of tactical value to the Communists, as it could be used to call for mass demonstrations. Moreover, the station had personally offended Marcos when it played the leaked audiotape of Marcos having sex with B-rate American actress Dovie Beams. Apart from sounds of intercourse, the tapes had Marcos singing Ilocano folk song Pamulinawen amid pleas for oral sex.[109] After only about three months, however, the *UP Collegian* resumed publication, without the same restraints placed on the student council.[110]

Student power would slowly reassert itself through student organizations associated with the university's colleges and departments. Groups like the Psychology and Political Science societies re-emerged ostensibly as benign social organizations, hosting sports festivals and dances. Government authorities, however, did not know that these efforts were being guided by underground operatives of the Communist Party, who aimed to use the student organizations as venues for political education.[111]

It was a dangerous endeavor. The new crop of student activists were operating in the open at the height of military rule and were easily subject to arrest. As a precaution, the Communist underground encouraged anti-dictatorship youth leaders with parents either in the military or in the Marcos government to lead their organizations. These students met under the protective auspices of Dean Malay's Office of Student Affairs, and would eventually launch an unelected and consultative committee called the Coordinating Committee on Student Affairs (CONCOMSA), which would serve as a liaison between the administration and the students.[112] SP authorized CONCOMSA's formation in September 1973, a full year after the declaration of martial law.[113]

When the students under Malay first broached the idea of a CONCOMSA to the Francophile SP, he replied with a quip: "CONCOMSA? That sounds like *comme ci comme ça!*"[114] It was, indeed, with the indifference of *comme ci comme ça* that SP treated the CONCOMSA, allowing them to operate under his protection, without intervening in its activities.

This passivity, however, was significant. During martial law, an authority figure's indifference to political organizing was almost equivalent to endorsement, leading the CONCOMSA members to suspect that SP was secretly on their side. Recalling her youthful naiveté and revolutionary optimism, CONCOMSA member Elizabeth Protacio-de Castro narrates that many of them thought that, with the proper education and exposure, they could "open" (*mulat*) SP's eyes and he would become a fellow Marxist.¹¹⁵

In any case, regardless of their political orientation, working under Malay and SP shielded the students from the increasing military surveillance on campus. Little did they know, however, that SP himself was being watched. Malay had long suspected that the military had imposed one of its on-campus allies as SP's assistant "to keep watch" on the university president, noting that this individual had become a very powerful person within the university administration.¹¹⁶ An anonymous source from SP's office also confirmed to me that this same person had been a military agent in charge of monitoring his activities. Examining administrative appointments during 1972, one notes that the same alleged agent was appointed his assistant almost immediately after the declaration of martial law.

Despite knowing that he was being watched, SP would test the waters around the military agent. At a party in December 1972, for instance, he cracked a joke about Marcos's alleged love affair with Dovie Beams. According to Malay, "[w]hen the recording of 'Pamulinawen,' the favorite Ilocano ditty was sung, SP shouted to all within hearing distance—'that's Marcos's song for Dovie Beams.'" The agent was aghast and claimed the remarks were communicated to Marcos or the military.¹¹⁷ SP was, thus, servile in public, but increasingly cynical in private. And this cynicism would slowly make its way into his public pronouncements.

THE UNIVERSALITY OF LIBERTY AND TYRANNY

WHILE IMPLEMENTING A neutered version of martial law on campus, SP found ways to obliquely criticize the Marcos administration in public. In December 1973, he delivered the keynote address to the UP Law Center on the issue of a new Philippine Constitution. Although a Constitutional Convention had been planning a shift to a parliamentary system of governance since 1971, it was only after martial law that Marcos was able to railroad a plebiscite that would ratify the new charter, according him the legal basis to stay in power indefinitely. SP's speech had originally been prepared for a postponed seminar in January 1972, prior to the declaration of martial law. Upon examining the original speech, however, he realized that "it would not be suitable to the present occasion" and that the original speech had "been overtaken by events."¹¹⁸

The speech does not mention martial law by name, but it references "the central problem of constitutionalism in our contemporary society," which involved balancing "the regulation of freedom in order to prevent anarchy" and "the limitation of power in order to prevent tyranny" on the other.[119] Since preventing anarchy was Marcos's avowed reason for declaring martial law, SP's audience would have certainly viewed the speech as a discussion of the president's emergency powers.

Having noted that Philippine constitutionalism was anchored on Western liberalism, he explained how this tradition was globally challenged by the "polarization of political forces into Left and Right."[120] In the 20th century, moreover, there was "everywhere a formidable residue of age-old inequalities, and a corresponding clamor for massive reforms." The result of these pressures was "a degree of government intervention in our lives unparalleled in human history."[121] It was, indeed, an age of extremes, and liberalism was in crisis.

This situation did not augur well for the "effective control of delegated power." "It is axiomatic," SP explained, "that an emergency creates emergency power, and recurrent emergencies tend to make power permanent," resulting in the "enlargement of executive discretion" and a receding of legal controls. And in a barely veiled reference to Marcos's manipulation of legal process, he claimed that, ultimately, "the courts themselves are called upon to validate the assertion and exercise of executive power in the emergency. The circle is complete."[122]

Naturally, the way forward for SP was liberty, his touch-point and the universal that grounded his politics. Western liberal democracy was not just appropriate for Europeans and Americans, and he believed its conception of freedom had "no nationality" for "neither has tyranny." "Both have occurred in all ages, all climates, all cultures, all civilizations. No race, nationality or society has had a monopoly on either." His remarks, SP concluded, were "less sanguine than expected." His purpose, however, was "not to depress your democratic hopes, but to invigorate them with a sense of sober realism."[122]

That sober realism became more pronounced in 1974—the year that would seal his future as a critic of the dictatorship. By that time, he already knew his politics had become fundamentally incompatible with the dictatorship, and his disdain for the regime was obvious to those around him. For SP, it was a year that had antecedents in his university's history.

In 1974, the UP observed the birth centenary of Rafael Palma—its fourth president and a personal hero of SP. If any UP President had faced a political climate similar to SP's, it was Palma. In 1933, Palma resigned from his post when President Manuel Quezon threatened to cut the UP budget after a bitter political feud. Like Marcos, Quezon wanted to stretch the powers of the presidency, and critics worried about the emergence of a potential dictator.

During a public tribute to Palma, SP himself selected excerpts of Palma's writings that many thought resonated with the times. SP watched as the excerpts were read on stage, the crowd around him growing increasingly tense. One of his seatmates alluded to the fact that Palma's comments, in the context of the present, would be considered subversive. Referring to the detention camps that were filled with Marcos critics, SP remarked, "[b]ring us food when we are inside."[124]

THE DILLINGHAM LECTURE

THUS FAR, SP'S public criticisms of martial law were veiled either in abstract discussions of constitutionalism or the ventriloquizing of predecessors. It was only a matter of time, however, before SP shifted from vagaries to specifics, from oblique allusions to naming names. The speech for the Law Center would, in effect, serve as the theoretical framework for his most controversial speech—a speech that would lead to his final break with Marcos. In that same year, he was invited to deliver a lecture at the University of Hawaiʻi's East-West Center on the topic of martial law. The East-West Center, whose board of governors includes appointees from the U.S. State Department, is a resource for official American policy thinking about Asia. Thus, although it was small, SP was talking before an influential American foreign policy elite, and only the foreign policy elite. The small group of anti-Marcos Filipino intellectuals who had taken refuge in the university were not invited to the event.[125]

Luis Teodoro was a leftwing English professor who was arrested after the declaration of martial law and brought into SP's office after his release. And it was Teodoro who was tasked to draft the East-West Center lecture.[126] His instructions were explicit; SP wanted to talk about what was really happening without covering up the facts or toeing the government line. They were marching orders that did not surprise Teodoro, as it was clear to him that his boss was never in favor of martial law to begin with.[127]

Whenever SP went off-script and ad-libbed sections of his speeches during martial law, he would declaim a favorite adage: "It is better to be silenced than to be silent."[128] His Hawai'i speech would be an affirmation of this, for it was a speech that Marcos would attempt to suppress.

SP must have felt relieved to deliver the speech, having bottled up his reservations for two years. A man renowned for transparent prose wilts when forced to obfuscate. On the day of the speech, he made a long-distance telephone call to his assistant (the suspected military agent), and he was described as sounding very relaxed.[129]

The speech itself rehashed many of the tropes from the Law Center keynote, from the universality of freedom and human rights to a discussion of the liberal tradition in the Philippines. In the beginning of the speech, SP framed martial law as the very collapse of this liberal, democratic tradition, asking:

> What made forty million Filipinos, among the most literate in Asia and accustomed for nearly three quarters of a century to the lusty ways of a freewheeling democracy, docilely accept one September day in 1972 the indefinite suspension of normal constitutional government and the curtailment of their civil and political rights? Was Philippine democracy so fragile that it could be toppled not by a show of armed force but by a mere presidential proclamation?[130]

He did not presume to have clear answers to this question, and he did not "pretend to be unbiased," because he was a liberal "and liberalism is itself a bias." And as a liberal, he was "not a fanatic of the absolute."[131]

After discussing the various problems of Philippine society leading up to martial law ("Factionalism, fragmentation, and extreme partisanship dominated the policy-making process of government, while the conduct of public affairs was vitiated by the inordinate politics of patronage and clientage."[132]), SP argued that martial law seemed like a small price to pay. "People," he said, "clung to the hope that there would finally be an end to the uncertainty and strife that had characterized life in the Philippines since the beginning of the decade." For them, "the temporary loss of a few freedoms, dramatized by the imposition of curfew hours, the closure of schools and newspapers, and the silence of the radio and television stations, would be a small price to pay for this."[133]

In the beginning, the widespread hope for reform appeared justified. The crime rate dropped, unlicensed arms were confiscated, corrupt officials were dismissed, tax collection increased, private armies were disbanded, and the military reported success against secessionists in the South. By decree, the entire country was also declared land reform area, and the government provided close to 180,000 tenant farmers certificates of land.[134] Finally, he noted the quick implementation of a bilingual educational policy and narrated with approval Marcos's intent to expand open diplomatic relations with Communist states.[135]

There were, therefore, various hints in the speech that SP was attempting to be fair to Marcos. SP wanted to first acknowledge the advances under martial law, "because there seems to be a view that President Marcos is motivated solely by the desire to perpetuate himself in power."[136] But the reforms Marcos wanted to implement needed perhaps too much time, since Filipinos would not give up their freedoms for very long.[137] "The Filipinos," he contended in an echo of his Law Center speech, "are running a race with catastrophe. For, it is far easier to lose freedom without bloodshed than to regain freedom without bloodshed." Radical therapies were not "without risk," and the government needed to ensure "that the deep-seated vices are eradicated without killing the patient."[138]

SP decried the curtailment of basic freedoms, from the censorship of the press, the prohibition of strikes and demonstrations, the indefinite detention of political prisoners, the erosion of constitutional government, and the constraints on academic freedom. "Prolonged repression," he argued, "tends to erode the support of the people and constrains them to remain silent when their voice most needs to be heard."[139] More, the holders of power "seduced by the attractions of unrestrained authority, may soon come to believe that the delegation of power to them is permanent." The situation could not last forever, and the people's "constitutional rights and liberties" had to be "restored sooner or later—preferably sooner than later."[140] The solutions, echoing his argument in the law center, were liberal democracy and human rights. As SP always noted, these were not constructs exclusive to the West.[141]

At the time, SP was still optimistic that the repression would not be indefinite. Filipinos and their president were too accustomed to democracy. For instance, he did not believe that the military had a "deliberate policy of physical torture."¹⁴² "If President Marcos is a dictator," he explained, "he is not ruthless enough to be an effective one. I suspect that he is a crypto-democrat—an authoritarian who can no quite get over his democratic upbringing."¹⁴³

Ultimately, SP's solution was clear: "A deliberate policy to lift martial law is clearly in order."¹⁴⁴ He called for the release of political prisoners, the restoration of a free press, and the holding of elections. ¹⁴⁵ While he accepted that the Constitution provided for martial law, he emphasized its nature as an emergency measure. "Martial law," he explained, is "a derogation of the Constitution which the Constitution itself permits; it is, in effect, an injury self-inflicted by the Constitution in order to prevent greater injury." If it is not "limited in scope and duration . . . the Constitution dies." More crucially, even if martial law were implemented for reform, it lacked the participatory processes necessary for sustainable change:

> In consequence of the need to forestall violent revolution, martial law may have provided the occasion to initiate a process; but it may not be indefinitely prolonged on the ground that it is needed to complete the process. Social transformation in a democracy is a long-term task of all the people living and acting together in freedom and responsibility.¹⁴⁶

In ending the speech, SP once again paid lip service to supporting Marcos's reforms. The failure of Marcos's reform program, he concluded, "would convince the people that there is no option left but the forcible seizure of political power in order that the goals of the social revolution which for centuries they have striven to achieve but which have repeatedly eluded them may finally be realized."¹⁴⁷ But despite the hedging, he had made his position clear. SP had finally outed himself as a critic of martial law, and there would be consequences.

DISMISSAL

TOWARDS THE END of 1974, it was clear that the Marcos military had lost all trust in SP. The agent in his office had grown increasingly overbearing, unabashedly telling people that the military had decided to keep SP traveling, so that the university could be run without its president.¹⁴⁸ This mistrust was likely buttressed by the publication of the East-West Center speech in pamphlet form by the University of the Philippines Press barely a month after its delivery.[149] Previous critics of martial law had either been leftwing activists or opposition politicians. Here, however, was a respected, non-partisan career bureaucrat (a close friend of Foreign Affairs Minister Romulo no less!) and scholar voicing his dissent.

The year was the last in SP's first term as UP President, and he was in a precarious position. Watching him up close, Malay was once again reminded of the idealist Palma. Like Palma, SP was "walking a tightrope bet. expedience and principles,"[150] and the pressure took its toll on him. In late November and early December, he seemed confused and irritable, likely because he was worried about his reappointment.[151] In retrospect, the chances for reappointment were always slim. Although he held on to the hope that Romulo would vouch for him with Marcos, his critique of martial law had already irked a vindictive dictator.[152]

The first indication that Marcos had taken note of SP's critique was in early December, when Marcos's brother-in-law, Benjamin "Kokoy" Romualdez dismissed the publisher of his *Times Journal*, ostensibly after the publication of an unexpurgated version of SP's Hawai'i speech.[153] Despite the controversy, he seemed resolved to continue raising objections about the dictatorship. On 5 December, he delivered a speech to the Manila Rotary Club, criticizing political interference in the University, after which he distributed copies of his "Martial Law in the Philippines." Three cabinet members were in attendance, and one was quoted as saying, "It's not every day you can hear a speech like that."[154]

Malay thought SP was being canny. "Is SP determined to force a showdown which will determine if he remains UP president or is replaced?" he asked. "If he is on his way out, why not go out fighting and be sacrificed as a martyr? On the other hand, can Marcos and military afford people saying SP was canned because he raised opposition to martial law? Either way, SP wins."

This suspicion was confirmed after a conversation with SP a week later. SP himself was unsure about his reappointment. "He [SP] said that a lot of people think he shouldn't wait to be ousted—or his term expire next month, why not quit now 'when he's ahead?'" wrote Malay. SP had described a game of cat and mouse between himself and the administration: the president and/or the military were waiting for him to resign or declare a lack of interest in reappointment. But SP refused to play the mouse. Perhaps, Malay mused, "he's waiting to be canned so he'd be like Palma. But the tension must be terrible!"[155]

Meanwhile, the Board of Regents, which was under the influence of Marcos appointees, was taking its time to decide. SP's term was ending on the 31st of the month, but they did not discuss his appointment in their 17 December meeting.[156] As the waiting game wore on, SP's student supporters began to organize. The editorial board of the *Philippine Collegian* published a statement entitled "Let Lopez Continue making the UP relevant," praising him for democratizing the university.[157] The CONCOMSA, under the supervision of Malay and his deputy Oscar Alfonso, had also begun drafting a resolution of support for their president. By this time, he had become more vocal about his desire to take on a second term. Previously, he was against any resolutions or statements advocating for his reappointment. By mid-December, however, he told Alfonso that he did not "care one way or the other."[158]

It was evident that SP, in the words of Malay, had now "set his heart on reappointment."[159] This much was clear when he hosted a dinner for university deans and directors at the University's Executive House. It was a sumptuous meal of baked ham, lumpia, and pancit. When he spoke, SP was both candid and conflicted. As an ex-poker player ("I only play mahjong, because I lost a lot of money on poker"), he thought of quitting while ahead. "The UP has never been in as good a shape as now, considering the (martial law) situation," he said. He had weathered both the heights of student militarism and the imposition of military rule.[160]

Once again, SP repeated that he initially discouraged campaigns for his reappointment, but no longer cared one way or another. He said that no student organization had lobbied for Romulo's reappointment, and proudly noted the *Collegian's* statement of support. Should he be retired, however, he was glad to leave UP in good physical and academic shape.[161] He did not know if he would have another chance to see deans and directors again, so he thanked them for helping him run the university over the last six years. The coming years would be critical for the university and the nation. Concluding, he claimed that he was glad to have spoken out against martial law, since someone had to do it. "Our University and the Church are now keeping alive the spirit of protest."[162]

Despite martial law, the University was a place of dissent. SP knew this, and it was his fortitude that earned him the respect of his students. Two days after, CONCOMSA handed him an open letter, which read:

As your present term draws to an end, the University indulges in the intellectual exercise of evaluating the President who has led the community through the travails of student unrest and martial law. In these five years you have pursued policies in accordance with the principles of the times—Filipinization, decolonization and the affirmation of the University's integrity.

In the same vein, the students have continued to fight for student rights and welfare—for the reactivation of the student council; representation in the Board of Regents and better University facilities—all of these in line with the principles of the times. Students have faced equal odds in their battles for the realization of these principles.

We hope you will be with us to face the tasks that are great and many. Much remains to be achieved. We cannot abandon our principles.[163]

The groundswell of support must have emboldened SP. Immediately after the holidays, he authorized the *Philippine Collegian* to invite Manila Archbishop Jaime Cardinal Sin to speak on campus about torture in the military, ignoring Malay's suggestion that they also invite a representative from the military to present the other side. Despite the precarious nature of his appointment, SP would not even accommodate the government line. Should he be reappointed, he told Malay, it would be on the understanding that he would continue to speak his mind as he had done in Hawai'i.[164]

SP's position would obviously be unacceptable to Marcos. By 13 January, as SP was about to leave for Kuala Lumpur, gossip (*chismis*) was already circulating through UP's fraternity networks that Marcos's former Minister of Education, Onofre D. Corpuz, would be the next president.[165] By 17 January, it was official: SP was out, and Corpuz would be his replacement. Malay was able to see SP that morning, prior to a meeting with the Vice Presidents and Deans. SP claimed he had never been more relieved in his life.[166] In the meeting, he told everyone to cooperate with Corpuz, and asked those whose terms coincided with his to tender their resignations. When the others offered to resign as well, SP stopped them, since he did not want UP to "grind to a halt."[167]

Teodoro went to visit SP after he heard the news, and found his boss preparing his things. SP's staff members at Quezon Hall (the administration building) were crying. It was clear to Teodoro that the East-West Center speech had caused his ouster, and Marcos was "tightening his grip" on the University by appointing a more pliant ally. Speaking to Teodoro, SP's conclusion was simple: "I guess our speech did something."[168]

SP wanted to stay in the university after the presidency. He had written Marcos in November, claiming he did not want to go back to the Foreign Service. He wanted to continue teaching graduate courses at UP.[169] By most accounts, he took his dismissal graciously, only nursing resentment towards Romulo, who failed to defend him before Marcos. When Teodoro saw SP a few months after, he noticed a "dejected" man who had nonetheless accepted the political reality of his situation. He let it slip, however, that he thought Romulo "let him down."[170]

Malay shares a similar story. "SP is sore with Carlos P. Romulo, who promised (but didn't) to help SP be given a reappointment," he wrote in February. "Romulo said however that before he could bat for SP, Marcos had exploded on the subject. . . . So CPR kept silent."[171]

The first few months after the presidency must have been a relief. In the months after the presidency, SP had begun to catch up on his reading and to organize his library "of about three thousand books which I had accumulated during the past thirty years and lugged along . . . from the United States to Europe, to the Philippines, then back to the States, and finally home to the Philippines in 1969."[172] Two assistants from the UP library helped him arrange the books according to the Dewey system. From his office in Quezon Hall, he moved to a new work desk in the basement of his home in the suburban enclave of West Triangle, Quezon City.[173] His description of his workspace, quoted here at length, reveals a loose, descriptive prose style, barely evident in his speeches as UP president:

> My basement study measures approximately 8 by 18 meters, with a ceiling three meters high. The sides are lined with bookshelves, and the fourth has shelves for music records and tape recordings. My working desk is close to one side at the center of the room, and the fourth has shelves for music records and tape recordings. My working desk is close to one side at the center of the room, and across from it is the stereo equipment. There is no television set. On top of the shelves are art objects of wood, metal, porcelain or crystal which I have picked up around the world, and on the walls are paintings of Manansala, Carlos Francisco, de Joya and Romeo Tabuena, as well as a set of fine colored prints of the great landmarks of Paris—the

> Notre Dame, the Madeleine, the Arc de Triomphe, the Place de la Concorde, etc. which I picked up in a little bookshop along the Seine. A door leads to a storeroom where I keep my collection of paintings in upright stacks as well as a small wine cellar where I keep some old bottles of liqueur, cognac and champagne as well as a few bottles of vintage Bordeaux and Burgundy. Seated at my desk, reading a book or listening to music, I could see through the windows which are level with the ground a part of the spacious garden where I grow vegetables—tomatoes, okra, eggplant, ampalaya, lettuce, and cucumber—as well as fruit trees—mango, coconut, chico, guava, caimito, atis, and duhat—and flowering plants—anteriums, bougainvillea, roses, sampaguita, kalachuchi, and orchids.[174]

A seemingly tranquil place for a tranquil retirement. A small liberal space in a country that had slid into extremes.

POSTSCRIPT TO UP: A GRAND OLD MAN

BUT SP'S RETIREMENT would not be tranquil. It was, indeed, still better to be silenced than be silent. His public life in the late 1970s and 1980s deserves a chapter of its own. It was in this period that he became the grand old man of liberalism and the anti-Marcos opposition, writing regular columns for the Catholic newspaper *Veritas* and, eventually, the anti-Marcos weekly *Mr. & Ms,* which would become the *Philippine Daily Inquirer*, the present day paper of record. He would also serve as the chairman of the Philippine PEN, where he developed a close relationship with its founder and fellow Marcos critic, novelist F. Sionil Jose. By his own account he wrote "with as much intensity as in 1933, but with a lot more care." Asked how he kept his verve and how he "conserved his powers," he replied: "Clean living and loving."[175]

SP remained under the careful watch of the military. In 1981, recalls Jose, SP heard rumors of him being on a military arrest list. SP, who had previously hid anti-Marcos activists in his own house, sought refuge at Jose's. At age 70, it was now his turn to hide. Upon finding SP in his house, Jose, who was also on the arrest list exclaimed: "SP, what are you doing here? If the military comes looking for a mouse, they will find a lion instead!"[176]

CONCLUSION

IN JANUARY 2012, the University of the Philippines held a daylong symposium on various aspects of SP's work, "from academic governance and foreign affairs to human rights and, of course, literature."¹⁷⁷ One of the speakers was Jose "Butch" Dalisay, a fictionist and critic. "I spoke that afternoon," he wrote, "as one of those noisy undergraduates who gave President Lopez a hard time at the barricades during the Diliman Commune of February 1971." "I was newly 17 then, and he was a few months short of 60. I've just turned 58, and having spent some time myself in university administration, I can now better appreciate the quandary of the classic liberal caught between two opposing sides."¹⁷⁸

He recalls that many writers of his generation were inspired by SP's *Literature and Society,* but soon outgrew him and became drawn to Mao and his *Talks at the Yenan Forum,* tossing aside SP's "terminal admonition to distinguish between art and propaganda." For them, "art *was* propaganda."¹⁷⁹ What they did not realize was that it was SP's own openness that allowed his students to outgrow their teacher.

Beyond remembering a great man, the SP tribute was also occasion for Dalisay to reflect on the trajectory of intellectuals from the First Quarter Storm (FQS) generation. Since the radical seventies, many of his cohort "have moved closer back to Lopez than to Mao—particularly the Lopez who was once quoted to have said that there were really only two things worth writing about: love and politics."¹⁸⁰ Detachment, disillusionment, and the simple passage of time returned the radicals to the liberalism of their parents' generation.

I have often asked if the Philippines had a "'68 generation," a generation that moved from student radicalism in the 1960s and 1970s to a disillusioned but idealistic leftwing liberalism after the Cold War.¹⁸¹ In the sense that the *annus mirabilis* of Philippine radicalism was 1970 and not 1968, the term "'68 generation" may be inapt. But in a more profound sense, it is an illustrative category, and it explains Dalisay's return to SP and his cautious liberalism. The '68-ers in Paris— neophilosophes like Andre Glucksman, Bernard Henri-Levi, and Pascal Bruckner—left Mao, Marx, and Sartre, only to return to the liberalism of the previously maligned Raymond Aron. Though many are loath to admit it, the '68-ers (or should I say the FQS generation?) of the Philippines have made a similar journey: from a desire to destroy the state to a commitment to its democratization and the strengthening of its institutions. It is a story that I have told before,¹⁸² and one that the more trenchant memoirists of the period have noted themselves.¹⁸³

Now that many of these older Marxists also believe in compromise, they are facing challenges similar to those SP confronted. Former Marxists are now cabinet members or members of parliament, and they are forced to listen to constituencies outside "the movement." They will inevitably rethink many of their positions. And they will be accused of being two-faced.

When liberals join institutions of power to serve as modus vivendi, they are immediately engaged in some form of hypocrisy. They cannot remain pure in their ideals because their primary goal is not to defend their beliefs but to reconcile those of others. They stop becoming the heroes. Instead, they enable the heroes to emerge, and, ironically, remain after these heroes fail or change their minds. SP could have quit the moment Marcos declared martial law, or he could have categorically taken the students' side. But this purity may have cost him his job, which would have left the student radicals without a protector. The liberal becomes a hypocrite so that others may be safe.

Hence the liberal must always ask: Where do I draw the line? When do I stop compromising? There is no answer to this question. But it needs to be continually asked since liberals chart unknown territories. The liberal's task is empirical. In this chapter, we saw how quickly SP's positions evolved based on student demands, pressure from the military, and the relative openness of a dictator at certain junctures. We saw how the republican duty of being a "political animal" required the ongoing reassessment of context-specific needs based on conflicting beliefs and interests. If there were given rules on how to compromise, liberalism would be nothing short of procedural. Yet SP believed in a liberty that emerges not through rules but through the practice of mediation.

For this reason, liberals will always upset those who seek clarity and certainty. They can be unpredictable. SP emphasized that one cannot place the liberal since liberal does not admire the absolute. As they adlib politics, liberals will change their minds, contradict themselves, and will often even fail. Yet their uncertainty guards them from the temptations of authoritarianism.

True liberals may be hypocrites, but they are never demagogues.

Conclusion
Postcolonial Liberalism, a Global Idea

Though the narrative of this work has been grounded in Philippine realities, it is intertwined with the major global events of the 20th century. Rarely, of course, do Filipinos discuss the Philippines in light of world history. Part of this phenomenon, as I alluded to earlier, stems from methodological nationalism, which dovetails easily with the impulse to write the history of "the Filipino people." It is also informed by narrow forms of regionalism, which only permit historians to locate the Philippines within Asia or the "Malayan world."[1] Amid this, I have sought through this work to trace forms of global, outward-looking, yet nationalist thinking within the Philippine liberal tradition. As we saw in the introduction, this globality was inherent from the very inception of Philippine liberalism, rooted in a tradition of what Megan Thomas calls "wordly colonials," who "constructed conceptions of history associated with colonial projects" but did so "on the colonized's terms."[2]

The liberals of the 20th century were continuing not only a 19th-century project but also a global one. As such, I hope that the attributes of postcolonial liberalism I outline have use outside the Philippines, for the rest of the world.

"Global history," of course, is not without its limits. Eurocentrism—a tendency to view history as emanating from the West—is present in most works with the Olympian hubris to write about the "world." *Mea culpa.* I cannot deny that much of this work has been about the interpretation of American and European ideas in a pro-American Southeast Asian state. For this lapse, my defense is straightforward: these four intellectuals *were* really inspired by "the West." More importantly, an honest assessment of ideas should examine their quality instead of their provenance. These ideas, regardless of where they came from, were germane for 20th-century Philippines and, beyond.

THE WORLD THROUGH FILIPINO EYES

CAMILO OSIAS BEGAN promoting internationalism after the Great War, a period that exposed the limits of narrow nationalism. A strong belief in the superiority of their individual nations' causes led the combatants of that war to the trenches, leaving millions dead in Europe. America, a belligerent that suffered less than the European states, absorbed some of the War's lessons while evading its trauma. This gave birth to John Dewey's optimistic vision of internationalism that eschewed jingoism even as it maintained the need for domestic state building. It was a liberal internationalism that was optimistic about the democratic nation-state. This optimism became part of early 20th-century attempts to define the future of independence of America's only colony, resurrecting late 19th-century visions of nationalist internationalism, while combining these with the postcolonial rhetoric of nation-building.

An economic crisis marked the gap between two world wars. The Great Depression forced Western economies to rethink the interaction of markets and the state. The war economies of the Second World War, moreover, led to a further validation of state intervention in the economy. Finally, the growing might of the Soviet Union and the threat of fascism forced non-Communists to seek alternatives to both the free market and the state-directed economy. These events informed the emergence of related economic visions: Keynesianism, New Deal liberalism, European social democracy, and the politically distinct Asian developmental state. Since liberalism was the predominant intellectual discourse of 20th-century Philippines, authoritarian developmentalism was not on the table (at least, not until the emergence of the Marcos dictatorship). Economic planners, therefore, looked once again to America. Salvador Araneta was one such economic planner, whose vision of development was anchored on a desire for the Philippines to join a global fraternity of industrialized states. This was, once again, a form of internationalism.

The immediate postwar world confronted two major phenomena: decolonization and the Cold War, creating a tripartite division of world politics. The antagonists of the Cold War divided into the first and second world, while the newly independent states became the third. In this era, the mantle of internationalism shifted to the Third World. Isolated from the United Nations Security Council, the Third World slowly asserted its voice in the UN's ever-growing General Assembly, whose president Carlos P. Romulo represented the emergent nations of Asia. At the Bandung conference, the Third World became the locus of liberal human rights, proving that this discourse was not exclusive to the West. Romulo once again became a key figure in this movement, insisting that the global third way should reject two assaults on human rights: First World imperialism and Second World Communist authoritarianism. Salvador "SP" Lopez, Romulo's protégé, continued this advocacy for human rights as Chair of the UN's Commission on Human Rights.

When SP returned to the Philippines, it was convulsed, like many other parts of the world, by the radicalism of the late 1960s/early 1970s. Like his fellow liberal educators from campuses in the U.S., France, Thailand, and Mexico, he confronted a youth that rejected not only his liberalism but also the ossified "old Left" of Soviet-oriented Communist Parties. This was a new phenomenon, and classic anti-Communist rhetoric could no longer be used to discredit it. The energy of the New Left placed global liberalism in crisis. In contrast to phenomena such as culturalist Maoism, liberalism seemed too timid to confront postwar dictatorships and autocracies. Liberals had to brace themselves and mediate, channeling the energy of the New Left into realistic political projects. To the New Left, of course, this represented liberalism's penchant for co-optation. But, for the liberal, it showcased liberalism as a modus vivendi, a method as opposed to a telos.

That the period of liberal experimentation in the Philippines coincided with these international events meant that, for much of the 20th century, it was liberalism that mediated between the Philippines and the world. The liberal mind was a window to the outside, and it bridged the nexus between local and international concerns. It is with this assumption of Philippine liberalism's globality that I propose the following definition of postcolonial liberalism.

POSTCOLONIAL LIBERALISM

POSTCOLONIAL LIBERALISM ESPOUSES an open-ended form of nationalism. The "nation" that postcolonial liberals have in mind, however, is not the essential given of cultural or racial nationalism. Rather, it is a nation-in-waiting, constructed through everyday political negotiation, consisting of various civic and cultural referents. It is closer to American patriotism, where the nation is not so much a primordial community as a never-ending experiment in self-governance. As Richard Rorty reminds us, American patriotism was shaped by a secular civic religion—a communitarian rhetoric that aided leftwing movements from Progressivism to New Deal liberalism.[3] That this vision often fails in its country of origin should not discount the saliency of the idea, and its possible application to postcolonies. Maybe it is postcolonial liberals who will resuscitate the liberal democratic experiment and unmoor it from imperialism. For should we not all aspire towards state experiments that transcend race and class? In the pragmatist tradition, this nationalism is dynamic and rejects the chauvinism that derives from the navel-gazing. Osias's internationalism insisted that a dynamic global shape an equally dynamic local. Similarly, Araneta called for a planned economy because he believed his country deserved to participate in an economic model that had benefited developed countries.

Postcolonial liberalism accepts its origins. As a product of the Enlightenment, it is futile to deny that most, though not all, of liberalism's canon was defined by privileged white males. None of this, however, should prevent its appropriation in postcolonial contexts. A good idea is a good idea regardless of where it comes from, and a postcolonial liberal refuses to get bogged down in debates about what is "authentically ours." Pascal Bruckner argues eloquently that, though rights-based liberal values were

> born on European soil, they are no longer Europe's exclusive property. Oppression has been carried out by Spain, Portugal, Holland, England, France, and the United States, but the moral progress made by these same nations is the property of all peoples. Individual rights, like scientific discovery, are neither Western nor Eastern, neither African nor American.[4]

Therefore, if "Western" liberalism has been hypocritically applied in the past, re-articulating it in the postcolony may purify its future. Advocates of postcolonial theory routinely absolve Marxism of its violences, because it has provided the grammar for anticolonial dissent. Years after decolonization, however, the Enlightenment discourse that we should "borrow" from the West may no longer be one of dissent, but one of mediation. Romulo and SP, for instance, saw in global human rights the best the Enlightenment has to offer, and sought to actualize those rights in the Philippines and the United Nations.

Postcolonial liberalism is a method of mediation and governance. In the past years, liberal democracy has been called arrogant, in part because Francis Fukuyama triumphantly proclaimed it "the end of history"—the best political model to emerge from the various contestations of human political development. But liberal democracy can only "end" history if one assumes that liberalism has a definite terminus. In other words, the end of history argument is illiberal by virtue of its totalizing *telos*. As a modus vivendi, liberalism is both a program and a method, and the processes it sets into motion are perpetually evolving. This point harkens back to my defense of pencil-pushing in the opening chapter. To balance plural interests in a democratic society, liberals espouse deliberation, and establish systems that facilitate this deliberation. Perhaps this is why all the liberals in this book were all at one point university presidents. The liberal university is the perfect representation of the institutionalized deliberation that the liberal aspires for. Academic freedom is a model for deliberation, as it enables open and free inquiry. In a free university, students are exposed to various ideas, enabling them to make up their own minds about politico-ethical issues. Discussion of these issues is enabled and delimited by various rules and procedures (tenure, ethical codes, pedagogical systems, and so on) that ideally promote democratic exchange. At times these processes may be long, boring, and tedious. Liberalism, however, is not a politics of revolutionary shortcuts.

Postcolonial liberalism seeks power to limit power. Liberals are not self-marginalizing, because they are willing to compromise. This willingness to get their hands dirty lands liberals in the halls of power. Once in positions of influence, however, liberals use power to diffuse it. Liberals are brave enough to test their own consciences in the field of political negotiation, knowing that they can return to first principles. This places liberals in stark contrast to Communists who seek great power because they are "principled," their earnest Marxist hearts precluding compromise, since "history" demands their ascension to power. But liberals accept that politics occurs after a fall from Eden, where all actors partake of democracy's original sin: the need to be a hypocrite. For how can one not be hypocritical in a context where one believes in things but is forced to respect contradictory thinking? Liberals know that this game of hypocrisy is, indeed, dangerous, and not everyone is able to conquer it. Carlos Romulo became addicted to bureaucratic power, failing to see that liberal deliberation was no longer possible in a dictatorship. SP knew better, treading a very fine line between mediation and criticism. Though their responses to dictatorship were different, both were liberals in that they engaged in a to and fro dance with power.

Postcolonial liberalism is a public politics conjoined with public accountability. If postcolonial liberals risk being judged by a political public, it is because they risk getting things done. And this risk comes with the knowledge that they can be held accountable, blamed by the constituencies they serve. Postcolonial liberalism listens to "the people," but does not view this entity as amorphous. It is a critique of both leftwing and rightwing populisms that assume the given interests of "the masses" against "the elite." Liberals eschew this simplification, believing that various constituencies need to be persuaded by leaders who set out clear visions for a society. This impulse is reflected in the liberal's lucid prose style: postcolonial liberals risk being understood, thus courting the kind of dissent and debate that they enjoy. Their rhetoric is in stark contrast to what usually passes today as theorizing from the postcolony. In the sense that much postcolonial philosophy is unintelligible, these works attenuate the problems of their societies: We already have to deal with the word vomit of political demagogues, so why must we deal with similar obfuscation from non-liberal academics and intellectuals? The postcolonial liberal's radical transparency is part of an equally radical attachment to a sense of the public. SP's commitment to proletarian literature and social relevance was more than a diatribe against dilettantism; it was also an acknowledgement of the intellectual's role within decolonizing contexts. Artistic production was a vehicle for common cultural referents that would create a common discourse, producing a shared public space. Similarly, Osias's focus on creating a dynamic literary canon, spread through a common public school system, envisioned a postcolony that was collectively reading, redefining its democracy as a national community.

Postcolonial liberalism confronts inequality. Free market liberalism, grotesque and simplistic in any context, is even more so in the formerly colonized states, where it becomes salt rubbed on deep wounds of poverty. A country like the Philippines confronts great inequality, but is bereft of the institutions that mitigate this inequality. In places like Europe and North America, conservatives are eroding welfare systems, and this is a tragedy of our times. But the farce of the 20th century is that these institutions never existed in most former colonies to begin with. Even more farcical is the fact that "revolutionaries" from Western liberal democracies, who benefit from their welfare systems, insist that postcolonies revolt against capitalism instead of forging the welfare institutions that have helped their Western "comrades." If liberalism is to re-emerge as a postcolonial politics, it must be indistinguishable from social democracy. As Tony Judt notes, "it was social democracy and the welfare state that bound the professional and commercial middle classes to liberal institutions in the wake of World War II."[5] Social democracy in postcolonies will not simply bind the middle classes to liberal institutions but will allow those liberal institutions to create those middle classes. At stake is not simply economic efficiency but the morality of postcolonial societies. Araneta was a thinker who could not divorce the wisdom of economic planning from his own morality as a socially conscious Christian. To a lesser extent, Romulo, who admired Araneta's ideas, became a late advocate of nationalist economics, inspired by Latin American dependency theory, which was then mainstreaming in the UN. Independent economics was part of anticolonialism's morality.

Finally: *Postcolonial liberalism is a gradualist philosophy that does not preclude change.* It is not the liberal's business to assess when, if, and how a large, amorphous, and barely definable system like "late capitalism" or "the system" will be destroyed. As far as liberals are concerned, revolutions that have aimed for total change have become total dictatorships. Again, postcolonial liberalism refuses an Edenic return, and insists on, dare I say, a conservative realism. Liberals are not risk takers when it comes to politics, because the stakes are too high. Conjuring a completely equal system or the death of wage labor may sound appealing, but can we risk such revolutionary projects when their failures could spell and have spelled the destruction of democratic institutions? Or even the death of millions in places like the Gulag? This cautiousness was the reason why all the intellectuals in this book were anti-Communists (with Romulo, of course, being the most vocal); they located themselves squarely against both fascism and Communism, viewing these as two sides of the same coin. None of this cynicism, however, precluded a belief in change. SP insisted that liberalism was a discourse of "the Left," because he saw liberalism as espousing gradual but dynamic reform. Progress that comes through slow deliberation is more sustainable than sudden raptures. If these seemingly glacial processes lead to the dismantling of capitalism or the present order sometime in the future, so be it. If it does not, liberals will continue to mediate. Ultimately, liberalism's gradualism draws from its fundamental humility: it cannot and will not claim to predict the future, for history is not on anyone's side.

LIBERALISM FOR THE PHILIPPINES

AT THIS POINT, I should state the obvious: I believe in this vision of liberalism. In the Philippines, it is a deep tradition that can be neither effaced by Marxism nor the anti-Western nationalism of the Diliman Consensus. It can be rediscovered, and our four protagonists may become relevant again. A renewal of their ideas is urgent.

I conclude this book at an uncertain period in our political history, barely a hundred days after the ascension to power of the populist strongman Rodrigo R. Duterte. The new president won the election amid popular disillusionment with the administration of the liberal-democrat Benigno Aquino III. Aquino and his Liberal Party prioritized slow, governance reforms that left many pining for an action-oriented mayor who would solve quotidian problems like criminality, traffic, and governmental red tape. More profoundly, 30 years of re-democratization after Marcos failed to deliver inclusive economic security, leading to the emergence of authoritarian nostalgia.

Duterte has turned liberalism into a dirty word. It was a feat achieved through virulent propaganda largely supported by the family of Ferdinand Marcos, who now hold significant sway over the new president. And completing the alliance of authoritarianisms from the left and the right, the president has appointed members of the Maoist Communist Party to his cabinet.

Duterte is currently waging a brutal war on drugs that has led to over 7,000 deaths of suspected pushers and users.[6] When U.S. president Barack Obama raised questions concerning human rights, Duterte told him to "go to hell." He gave the dirty finger to the E.U. for raising similar concerns, and, fearing that the UN would be used as a venue to challenge his drug war, he questioned the contributions of the UN to the Philippines. Human rights are currently portrayed as anathema to governance. They have become, despite the legacies of SP and Romulo, "Western values."

Duterte claims to have crossed an "ideological Rubicon" domestically and internationally. Instead of continuing the country's close ties with the United States, he wishes to reach out to Russia and China. One is never sure if Duterte's words constitute mere bluster or represent a real political shift. Yet recent events are enough to petrify liberals like myself. In this sense, we are no different from panicked liberals in the U.S., Europe, Turkey, and other places beset by 21st-century illiberal populism.

Will our liberal institutions survive the assault from 21st-century populism? Despite the many failures of post-Marcos liberal democracy now being exposed by Duterte, the present system has deliberative potential, which could blunt the appeal of populism in the long run. Sociologist Nicole Curato notes that "Discourses in the public space are free and wide-ranging, where views even of marginalised sectors have been articulated, contested, revised and reconsidered." The challenge, she explains, is for these varied discourses to create an "empowered space," where they affect political decision making.[7] Similarly, political scientist Nathan Quimpo argues that democratic consolidation has occurred because a growing number of non-Communist leftists seek not to weaken state institutions but to strengthen them.[8] Quimpo believes that post-Marcos Philippines is a "contested democracy," where democratization from below is still possible. Philippine liberalism will live or die on the creation of Curato's "empowered space." And Quimpo's grassroots movements, his modern "Left," will be the ballasts of a liberal democracy under assault.

Have these efforts at liberal consolidation been enough? Or will we become incredulous once again—like SP Lopez at the beginning of martial law—at how quickly the tide turns? At how easily Filipinos trade freedoms for a perception of security? The postwar liberal experiment in self-government lasted over thirty years, until Marcos's rule ended it. Today, it has been thirty years after the "restoration" of democracy after Marcos, and one wonders if liberal-democratic experiments in the Philippines have 30-year expiration dates. I have neither the temerity nor the capacity to predict how this political juncture will unfold.

The historian, working in the past, has the luxury to equivocate about the present. But the citizen and the patriot, inevitably embroiled in exigencies of the present politics, has no choice but to hope.

Rita D. Estrada, a lesser known mid-century liberal.

Afterword
A Fifth Liberal

I noticed halfway into this project that I was writing a prequel. My first book, *Taming People's Power: The EDSA Revolutions and their Contradictions*, was about my parents' generation—the generation of Marxist activists who opposed the Marcos dictatorship through armed and political struggles. In that book, I spoke about my vexed relationship with the Maoism of my parents and their comrades, tracing that movement's rise and what I now consider to be its ultimate failure. The autobiographical impulse of that book was explicit, and it embraced the cliché of tracing one's roots.

I thought this work would be less parochial. Alas, it is informed by the same cliché, for these pages are about the generation of my grandparents, the generation that collectively participated in the liberal experiment. I realized this as I was looking through my maternal grandparents' old bookshelf. Though many of their books have been lost over the years, my family still has a few titles: works by William James, a first edition of Rizal's letters edited by Wenceslao Retana, signed copies of Cesar Majul's work on Muslim Filipinos, the anti-Communist essays of Milovan Dilas, and numerous tomes of their hero, Bertrand Russell. These books would not have been out of place in the shelves of Osias, Araneta, Romulo, or SP.

My grandmother, Rita Estrada, was a philosopher and psychologist while my grandfather, Horacio Estrada, was a pharmacologist. Both taught at the University of the Philippines. And, although Lolo Horacio was a natural scientist, he shared Lola Rita's broad interest in philosophy, history, and the social sciences.

I knew them well, growing up in their faculty housing at UP's sprawling Diliman campus. They were my second parents, doting on me as their first grandchild. Through them and my parents, I experienced a childhood canopied by Acacia trees, embraced by familial warmth, flanked by liberal intellectuals. We lived in a bungalow with a large porch and a modest backyard. The house, on the far end of Agoncillo Street (a five-minute walk from the university infirmary), was one of the oldest on campus, built shortly after the university relocated to its sprawling grounds in Quezon City, in the north of Metro Manila. My fondest childhood memories are of Sunday mornings watching my grandparents playing bridge with neighboring professors from different colleges, my grandmother serving dishes like baked beans or a New England broiled dinner.

Since they died before I became a historian, it is only belatedly that I have started to understand them as intellectuals. My grandparents, though decades younger, were of the same liberal ilk as the intellectuals in this book. I will never know for sure, but they were likely raised on Osias's *Philippine Readers*; they most definitely would have lived through the economic debates of Salvador Araneta; and more importantly, they were professors in the university run by Romulo and SP (Mama tells me that Romulo was once their dinner guest.).

As a pharmacologist, Lolo Horacio spent his career testing the efficaciousness of local herbs and plants reputed to have medicinal properties. In many ways, his work was the medical equivalent of Osias's *Filipinismo*: Lolo was involved in a collective effort within UP to create a canon of local medicinal plants. Early in his career, he was offered a tenure track position at the University of Pennsylvania but he turned it down, believing that his medical research needed to benefit Filipinos. Like other doctors of his era, he saw himself as part of the nation-building project. And he imparted some of what he learned to us. Until now, upon contracting a minor cough, I buy tablets made from the *lagundi* plant—an herb tested in Lolo's UP College of Medicine lab, instead of the cough medicines peddled by international pharma.

Let me, however, focus on Lola, who, through this postscript, will serve as our fifth liberal intellectual. I have been remiss in writing a book completely about men, and I offer this afterword as a minor corrective; it is a short story about a female liberal, who was also a feminist.

Rita Maurat Domingo was born in Manila on 29 March 1925 to Vitaliano Domingo and Julia Maurat. Neither my mother nor my aunt remember what Vitaliano did for a living (he died when Lola was young), but Julia was a fishmonger, and she raised Rita in poverty. Julia did not value Rita's education much, insisting that selling fish was more productive than reading. The teenage Rita, in fact, had to hide in her closet to read Tagalog fiction and *komiks* from the weekly magazine *Liwayway*. When she was caught, she would be made to kneel on mongo seeds. At times, she would even be physically restrained, tied up so she would be unable to grab books. Later in life, when Lola hoarded cheap romance novels from book sales, she would remind Mama that pleasure reading still felt like a privilege.

Rita did not have to become a scholar. She was a mestiza, with round eyes, thick brown hair, a narrow nose, and slender lips—features probably inherited from her maternal grandfather, who was a deserter from the French army. Before the war, Sampaguita Pictures—the largest film studio in the country—offered her to join their stable of actresses. And during the war, she received numerous marriage proposals from GIs who wanted to take her to America. Her numerous admirers also included scions of Manila's wealthiest families, most notably the son of Maximo Viola—the funder of Rizal's novels. Yet high society life did not interest Rita, who wanted to become a scholar.

Julia agreed to send Rita to high school, but refused to spend a cent on college, forcing Rita to look for a scholarship, which she found at the Far Eastern University (FEU). But the scholarship was competitive, and a tuition waiver was granted to only the top student of the cohort. Rita had to be number one lest she lose her financial assistance. So she remained at the top of her class until graduation.

She completed her undergraduate studies in Philosophy and English (disciplines reflective of her love for reading) in 1948, and moved on to complete an MA in Philosophy (also at FEU) in 1954. While a graduate student, she met and married a medical student, Horacio R. Estrada, a member of Central Luzon's landowning elite, whose family looked down on marrying below one's class. Lolo was a low-level class traitor, and academia would become his refuge from his family. As for Lola, academia would let her read. She believed so much in the joys of reading that she put her two younger siblings through college.

After teaching philosophy in FEU for fifteen years, she was recruited by the chair of UP Diliman's Psychology Department—then a very young department that was only beginning to establish its disciplinary boundaries. That a philosopher would be hired to work in a psychology department only reflected the porosity of the two disciplines at the time. I suspect Lola read William James, because pragmatism provided a common discourse for experimental psychology and philosophy.

Lola would become one of the department's institution builders, serving in various administrative positions. She also became a beloved teacher. Even before meeting my mother, my father, then a Maoist student activist, already considered Rita Estrada one of his favorite teachers: She sat on her desk, spoke off the top of her head, digressed, and cracked a lot of jokes.[1] Despite what initially felt like rambling, Papa learned a lot.

Papa remembers how Prof. Estrada looked kindly towards student activists (perhaps because her own daughter was one), though she never publicly proclaimed support for the Maoists. Even if her favorite philosopher was the anti-Communist Bertrand Russell, this did not prevent her from feeling the same elderly beneficence that SP felt for his students. In her old files, my aunt found a jailhouse letter from Lean Alejandro, one of the great martyrs of the Communist Left, calling Lola a "fellow traveler" in the struggle against Marcos. She was one of Alejandro's favorite teachers, and, in his letter, he recalled meals in our house, where they spoke of J.R.R. Tolkien's *Lord of the Rings* and national liberation. Marcos, for Alejandro, was the Sauron—the Dark Lord—of their times.

Lola's sympathies for her students were evident to anyone who lived through the dictatorship. Like SP, Lola took the students' side against Marcos during the Diliman Commune. Like SP, she lived on campus, and saw the police assault as an attack on her community, the Diliman Republic. And like SP, she visited her students in the barricades, offering them encouragement and support. As a skilled cook and baker, she had the additional advantage of being able to offer them sandwiches and juice.

Lola was primarily a pedagogue, and the pressure for Filipino academics to publish during her time was not pronounced as it is today. As a consequence, my family does not have a lot of her written work. I have, however, found a very strange document in our shelves: her 1981 MA Psychology thesis entitled "An Inquiry into Sexism in the Tagalog Language." She was fifty-six when she completed it.

By the late 1970s, the Department of Psychology began to have a greater sense of its disciplinal boundaries, which must have forced Lola, a philosopher, to earn credentials in the discipline. She had already commenced a doctorate in psychology at the University of Kansas in 1963, but returned to the Philippines after a year of missing her three kids.

The master's degree was just a box she had to tick. It must have been strange for her being taught by peers and colleagues whom she had worked with for so long. When she began work on the thesis, she was already an Associate Professor and Assistant Chair of the Department. Her adviser, moreover, was someone almost twenty years her junior: Virgilio "Ver" Enriquez—the man who would later be called the father of Filipino indigenous psychology.

Even intellectually, Enriquez was from a different generation. In the field of psychology, he was the personification of the inward-looking nationalism of the Diliman Consensus. Filipino indigenous psychology—Sikolohiyang Pilipino—like its sibling, Pantayong Pananaw (see introduction), sought to discover and liberate "Filipino" subjectivity by unshackling it from "Western" categories. It is a disciplinal orientation that continues to dominate UP Diliman's Psychology Department.

Ostensibly, Lola's topic fit into the ethos of Sikolohiyang Pilipino, as it mined linguistic structures for insights about the "Filipino psyche." In a significant way, however, it did not. For one, the work is explicitly, if crudely, feminist at a time when no work in Filipino indigenous psychology (then a very young undertaking) had attempted to merge the subfield with feminist critique. Lola's work itself did not have ambitions of revising Sikolohiyang Pilipino's foundational theories to include gender analysis. That would come more than a decade later when, in 1996, Lola's daughter, Sylvia (Mama), completed her dissertation *"Sekswalidad, Pagkababae, at Pagkatao: Isang Panimulang Pagsisiyasat sa Konstruksyon ng Pagkababae sa Kulturang Pilipino"* [Sexuality, Femininity, and Personhood: A Primary Investigation into the Construction of Femininity in Filipino Culture].

Lola's thesis, unlike the jargon-laden pseudo-scientific works of contemporary psychology, was written like an essay, and its "methodology" was the well-written argument. Its prose was unencumbered, since it did not have a ghastly section called the "theoretical and analytical framework."

More importantly, the thesis was bereft of the nationalist earnestness of other works in Sikolohiyang Pilipino—including her daughter's. Mama wrote her dissertation only a few years after leaving the Maoist underground; she also completed it in the year that Lola died. It is, thus, a serious and scholarly treatise that dissects constructions of Filipina femininity in newspaper rape narratives and popular love stories. Its goal was explicitly emancipatory, seeking to challenge Filipina femininity to forge it anew.

Lola's goal, however, was not liberation. The thesis had a clear audience and a clear intention of what it had to tell this audience:

> The audience I had in mind, for this thesis is (I hope) the literate, US-type-educated Filipino of this era who may find this work interesting, even enjoyable and afford him/her insight, through language, into the workings of the Filipino psyche and perhaps laugh with the author at ourselves.[2]

Laughter, indeed, was part of her work. To wit, one section of the thesis makes a point about finding a unique worldview offered by Tagalog. She does this by jesting about the impossibility of translation between two languages:

> Translation, of course, between such disparate languages as English and Tagalog is not for the faint-hearted or the weakminded [sic]. Someday, some brave soul may tackle "I told you to not and then you again" or the present horrors "kadiri to death" [gross to the death] or "how baboy naman the pig" [how pig-like the pig] and relate it all to a Weltanschauung peculiarly Filipino moderne![3]

When Lola allowed herself some of Sikolohiyang Pilipino's nativism by romanticizing "native" culture, she did so through the lens of a 20th-century Filipino liberal. She celebrates, for instance, Tagalog's capacity to express "events sans a subject-predicate formulation" ("*umuulan*" as opposed to "It's raining outside"). Using terms practically lifted from pragmatist philosophy, she claimed that:

> Tagalog hews closer to the modern physicist's conception of the reality—that this is indeed a world of events, processes and continually changing

phenomena. One can imagine Heraclitus, five centuries before Christ, would have found Tagalog his language of choice as it can express realistically his universe of eternal flux. [4]

Forgive the bias, but Camilo Osias could not have phrased an argument for the world's dynamism better. Indeed, Lola's point is a kind of Osias-style internationalism: The beauty of the Tagalog language is not only a function of what it says about Filipinos, but what it allows us to say about the world. Like Osias, Lola, too, made mention of "narrow nationalism" and its blinders.[5]

The broad point of the work, however, concerned female empowerment and rights. In " the civilized world," she claimed, "we demand the right of human beings to be treated strictly according to their merit without regard or reference to such accidents as race, creed (religious or political) or place of origin." "To this list," she added, human rights discourse has "added sex, and, in the wake of homosexual and ambisexual revolution, sexual preference." These values "are, for the most part, the values of the West." This fact, however, was a not a concern since they are values that "educated Filipinos accept, or at the very least, pay lip service to."[6]

Tagalog passes this liberal criteria. Unlike Western languages like English or Spanish, Tagalog, which has very few gendered signifiers, "need not go through" a "tortuous purge" in order to remove a "heavily masculine bias."[7] "There is something to be said," she joked, "for a childhood where one's concerns did not include the sex of water (el agua) or table (la mesa) [sic]." "This is really innocence!"

The thesis makes a modest, even simplistic, point about equality ("As such, Tagalog qualifies as a communication medium for an androgynous society where sexual egalitarianism, at least in language, is realizable as an ideal"),[8] and the work has no revolutionary implications; in fact, it distances itself from Marxist rhetoric through what I suspect was a snide rephrasing of stale Maoist slogans: "Whether women of this nation are disadvantaged or not in the present semi-technological semi-agricultural more than semi-colonial country we live in is for other disciplines to establish."[9]

The modest point of the thesis was to begin a dynamic conversation about a dynamic nation, in order to "forge a society that embodies all the goodness of its past and the lessons, painful and otherwise of its present and the promise of realization of its aspirations and visions of its future."[10] It was a future-oriented view of nation and state building.

My reason for writing about Lola is as modest as her thesis. I do not think she impacted Filipino intellectual life the way Osias, Araneta, Romulo, or SP did. She was a humble professor, tucked away in Diliman campus. She was also a woman in a masculine intellectual world. But her story exemplifies how liberalism suffused the lives, thinking, and actions of an entire generation of intellectuals. And her relationship with her daughter, my mother, reflected the elderly beneficence of her liberal generation: Mama was allowed her forays into radicalism and nativist nationalism, because liberals let you discover the values of liberalism for yourself. They will not convince you immediately, as appreciating moderation requires playing with fire first.

Recently, Mama has started to resemble the Lola I remember not just physically but also intellectually. While writing this, I have pressed numerous books into her hands, most of them tracts on liberal politics. Interestingly, the ex-Maoist has had a very congenial relationship with these works, and has begun quoting them in her own writings. They are familiar to her because they are vestiges of her youth. As the daughter of Rita Estrada, she has liberalism in her political DNA. In the past few years, she, too, has come out as a liberal, while maintaining her roots in the women's and reproductive health movement.

A part of her never gave up on liberalism anyway. She has always parented as a liberal, raising me in a house bereft of a party line (she even let me attend what she considered a conservative Catholic university, and paid for it to boot!). But now her private liberal parenting coincides perfectly with her outward liberal politics, making her personal truly political.

The shift is most perceptible in her writing, which these days has been increasingly funnier—unsurprising for someone whose first writing teacher was Rita Estrada. Last year Mama published her second book—a series of essays on her life as a rape and domestic violence counselor. The topic is, naturally, grim, but the prose is ebullient, warm, joyful, and transparent. A humanist text, it is about the moments of laughter, even humor, amid suffering. It is called *And then She Laughed*.

We may kill our Marxist fathers, but we become our liberal mothers.

Notes

INTRODUCTION: LIBERALISM ASKANCE

1. Arjun Appadurai, "Diversity and Disciplinarity as Cultural Artifacts," in *Race, Identity and Representation in Education*, ed. Cameron McCarthy et al. (New York: Routledge, 2005), 434.
2. Ibid., 435.
3. Dipesh Chakrabarty, "Notes Toward a Conversation Between Area Studies and Diasporic Studies," in *Orientations: Mapping Studies in the Asian Diaspora*, ed. Kandice Chuh and Karen Shimakawa (Durham: Duke University Press, 2001), 126.
4. Adam Kirsch, "Melancholy Liberalism," *City Journal*, Winter 2016. http://www.city-journal.org/2016/26_1_melancholy-liberalism.html, accessed 26 January 2016.
5. For examples of how liberalism has been pilloried by postcolonial thought, see Bhikku Parekh, "Liberalism and Colonialism: A Critique of Locke and Mill," in *The Decolonization of Imagination: Culture, Knowledge and Power*, ed. Jan Nederveen Pieterse and Bhikku Parekh (London: Zed Books, 1995); Uday Singh Mehta, *Liberalism and Empire* (Chicago and London: University Of Chicago Press, 1999); Karuna Mantena, *Alibis of Empire: Henry Maine and the Ends of Liberal Imperialism* (Princeton: Princeton University Press, 2010). According to Andrew Fitzmaurice, it was Edward Said's *Orientalism* that started the trend of historians exposing "liberalism's complicity in empire." See "Liberalism and Empire in Nineteenth-Century International Law," *The American Historical Review* 117, no. 1 (February 2012): 122–40.
6. Mehta, *Liberalism and Empire*, 7.
7. Ibid., 12.
8. Jean Comaroff and John L. Comaroff, *Theory from the South: Or, How Euro-America is Evolving Toward Africa* (Boulder and London: Paradigm Publishers, 2012), 23.
9. Boaventura de Sousa Santos, *Epistemologies of the South: Justice against Epistemicide* (Boulder and London: Paradigm Publishers, 2014), 238.
10. Ibid., 160.
11. For a critique of this tendency, see Pascal Bruckner, *The Tears of the White Man: Compassion as Contempt*, trans. William R. Beer (New York: The Free Press, 1986). In the 1960s, the emergence of the "New Left" occurred as Trotskyites and Maoists in places like Paris and Berkeley discovered the guerrilla Communisms of the developing world, turning those struggles into

"Rorschach tests" for the revolution they wished to see at home, but could only find abroad. See Richard Wolin, *The Wind from the East: French Intellectuals, the Cultural Revolution, and the Legacy of the 1960s* (Princeton: Princeton University Press, 2010).

12 Eric Hobsbawm, *The Age of Extremes: A History of the World, 1914–1991* (New York: Vintage Books, 1996), 563.
13 Francois Furet, *The Passing of an Illusion: The Idea of Communism in the Twentieth Century*, trans. Deborah Furet (Chicago and London: University Of Chicago Press, 2000), 11.
14 Ibid., 24.
15 John Gray, *Two Faces of Liberalism* (New York: The New Press, 2000), 2.
16 Neil Lazarus, "The Fetish of 'the West' in Postcolonial Theory," in *Marxism, Modernity, and Postcolonial Studies*, ed. Crystal Bartolovich and Neil Lazarus (Cambridge: Cambridge University Press, 2002), 43–64.
17 Ibid., 52.
18 Vivek Chibber, *Postcolonial Theory and the Specter of Capital* (London and New York: Verso, 2013), 23. I am aware the both Chibber and Lazarus defend the Enlightenment not as liberals but as Marxists. Nonetheless, a liberal may level the same critique at postcolonial theory. For, indeed, Marxism and liberalism have common roots in the Enlightenment.
19 Gray, *Two Faces of Liberalism*, 2.
20 Thomas Nagel, *The View From Nowhere* (New York and Oxford: Oxford University Press, 1989).
21 Amartya Sen, *The Idea of Justice* (London: Penguin Books, 2011), 6.
22 Ibid.
23 Michael Sandel, *Democracy's Discontent: America in Search of a Public Philosophy* (Cambridge and London: The Belknap Press of Harvard University, 1996), 4.
24 Sen, *The Idea of Justice*, 18.
25 Sandel, *Democracy's Discontent*, 26.
26 Lisandro E. Claudio, "Locating the Global South," in *The Sage Handbook of Globalization*, ed. Manfred B. Steger, Paul Battersby, and Joe Siracusa (Thousand Oaks: Sage, 2014), 185–99.
27 Alan Ryan, *The Making of Modern Liberalism* (Princeton and Oxford: Princeton University Press, 2012), 28.
28 Edmund Fawcett, *Liberalism: The Life of an Idea* (Princeton and Oxford: Princeton University Press, 2014), 143.
29 Ibid., 144.
30 Ramachandra Guha, "The Absent Liberal: An Essay on Politics and Intellectual Life," *Economic and Political Weekly* 36, no. 50 (15 December 2001): 4663.
31 Ibid., 4664.
32 Ibid.
33 Ibid.

34 Ibid., 4665.
35 Teodoro A. Agoncillo, *The Revolt of the Masses* (Quezon City: University of the Philippines, 1956).
36 Reynaldo C. Ileto, *Pasyon and Revolution: Popular Movements in the Philippines, 1840–1910* (Quezon City: Ateneo de Manila University Press, 1979).
37 Jim Richardson, *The Light of Liberty: Documents and Studies on the Katipunan, 1892–1897.* (Quezon City: Ateneo de Manila University Press, 2013), 406.
38 Caroline Sy Hau, "'Patria é intereses': Reflections on the Origins and Changing Meanings of Ilustrado," *Philippine Studies: Historical and Ethnographic Viewpoints* 59, no. 1 (March 2011): 3–54.
39 Nick Joaquin, *A Question of Heroes* (Pasig City: Anvil Publishing Inc., 2005), 25. The transatlantic and global influence of universal liberty and rights in the wake of the twin revolutions in France and America have now been given a more in-depth exploration. Prior to socialist internationalism, it was liberalism that provided a framework for global brotherhood and solidarity. See Janet Polansky, *Revolutions Without Borders: The Call to Liberty in the Atlantic World* (New Haven: Yale University Press, 2015). Through the work of Benedict Anderson, we know that it was early Creole nationalism that allowed liberal ideas to be articulated through the language of anticolonial nationalism. *Imagined Communities : Reflections on the Origin and Spread of Nationalism* (London and New York: Verso, 1983), 50–65.
40 Joaquin, *A Question of Heroes*, 25.
41 Ibid., 29.
42 Parishes in the Philippines, in violation of canon law, were run by friar orders (Dominicans, Franciscans, etc.) as opposed to "secular" priests under the hierarchy of the Vatican. That many secular priests were creoles heightened the tension surrounding the issue.
43 Joaquin, *A Question of Heroes*, 25.
44 Ibid., 30.
45 The more reactionary Carlists forced Maria Cristina (on behalf of her daughter) to forge alliances with moderate liberals. See Isabel Burdiel, "Myths of Failure, Myths of Success: New Perspectives on Nineteenth-Century Spanish Liberalism," *The Journal of Modern History* 70, no. 4 (December 1998): 903–904.
46 John N. Schumacher, *The Propaganda Movement: 1880–1895: The Creation of a Filipino Consciousness, the Making of a Revolution* (Quezon City: Ateneo de Manila University Press, 1997), 11.
47 Ibid., 5.
48 Megan C. Thomas, *Orientalists, Propagandists, and Ilustrados: Filipino Scholarship and the End of Spanish Colonialism* (Minneapolis and London: University of Minnesota Press, 2012), 11. See also Benedict Anderson, *Under Three Flags: Anarchism and the Anti-Colonial Imagination* (London: Verso, 2007), 56–57.

49   Schumacher, *The Propaganda Movement*, 8.
50   Joaquin, *A Question of Heroes*, 22.
51   Filomeno V. Aguilar, "Filibustero, Rizal, and the Manilamen of the Nineteenth Century," *Philippine Studies* 59, no. 4 (2011): 431.
52   Ibid., 36.
53   Filomeno V. Aguilar, "Tracing Origins: Ilustrado Nationalism and the Racial Science of Migration Waves," *The Journal of Asian Studies* 64, no. 3 (2005): 627.
54   Anderson, *Under Three Flags*.
55   Schumacher, *The Propaganda Movement*, 171.
56   Ibid., 308.
57   Ileto, *Pasyon and Revolution*; Agoncillo, *The Revolt of the Masses*.
58   Michael Cullinane, *Arenas of Conspiracy and Rebellion in Late Nineteenth-Century Philippines: The Case of the April 1898 Uprising in Cebu* (Quezon City: Ateneo de Manila University Press, 2014), xvii.
59   Michael Cullinane, *Ilustrado Politics: Filipino Elite Responses to American Rule, 1898–1908* (Quezon City: Ateneo de Manila University Press, 2003), 42.
60   Richardson, *The Light of Liberty*, 462.
61   This bifurcation and the debates within the ilustrado class are explored in Milagros Camayon Guerrero, *Luzon at War: Contradictions in Philippine Society, 1898–1902* (Pasig City: Anvil Publishing Inc., 2015).
62   Cullinane, *Ilustrado Politics*, 53.
63   Ruby Rivera Paredes, "The Partido Federal, 1900–1907: Political Collaboration in Colonial Manila," (Doctoral Dissertation, The University of Michigan, 1990), 165.
64   Resil B. Mojares, *Brains of the Nation: Pedro Paterno, T. H. Pardo de Tavera, Isabelo de Los Reyes and the Production of Modern Knowledge* (Quezon City: Ateneo de Manila University Press, 2006), 180.
65   Ibid., 186. For an analysis of the varying degrees of secularism among Filipino nationalists in this period, see Filomeno V. Aguilar Jr., "Church-State Relations in the 1899 Malolos Constitution: Filipinization and Visions of National Community," *Southeast Asian Studies* 4, no. 2 (August 2015): 279–311.
66   Resil B. Mojares, "Reinventing the Revolution: Sergio Osmeña and Post-Revolutionary Intellectuals in the Philippines," *Philippine Quarterly of Culture & Society* 24 (1996): 278.
67   Bonifacio's successor as the leader of the revolutionary Katipunan, Emilio Aguinaldo was proclaimed the president of an early Philippine Republic in 1898, but this soon became a government on the run. Moreover, regional elites only gave it provisional support, hedging their bets by remaining open to American governance. As such, Aguinaldo can hardly be considered a state-builder.
68   I use the term "consensus" loosely, of course, knowing full well that it has been challenged at various points—most notably by the historical work of Nick Joaquin—and that its fortunes have varied over the years. I also do not wish to indicate that this phenomenon was limited to the Diliman campus or to the University of the Philippines. Despite my slightly facetious and polemical

use of the term, it has served as an efficient shorthand that distills a broad, complex trend.

69 For works that examine the impact the book has had on postwar Philippine nationalism, see Rommel Curaming, "When Clio Meets the Titans: Re-Thinking State-Historian Relations in Indonesia and the Philippines" (Ph.D Thesis, Australian National University, 2006), 99; Neferti Xina M. Tadiar, *Fantasy-Production: Sexual Economies and Other Philippine Consequences for the New World Order* (Quezon City: Ateneo de Manila University Press, 2004), 160; Reynaldo C. Ileto, *Filipinos and Their Revolution: Event, Discourse, and Historiography* (Quezon City: Ateneo de Manila University Press, 1998), 185–86; Reynaldo C. Ileto, "Reflections on Agoncillo's *The Revolt of the Masses* and the Politics of History," *Southeast Asian Studies* 49, no. 3 (December 31, 2011): 496–520.
70 Ileto, "Reflections on Agoncillo's *The Revolt of the Masses*."
71 Ibid., 512.
72 Curaming, "When Clio Meets the Titans," 99.
73 Ibid.
74 See Vernon R. Totanes, "'History of the Filipino People' and Martial Law: A Forgotten Chapter in the History of a History Book, 1960–2010," *Philippine Studies* 58, no. 3 (2010): 313–48 for a history of Agoncillo's tome and its multiple editions.
75 Lisandro E. Claudio, "Postcolonial Fissures and the Contingent Nation: An Antinationalist Critique of Philippine Historiography," *Philippine Studies: Historical and Ethnographic Viewpoints* 61, no. 1 (2013): 45–75.
76 Patricio Abinales, however, has shown that even Maoist nationalism in the Philippines drew heavily from postwar liberal traditions. See his *Fellow Traveler: Essays on Filipino Communism* (Quezon City: University of the Philippines Press, 2001), 201.
77 Yusuke Takagi, "Nationalism in Philippine State Building: The Politics of the Central Bank, 1933–1964" (Doctoral Dissertation, Keio University, 2014), 22.
78 Caroline S. Hau, "Sins of the Fathers: The Elite in Philippine Literature," *The Manila Review*, February 2014, http://themanilareview.com/issues/view/sins-of-the-fathers-the-elite-in-philippine-literature, accessed 2 November 2015.
79 Hau, "'Patria é intereses,'" 23.
80 Ibid., 25.
81 Vicente L. Rafael, "Introduction: Revolutionary Contradictions," in *Luzon at War: Contradictions in Philippine Society, 1898–1902*, by Milagros Camayon Guerrero (Pasig: Anvil Publishing, Inc., 2015), 7.
82 Ibid., 8.
83 Ibid.
84 Ibid., 13.
85 Ibid.
86 Ibid.
87 Cited in ibid., 1.
88 Ibid., 5.

89 Ibid.
90 Manfred Hildermeier, *The Russian Socialist Revolutionary Party Before the First World War* (New York: St. Martin's Press, Inc., 2000), 34.
91 Hau, "'Patria é interesses,'" 23.
92 Chibber, *Postcolonial Theory and The Specter of Capital*, 53.
93 Francois Furet, "The Terror," in Francois Furet and Mona Ozouf, eds., *A Critical Dictionary of the French Revolution*, trans., Arthur Goldhammer (Cambridge: Harvard University Press, 1989), 66.
94 Tony Judt, *When the Facts Change: Essays 1995–2010* (New York: Penguin Press, 2015), 348.
95 Eric J. Hobsbawm, "The Future of the State," *Development and Change* 27, no. 2 (1996): 269.
96 It is because of this that I have deliberately parked any discussion of the Liberal Party (LP) of the Philippines. The LP was founded in 1945 by a breakaway group from the dominant Nacionalista Party (NP) led by Manuel Roxas. The breakaway faction claimed to be more liberal than the conservatives who had led the NP. However, the ideological coherence of both the NP and the LP for most of the 20th century is questionable, as evidenced by the historical number of turncoats from both parties. Moreover, their constituencies have never been stable, as voting patterns evidence loyalties to personalities rather than to parties. To the LP's credit, it did become the major legal opposition party to the Marcos regime, and it is currently the most programmatic of the major political parties (a low bar in the Philippines where parties barely matter). This has not meant, however, that it has done much to articulate the ideas of Philippine liberalism. This work is more concerned about liberalism as nation-building discourse as opposed to its role in electoral politics. I hope to show that the best liberal intellectuals were bureaucrats and not elected officials.

CHAPTER 1: CAMILO OSIAS AND THE NATIONALIST INTERNATIONAL

1 Renato Constantino, "The Mis-Education of the Filipino," *Journal of Contemporary Asia* 1, no. 1 (1970): 20–36. The original was published in the *Philippine Graphic* in 1966. I will, however, cite the 1970 republished version, as it is more readily accessible.
2 Ibid., 36.
3 Ibid., 37.
4 Ibid., 38.
5 Ibid.
6 Maria Guillen Acierto, "American Influence in Shaping Philippine Secondary Education: An Historical Perspective, 1898–1978" (Ph.D. dissertation, Loyola University of Chicago, 1980), 65.
7 Florencio P. Fresnoza, *Essentials of the Philippine Educational System* (Manila: Abiva Publishing, 1950).
8 Ibid., 245.

9   Camilo Osias, *The Story of a Long Career of Varied Tasks* (Quezon City: Manlapaz Publishing Company, 1971), 15.
10 Ibid.
11 Ibid., 42.
12 Ibid., 48.
13 See Vernon R. Totanes, "History of the Filipino History Book" (Ph.D. dissertation, University of Toronto, 2012), 77–110.
14 The controversies surrounding collaboration with the Japanese are too complex to explain here. For an account of why and how pro-American bureaucrats like Osias cooperated with the Japanese colonial government, see Satoshi Nakano, "Appeasement and Coercion," in *The Philippines Under Japan: Occupation Policy and Reaction*, edited by Setsuho Ikehata and Ricardo Trota Jose, 21–58 (Quezon City: Ateneo de Manila University Press, 1999).
15 The two sources of Osias's biography are his memoirs and a sycophantic biography (typical of the biographies of elite politicians) by Bananal. Osias, *The Story of a Long Career;* Eduardo Bananal, *Camilo Osias, Educator and Statesman* (Quezon City: Manlapaz Publishing Company, 1974).
16 In this chapter, I am concerned more with Osias's thoughts on internationalism and nationalism than with secularism. Anyone interested in this aspect of Osias's thinking should see Camilo Osias, *Separation of Church and State* (Manila: S.N. [Probably self-published], 1934). A copy may be found in Ateneo de Manila University's Filipiniana collection.
17 Camilo Osias, "Rizal: Pioneer Nationalist and Internationalist," *Historical Bulletin* IV, no. 2 (1960): 39. I thank Jun Aguilar for finding this article.
18 Ibid., 49.
19 Ibid., 48.
20 Resil B. Mojares, *Waiting for Mariang Makiling: Essays on Philippine Cultural History* (Quezon City: Ateneo de Manila University Press, 2002), 270–96; Resil B. Mojares, *Brains of the Nation: Pedro Paterno, T. H. Pardo de Tavera, Isabelo de Los Reyes and the Production of Modern Knowledge* (Quezon City: Ateneo de Manila University Press, 2006), 467–505; Resil B. Mojares, *Isabelo's Archive* (Pasig: Anvil Publishing Inc., 2013), 235–48.
21 Mojares, *Isabelo's Archive*, 245.
22 Mojares, *Brains of the Nation*, 495.
23 Mojares, *Waiting for Mariang Makiling*, 26.
24 Patricia May B. Jurilla, *Tagalog Bestsellers of the Twentieth Century: A History of the Book in the Philippines* (Quezon City: Ateneo de Manila University Press, 2008), 35–56.
25 Roland Sintos Coloma, "Disidentifying Nationalism: Camilo Osias and Filipino Education in the Early 20th Century," in *Revolution and Pedagogy: Interdisciplinary and Transnational Perspectives on Educational Foundations*, ed. E. Thomas Ewing (New York: Palgrave Macmillan, 2005), 20.
26 Roland Sintos Coloma, "Care of the Postcolonial Self: Cultivating Nationalism

in The Philippine Readers," *Qualitative Research in Education* 2, no. 3 (October 2013): 323.

27 Ibid.

28 Malini Johar Schueller, "Colonial Management, Collaborative Dissent: English Readers in the Philippines and Camilo Osias, 1905–1932," *Journal of Asian American Studies* 17, no. 2 (2014): 162. It should be noted that Scott's notion of hidden transcripts was conceived in the context of subordinated and silenced groups like peasants, prisoners, and slaves. An elite intellectual like Osias, who rose within the colonial bureaucracy, was hardly rendered inarticulate by the colonial experience. In fact, it was the very engagement with the power of colonialism that gave Osias a voice. See James C. Scott, *Domination and the Arts of Resistance: Hidden Transcripts* (New Haven: Yale University Press, 1990).

29 Another reservation with critiques of empire by Western scholars (and their "Third World" allies such as Constantino) is their tendency to view colonialism as merely suppressing a local culture. However, as Pascal Bruckner notes, "What was quickly forgotten was that the respect for cultural differences had long been a colonialist argument in favor of a policy toward the natives, as Durkheim argued, or for indirect administration that gave much leeway to local practices.... Also quickly forgotten was that the right of people to cultural diversity had been demanded not only by anti-colonialists in their exhortations to Europe to withdraw, but also by the colonialists themselves to justify a policy of nonassimilation." *The Tears of the White Man: Compassion as Contempt*, trans. William R. Beer (New York: The Free Press, 1986), 28.

30 Thus, domestic phenomena, instead of being understood on their own terms, become allegories for the multicultural struggles of ethnic minorities in America.

31 It is once again Mojares's work that exposes the provincialism of a narrow focus on American empire. Mojares explores the cosmopolitan grounding of turn-of-the-century Filipino intellectuals, who deftly navigated intellectual trends in Europe and America while integrating local knowledge about various regions in the Philippines. Mojares, *Brains of the Nation*, 495–505.

32 "Private Schools in Philippine Education," *Philippine Journal of Education*, November 1927, 22.

33 This fraught attempt at canon-formation was evident very early on in the development of a Philippine literary tradition in English (see Isabel P. Martin, "Longfellow's Legacy: Education and the Shaping of Philippine Writing," *World Englishes* 23, no. 1 [2004]: 129–39).Thus the Philippine experience with English-language education cannot be compared, for instance, to the Indian experience, which was less about domestic canon-formation than about the demands of imperial governance. See Gauri Viswanathan, *Masks of Conquest: Literary Study and British Rule in India* (New York: Columbia University Press, 1989).

34 Camilo Osias, "Appendix A: Inaugural Address of Camilo Osias as First President of National University Delivered at the Manila Grand Opera House,"

in *Camilo Osias: Educator and Statesman*, by Eduardo Bananal (Quezon City: Manlapaz Publishing Company, 1974), 147–56.

35 Mark Mazower, *Governing the World: The History of an Idea* (New York: Penguin Press, 2012), 48.

36 Ibid.

37 See Andrew E. Johnstone, *Dilemmas of Internationalism: The American Association for the United Nations and US Foreign Policy, 1941–1948* (Surrey: Ashgate, 2009).

38 See Louis Menand, *The Metaphysical Club: A Story of Ideas in America* (New York: Farrar, Straus and Giroux, 2001) for a readable intellectual history of pragmatism. See Alan Ryan, *John Dewey and the High Tide of American Liberalism* (New York: W.W. Norton, 1995), 135–53, for an account of Dewey's time in the Teacher's College.

39 See Ronald K. Goodenow, "The Progressive Educator and the Third World: A Look at John Dewey," *History of Education* 19, no. 1 (1990): 23–40; Ronald K. Goodenow, "To Build a New World: Toward Two Case Studies on Transfer in the Twentieth Century," *Compare: A Journal of Comparative and International Education* 13, no. 1 (January 1983): 43–59; Ronald K. Goodenow and Robert Cowen, "The American School of Education and the Third World in the Twentieth Century: Teachers College and Africa, 1920–1950," *History of Education* 15, no. 4 (December 1986): 271–89.

40 Goodenow, "The Progressive Educator and the Third World: A Look at John Dewey," 30.

41 Apart from Osias, two other notable Filipino educators attended Columbia. Osias's classmate, Francisco Benitez finished his undergraduate studies there in 1910 and his MA in 1914 (see Priscila S. Manalang, "Francisco Benitez," *Philippine Journal of Education* XXX, no. 2 (August 1951): 81, 114, for an account of Benitez's early education). Florentino Cayco—founder of Arellano University—obtained an MA in 1922. In the late 1920s all three educators were frequent contributors to the *Philippine Journal of Education*, which Benitez edited from 1921 until his death in 1951. Two further lines of inquiry (which are outside the ambit of this chapter) may be pursued in this regard. First, research in the archives of Columbia University could be conducted to trace the connections between Filipino educators and others from the global south. Second, it may be interesting for other intellectual historians to write about the history of the *Philippine Journal of Education*. I may pursue these topics myself in the future. Another important connection of Dewey to the Philippines can be gleaned from the fact that Dewey was strongly considered to serve as the president of the University of the Philippines in 1920. See Cristino Jamias, *The University of the Philippines: The First Half-Century* (Quezon City: University of the Philippines, 1962), 123–27. I thank Resil Mojares for alerting me to this story and this source.

42 Camilo Osias, *The Story of a Long Career of Varied Tasks* (Quezon City: Manlapaz Publishing Company, 1971), 109.

43 Camilo Osias, *Life-Centered Education* (Quezon City: Bustamante Press, 1954), 151.
44 Camilo Osias, "Appendix A: Inaugural Address of Camilo Osias as First President of National University Delivered at the Manila Grand Opera House," in *Camilo Osias: Educator and Statesman*, by Eduardo Bananal (Quezon City: Manlapaz Publishing Company, 1974), 151.
45 Ibid.
46 The same internationalist mindset even permeated his masonry. In Osias's inaugural address as grand master in 1955, he claimed "The Cosmopolitan composition of our Ancient and Venerable Fraternity is a positive attestation of the widespread appeal and the universal character of Freemasonry." Quoted in "MW Camilo Osias," *The Most Worshipful Grand Lodge of Free and Accepted Masons of the Philippines*, n.d, accessed 4 November 2015.
47 Camilo Osias, "Education for New Japan," *Philippine Economy Review* 5, no. 6 (1959): 9.
48 Ibid.
49 Camilo Osias, "Education: An Instrument of National Goals" (Lecture, Philippine Women's University, Ramona S. Tirona Memorial Lecture Series, Manila, 20 May 1967), 13. This talk was delivered at around the time Constantino was criticizing Osias's generation of thinkers. Apart from a new emphasis on economic independence (pp. 5–6 of the document)—Osias called it "economic democracy"—there is no evidence that Osias felt the need to allude to or refute Constantino. The new emphasis on economic independence could have been a reaction to Constantino's and his cohort's arguments concerning neo-imperialism's effects on the domestic economy. My suspicion, however, is that Osias had merely absorbed the broader emphasis on economic planning and import substitution that emerged from the 1950s onward. It is worth noting that Osias was a contributor to the *Philippine Economy Review* in the 1950s, sharing its pages with prominent advocates of import substitution such as the industrialist Salvador Araneta.
50 Camilo Osias, *The Filipino Way of Life* (Boston: Ginn and Company, 1940), x.
51 Although they are intellectually from different generations, De los Reyes and Osias knew each other as they both served in the Philippine Senate in the 1920s. Osias's love for folklore, evidenced in the *Philippine Readers*, also dovetails with De los Reyes's thinking, as the former began his career as a folklorist.
52 Osias, *The Filipino Way of Life*, xii.
53 Quoted in Menand, *The Metaphysical Club*, 319.
54 Quoted in ibid., 320.
55 Quoted in ibid.
56 Salvador P. Lopez, *Literature and Society: Essays on Life and Letters* (Manila: University Publishing Company, 1941).
57 Warren D. Smith, "Book Review: The Filipino Way of Life by Camilo Osias," *Pacific Affairs* 13, no. 4 (December 1940): 494.
58 Ibid., 495.

59 Ibid.
60 Coloma, "Empire and Education," 104.
61 Joe R. Burnett, "Preface," in *The School and Society*, by John Dewey, ed. Jo Ann Boydston (London and Amsterdam: Southern Illinois University Press, Carbondale and Edwardsville, 1980), vi.
62 John Dewey, *The School and Society*, ed. Jo Ann Boydston (London and Amsterdam: Southern Illinois University Press, Carbondale and Edwardsville, 1980), 10.
63 Ibid., 105.
64 Richard Rorty, *Achieving Our Country: Leftist Thought in Twentieth-Century America* (Cambridge, Mass: Harvard University Press, 1997), 23.
65 Menand has traced this tendency in pragmatism to the probabilistic bent of late 19th-century statistical theory. Provided a larger sample size, one could grasp a more accurate mean. "Truth," then, was also a matter of what pattern emerged based on trial and error. Menand, *The Metaphysical Club*, 431–32.
66 Osias, *The Filipino Way of Life*, 7. In this regard, Osias's philosophy predates Zeus Salazar's Pantayong Pananaw school of indigenous historiography (discussed in introduction)—a perspective also anchored on the concept of "tayo." Like Osias, Salazar contrasts "kami" (an exclusive us) to "tayo" (an inclusive us). The telos of "tayo" for Salazar, however, is the "holy task (*banal na gawain*)" of nation-formation. Taken from Osias's perspective, however, Salazar's "tayo" becomes another form of "kami," as nation-formation is only an intermediate step toward an internationalist ethics. See Zeus A. Salazar, "Wika ng Himagsikan, Lengguwahe ng Rebolusyon: Mga Suliranin ng Pagpapakahulugan Sa Pagbuo ng Bansa," in *Journal Launching of Bagong Kasaysayan* (DAPP-AVR, Bulwagang Palma Silid, U.P. Diliman, 1998), 92.
67 Osias, *The Filipino Way of Life*, 58.
68 Ibid., 38.
69 Osias, "Inaugural Address of Camilo Osias as First President of National University," 154.
70 Ibid.
71 Goodenow, "To Build a New World," 44.
72 Osias, *The Filipino Way of Life*, 269.
73 Bryan Turner, "Democracy in One Country? Reflections on Patriotism, Politics and Pragmatism," *European Journal of Social Theory* 7, no. 3 (August 2004): 285.
74 Francisco Benitez, "The Contributions of America to Filipino Life," *Philippine Journal of Education* X, no. 7 (December 1927): 4.
75 Benigno Aldana, *The Educational System of the Philippines* (Manila: University Publishing Company, 1949), 164.
76 Ibid.
77 Francisco Paulino Cayco, "Introduction," in *The Magus of Progressive Education: The Writings of Florentino Cayco*, ed. Merlita Lorena Tariman (Manila: Arellano University, 2007), ix.

78 Florentino Cayco, "The Role of Youth," in *The Magus of Progressive Education*, 77.
79 Florentino Cayco, "Democracy and Nationalism," in *The Magus of Progressive Education*, 155.
80 Ibid.
81 Constantino, "The Mis-Education of the Filipino," 436.
82 Ibid.
83 These publication dates were compiled from the copyright pages of multiple printings of the readers from four sources: The Ambeth Ocampo collection in Kyoto University's Center for Southeast Asian Studies, the Philippine National Library, the Library of Congress, and the Mario Feir collection.
84 Totanes, "History of the Filipino History Book," 103.
85 Salud M. Parayno, *Children's Literature*, Revised (Quezon City: Katha Publishing Co., Inc., 1997), 19.
86 See Dominador D. Buhain, *A History of Publishing in the Philippines* (Quezon City: Rex Printing Company Inc., 1998), 77. As this chapter is mostly focused on intellectual trends in Philippine education, I have only introduced this very partial book history of *The Philippine Readers*. Future research, however, may wish to look at the policy decisions surrounding the books and how these affected their publication and production. Despite their relevance, there has not been a book history of *The Philippine Readers*.
87 Renato Constantino, *A History of the Philippines: From Spanish Colonization to the Second World War* (New York: Monthly Review Press, 1975), 314. For the latest scholarship on the Sakdal movement, see Motoe Terami-Wada, *Sakdalistas' Struggle for Philippine Independence 1930–1945* (Quezon City: Ateneo de Manila University Press, 2014).
88 Reinerio A. Alba, "Nurturing Children's Literature in the Philippines" (National Commission for Culture and the Arts, 28 July 2003), http://www.ncca.gov.ph/about-culture-and-arts/articles-on-c-n-a/article.php?i=63&subcat=13, accessed 29 August 2014.
89 Martin, "Longfellow's Legacy," 130.
90 Bonifacio P. Sibayan, "Becoming Bilingual in English in a Non-English Environment (retrospective Essay in Honor of Joshua A. Fishman)," in *Focus on Bilingual Education: Essays in Honor of Joshua A. Fishman*, ed. Ofelia Garcia (Amsterdam: John Benjamins Publishing Company, 1991), 290.
91 Camilo Osias, *The Philippine Readers, Book 4* (Boston: Ginn and Company, 1922).
92 Ibid, 5.
93 Benedict Anderson, *The Spectre of Comparisons: Nationalism, Southeast Asia, and the World* (New York: Verso, 1998), 2.
94 Camilo Osias, *The Philippine Readers, Book 7* (Boston: Ginn and Company, 1932), iii.
95 Ibid, 315.
96 Ibid, 317.

97 See Patricio N. Abinales, "Absent Characters in the National Story," *The Manila Review*, September 2014, accessed 4 April 2015.
98 David Michael M. San Juan, "12 Reasons to Save the National Language," *Rappler*, 10 August 2014, sec. Ispeak, 20, http://www.rappler.com/move-ph/ispeak/65545-san-juan-save-national-language; Antonio P. Contreras, "Betraying the Filipino Language," *GMA News Online*, 17 June 2014, sec. Opinion, Blogs, http://www.gmanetwork.com/news/story/366049/opinion/blogs/betraying-the-filipino-language; Teo Marasigan, "Ang Hindi Magmahal," *Pinoy Weekly*, accessed 29 August 2014, http://pinoyweekly.org/new/2014/06/ang-hindi-magmahal/.
99 Ronald K. Goodenow, "The Progressive Educator and the Third World: A Look at John Dewey," *History of Education* 19, no. 1 (1990): 23–40.

CHAPTER 2: SALVADOR ARANETA AND THE FILIPINO NEW DEAL

1 Edmund Fawcett, *Liberalism: The Life of an Idea* (Princeton and Oxford: Princeton University Press, 2014), 288.
2 Eric J. Hobsbawm, *The Age of Extremes: A History of the World, 1914–1991*, 1st Vintage Books (New York: Vintage Books, 1996), 94.
3 This is, of course, a broad categorization of post New Deal liberalism. For the nuances of this liberalism, see Alan Brinkley, *The End of Reform: New Deal Liberalism in Recession and War* (Reprint, New York: Vintage, 2011) and Jason Scott Smith, *Building New Deal Liberalism: The Political Economy of Public Works, 1933–1956* (New York: Cambridge University Press, 2009).
4 Mark Blyth, *Austerity: The History of a Dangerous Idea* (New York: Oxford University Press, 2013), 126.
5 Tony Judt, *Postwar: A History of Europe Since 1945* (London: Vintage, 2005), 69.
6 Nils Gilman, *Mandarins of the Future: Modernization Theory in Cold War America* (Baltimore and London: The Johns Hopkins University Press, 2003).
7 Yusuke Takagi, "Politics of the Great Debate in the 1950s: Revisiting Economic Decolonization in the Philippines," *Kasarinlan: Philippine Journal of Third World Studies* 23, no. 1 (2008): 91–114.
8 See Blyth, *Austerity*, for an intellectual history of austerity economics.
9 George Packer, *Blood of the Liberals* (New York: Farrar, Straus and Giroux, 2000), 94–130.
10 Michael Cullinane, *Ilustrado Politics: Filipino Elite Responses to American Rule, 1898–1908* (Quezon City: Ateneo de Manila University Press, 2003), 57.
11 Salvador Araneta, "Life with Father by His Son, Salvador," in *A Molave for His Country*, ed. Salvador Araneta (Malabon, Rizal: AIA Inc. Press, 1970), ix.
12 Ibid., 143.
13 See Alfred W. McCoy, "Rent-Seeking Families and the Philippine State: A History of the Lopez Family," in *An Anarchy of Families: State and Family in the Philippines* (Quezon City, 1994), 429–536.
14 Jose V. Abueva, *Eugenio H. Lopez, Sr.: Pioneering Entrepreneur and Business

	Leader (Leadership, Citizenship and Democracy Program, College of Public Administration, University of the Philippines, 1998), 56.
15	Ma. Lina Araneta Santiago, *Salvador Araneta: A Man Ahead of His Time* (Malabon, Metro Manila: A.I.A. Inc. Press., 1986), 10. It is typical for family-published biographies of elite politicians in the Philippines to brag about education in the Ivy League even if, as in this case, the politician merely audited classes and did not receive a degree.
16	From the front flap of Salvador Araneta, *Bayanikasan: The Effective Democracy for All* (Malabon, Metro Manila: The Bayanikasan Research Foundation, 1976).
17	By this, Kelso referred to laborers becoming capital workers. The laborers receive credit from the corporation, which they then use to buy stock. By 1976, Araneta was describing his own works "Kelsonian." See Araneta, *Bayanikasan: The Effective Democracy for All*.
18	National Historical Institute, *Filipinos in History*, vol. 3 (Manila: National Historical Institute, 1992), 22.
19	Frank H. Golay, *Face of Empire: United States-Philippine Relations, 1898–1946* (Quezon City: Ateneo de Manila University Press, 1997), 377–78.
20	Takagi, "Politics of the Great Debate," 99.
21	At the time, sugar prices in the United States were lower than the global price. Quirino wished to export to Japan to fetch the higher price, while Araneta insisted that the Philippines had a commitment to fulfill sugar export quotas to the United States. The disagreement caused a confrontation between the president and Araneta, which resulted in Araneta tendering his resignation. "Frankly, I didn't like his raised voiced at me," Araneta would remark years later. Araneta felt eventually vindicated because Quirino reversed his decision a month later. Salvador Araneta, *Salvador Araneta: Reflections of a Filipino Exile*, editor and interviewer Michael P. Onorato (Fullerton: The Oral History Program, California State University, 1979), 17–18.
22	Ibid., 19–20. Araneta advocated for a flexible minimum wage, which, as we shall see below, was integral to his proposal for full employment.
23	Ibid., 20.
24	Takagi, "Politics of the Great Debate," 108.
25	"Biodata of Dr. Salvador Araneta," 14 January 1971, Folders marked "Salvador Araneta," Lopez Museum and Library. It is perhaps because of these vast business interests that Araneta has been easily dismissed as a rent-seeker. Indeed, as an industrialist, he would have directly benefited from the many policies that he advocated. This fact, however, should not prevent us from examining the quality of his proposals.
26	National Historical Institute, *Filipinos in History*, 22.
27	When Araneta suffered a fatal heart attack in 1982, for instance, he told his daughter "No te veo" (I can't see you). See Araneta Santiago, *Salvador Araneta—A Man Ahead of his Time*, 12.
28	Araneta, *Reflections of a Filipino in Exile*, 17–18.

29 Quoted in Araneta Santiago, *Salvador Araneta: A Man Ahead of His Time*, 13.
30 Nick Cullather, *Illusions of Influence: The Political Economy of United State-Philippines Relations, 1942, 1960* (Stanford, California: Stanford University Press, 1994), 127.
31 Amando Doronila, *The State, Economic Transformation, and Political Change in the Philippines: 1946–1972* (Singapore, Oxford, and New York: Oxford University Press, 1992), 99.
32 Paul D. Hutchcroft, *Booty Capitalism: The Politics of Banking in the Philippines* (Ithaca and London: Cornell University Press, 1998), 76–77. In the critique of Araneta, we once again see an image of a homogenous elite, sharing common macroeconomic interests, exhibiting close to no ideological difference. As we saw in the introduction, however, the elite play a to and fro dance with popular and grassroots politics. Moreover, as the case of Araneta will show, the elite's macroeconomic interests vary significantly. In Araneta's case, his position as an exporter made his economics very different from other elites, who were import-dependent.
33 Yusuke Takagi, "Nationalism in Philippine State Building: The Politics of the Central Bank, 1933–1964" (Doctoral Dissertation, Keio University, 2014), 264.
34 Patricio N. Abinales and Donna J. Amoroso, *State and Society in the Philippines* (Lanham, MD: Rowman & Littlefield, 2005), 183–84.
35 This was when, as Central Bank Governor, he allocated limited dollar reserves to the Cojuangco family, allowing them to purchase the sugar plantation Hacienda Luisita. Prior to working for the Central Bank, Cuaderno was the head of a commercial bank owned by the Cojuangcos. See Lisandro E. Claudio, *Taming People's Power: The EDSA Revolutions and Their Contradictions* (Quezon City: Ateneo de Manila University Press, 2013), 92–93.
36 Steven Dale MacIsaac, "Nationalists, Expansionists and Internationalists: American Interests and the Struggle for National Economic Development in the Philippines, 1937–1950" (Ph.D Dissertation, University of Washington, 1993), 18.
37 Ibid., 519.
38 Frank H. Golay, *The Philippines: Public Policy and National Economic Development* (Ithaca, New York: Cornell University Press, 1961), 40.
39 Ibid., 50.
40 Ibid.
41 Vicente B. Valdepeñas, Jr. and Germelino M. Bautista, *The Emergence of the Philippine Economy* (Manila: Papyrus Press, 1977), 206. I also looked at official statistics from the various bulletins of the Central Bank from this period. The data includes number of employed, but does not include number of unemployed.
42 Takagi, "Nationalism in Philippine State Building"; Allan E. S. Lumba, "Materializing the Central Bank of the Philippines: The Uncanny Postwar History of Money and Modernity" (International Studies Association Annual Convention, Hilton, San Francisco, San Francisco, CA, 2008).

43 John H. Power and Gerardo P. Sicat, *The Philippines: Industrialization and Trade Policies* (London, New York, and Kuala Lumpur: Oxford University Press, 1971), 73.
44 Ibid.
45 Teresa Tadem, "Social Capital and the Martial Law Technocracy: The Making and Unmaking of a Power Elite," *Kritika Kultura*, no. 20 (April 2013): 78.
46 Raul V. Fabella and Emmanuel de Dios, "Introduction," in *Choice, Growth and Development: Emerging and Enduring Issues: Essays in Honor of Jose Encarnacion*, ed. Emmanuel de Dios and Raul V. Fabella (Quezon City: University of the Philippines Press and the School of Economics, University of the Philippines, 1996), xxvii.
47 Department of Economics, Ateneo de Manila University, "About," accessed 6 November 2015, http://www.ateneo.edu/ls/soss/economics/about-us.
48 Fabella and de Dios, "Introduction," xxvii.
49 Cuaderno, for instance, learned banking as a working student in Hong Kong and, eventually, as a lawyer who assisted with the cases of the Philippine National Bank. Yusuke Takagi, "Beyond the Colonial State: Central Bank Making as State Building in the 1930s," *Southeast Asian Studies* 3, no. 1 (April 2014): 100.
50 Takagi, "Politics of the Great Debate," 105.
51 Ibid., 109.
52 "New Deal for PI," *The Manila Chronicle*, 21 April 1952. Indeed, import controls were not used to boost industrial production. As I have previously shown, this system was subject to rent-seeking, which allowed Cuaderno to allocate millions for the acquisition of a sugar plantation in Central Luzon (see footnote 15).
53 "Salvador Araneta Hits Balanced Budget Policy," *The Manila Times*, 9 February 1955.
54 It is common for historians of this period to refer to the "era of controls" or debates around "controls." These categorizations only lead to confusion. It is necessary to specify the type of control.
55 He often admitted that his pro-export policy was a function of his being an industrialist. He also did not deny that his support for exporters also initially came from his connections with the Negros sugar industry, which would, indeed, benefit from pro-export policy. Araneta was candid about his belief that the interests of industrialists like him were similar to the interests of the country as a whole.
56 Salvador Araneta, "Footnotes on Revaluation," *The Manila Times*, 28 July 1954.
57 "Araneta Urges Unpegging of Peso from U.S. Dollar," *Daily Mirror*, 23 February 1956.
58 Ibid. It is this analysis that allows us to contest Abinales and Amoroso's earlier claim (see above) that Cuaderno's policies involved a battle against rent-seekers who were challenging import controls. First, Araneta and his allies were critical of the Central Bank's capacity to allocate dollars precisely because this process was subject to too much discretion, and, thus open to rent-seeking.

Second, Cuaderno's opponents were, in fact, more consistent on the issue of protecting against imports. However, they believed that the best way to do this was through increasing import prices by devaluing the peso, rather than simple dollar allocations. Cuaderno, on the other hand, was inconsistent, as he wanted to defend exporters through the import control law, while simultaneously disadvantaging them through the pegged exchange rate.

59 "PI's Dollar Policy Hit: S. Araneta Proposes Realistic Study of Foreign Exchanges," *The Manila Times*, 15 September 1958.
60 Salvador Araneta, *Christian Democracy for the Philippines: A Re-Examination of Attitudes and Views* (Malabon, Rizal: Araneta University Press, 1958), 172.
61 Ibid., 182.
62 Ibid.
63 Ibid., 236.
64 Ibid., 235.
65 Quoted in "Araneta on Economy: Former Secretary Urges Production of Local Goods to Replace Imported US Commodities," *The Manila Times*, 5 November 1956. For an analysis of how this Rectonian rhetoric merged with Maoist anti-imperialism, see Patricio N. Abinales, *Fellow Traveler: Essays on Filipino Communism* (Quezon City: University of the Philippines Press, 2001), 201.
66 Araneta, *Reflections of a Filipino in Exile*, 36. Of Osias, he said: "A nice fellow. He was a brilliant speaker. He was my neighbor during the Japanese occupation. We became very close. He was the first Filipino academician to become president of a university. I recall very well that his inaugural address was well received. I was a young student then. He got a lot of political training as resident commissioner in Washington. He was not profound but was an excellent and witty public speaker with a perfect command of English. He was a patriot."
67 Araneta, *Christian Democracy for the Philippines*, 12. Unlike Osias, however, Araneta foregrounded the Christian undertones of the "brotherhood of man." It was part of his broader project to promote a "Christian Democracy" in the Philippines, similar to the Christian socialists of Europe. Araneta was not ashamed to refer to the Philippines as a "Christian country."
68 Ibid., 13.
69 Quoted in Claro M. Recto, "Foreword," in *Christian Democracy for the Philippines: A Re-Examination of Attitudes and Views* (Malabon, Rizal: Araneta University Press, 1958), vii.
70 Araneta, *Christian Democracy for the Philippines: A Re-Examination of Attitudes and Views*, x.
71 "Araneta Extols Japan's Industrial Development," *The Manila Times*, 21 November 1960.
72 Maria R. Tagle, "Japan as Economic Example to PI Cited," *Daily Mirror*, 22 June 1961.
73 See Yoshiko Nagano, *State and Finance in the Philippines, 1898–1941: The Mismanagement of an American Colony* (Quezon City: Ateneo de Manila University Press, 2015).

74 Miguel Cuaderno Sr., "My Solution to the Present Economic Crisis," *Philippine Economy Review*, April 1958, 30.
75 Takagi, "Politics of the Great Debate," 104.
76 Frank H. Golay, "The Philippine Monetary Policy Debate," *Pacific Affairs* 29, no. 3 (September 1956): 253.
77 Power and Sicat, "The Philippines," 41.
78 Ibid.
79 Araneta, *Christian Democracy for the Philippines*, 393.
80 Benn Steil, *The Battle of Bretton Woods: John Maynard Keynes, Harry Dexter White, and the Making of a New World Order* (Princeton and Oxford: Princeton University Press, 2013), 76.
81 Ibid., 84.
82 John Maynard Keynes, *The Collected Writings of John Maynard Keynes*, ed. Elizabeth S. Johnson and D. E. Moggridge, vol. 4 (London: Macmillan, 1971), 35.
83 Ibid., 4:36.
84 Ibid., 4:37.
85 Ibid., 4:39–40.
86 Ibid., 4:43.
87 Ibid., 4:36.
88 The toothless NEC is, of course, best contrasted with Japan's famous Ministry of Trade and Industry, which was, in many ways, institutionally stronger than the Japanese Central Bank. See the classic work by Chalmers Johnson, *MITI and the Japanese Miracle: The Growth of Industrial Policy : 1925–1975* (Stanford: Stanford University Press, 1982).
89 The argument for expansionary economic policies was easier to make for Roosevelt and the New Dealers in the United States, as that country's economic populism featured a clearly-articulated defense of inflation and devaluation. In the late 19th century, populist agrarian movements united around the "Greenbacker" movement, which argued against the high price of the dollar. By depreciating the dollar and allowing for inflation, the debts of poor farmers would, in effect, cost less. A high dollar and minimal inflation, on the other hand, would benefit bankers and other creditors. This tradition would become the basis of the country's economic populism, which continued into the late 19th century, with William Jennings Bryan advocating for silver dollars and inflation. By the time of the New Deal Roosevelt not only faced a crisis that allowed for bolder measures, he also had this tradition to tap into. Despite this, however, there were pro-business, anti-inflation crusaders within the New Deal, like treasury secretary Henry Morgenthau.
90 Miguel Cuaderno, *Guidelines to Economic Stability and Progress: A Selection of the Speeches and Articles of Miguel Cuaderno Sr. Governor of the Central Bank of the Philippines* (Manila: Central Bank of the Philippines, 1960), 65.
91 Ibid., 90.
92 Ibid., 310.

93 Christina D. Romer, "What Ended the Great Depression," *The Journal of Economic History* 52, no. 4 (December 1992): 782.
94 Brinkley, *The End of Reform*, 15-30.
95 Golay, *The Philippines: Public Policy and National Economic Development*, 118.
96 Ibid., 104.
97 Ibid., 118–19.
98 Ibid., 118.
99 Power and Sicat, "The Philippines," 127.
100 Ibid.
101 "New Deal for PI."
102 Salvador Araneta, "The Central Bank and Our Production Program," *Philippine Economy Review*, April 1958, 54.
103 Salvador Araneta, *Economic Nationalism & Capitalism for All in a Directed Economy* (Rizal: Araneta University Press, 1965), 201.
104 Dotsey and Stark argue that "it is quite possible that both inflation and capacity utilization are driven by more fundamental factors, such as changes in productivity or monetary policy. Moreover, the relationship between utilization and inflation could be sensitive to which fundamental factor is driving the economy and the way in which monetary policy responds to those fundamentals, making the relationship quite complex and conditional on economic circumstances." Put simply, both Cuaderno and Araneta were basing their arguments on what was then and continues to be empirically thin ground. Michael Dotsey and Thomas Stark, "The Relationship Between Capacity Utilization and Inflation," *Business Review*, no. Q2 (2005): 16.
105 Araneta, *Christian Democracy for the Philippines*, 401.
106 A. W. Phillips, "The Relation between Unemployment and the Rate of Change of Money Wage Rates in the United Kingdom, 1861–1957," *Economica* 25, no. 100 (1958): 283–99.
107 Though the Phillips curve would be severely challenged by Milton Friedman in the 1970s, during the period of "stagflation" in the 1970s (when high inflation went alongside less growth and employment), the Great Debate occurred decades before. Araneta was advanced, but he was not advanced enough.
108 Gerardo P. Sicat, "A Historical and Current Perspective of Philippine Economic Problems" (Philippine Institute for Development Studies, 1986), 12, http://opendocs.ids.ac.uk/opendocs/handle/123456789/3476.
109 Ibid., 11.
110 Ibid., 18.
111 Valdepeñas, Jr. and Bautista, *The Emergence of the Philippine Economy*, 183.
112 Cayetano Paderanga, "The Macroeconomic Dimensions of Philippine Development" (Philippine Studies Conference in Japan [PSCJ], Center for Southeast Asian Studies, Kyoto University, 2014).
113 Fumitaka Furuoka, Qaiser Munir, and Hanafiah Harvey, "Does the Phillips Curve Exist in the Philippines?," *Economics Bulletin* 33, no. 3 (2013): 2009.

114 Ibid., 19.
115 Ibid., 22.
116 Ibid., 23.
117 Caroline S. Hau, "Elites and Ilustrados" (Unpublished manuscript), 282. I thank the author for providing me access to this work.
118 Ibid., 284.
119 Araneta and Onorato, *Reflections of a Filipino Exile*, 11.
120 Ibid., 22.
121 Ibid., 32.
122 See Alfred W. McCoy, ed., *An Anarchy of Families: State and Family in the Philippines* (Quezon City: Ateneo de Manila University Press, 1994); Benedict Anderson, "Cacique Democracy in the Philippines: Origins and Dreams," *New Left Review* 169, no. 3 (1988): 3–31.
123 As indicated above, Araneta was a proud alumnus of the Jesuit institution, Ateneo de Manila University. In many ways, what was labeled "social democracy" in the Philippines was closer to European Christian democracy, inspired as it was by the blossoming of Catholic social teaching after Vatican 2. See Benjamin T. Tolosa Jr., ed., *Socdem: Filipino Social Democracy in a Time of Turmoil and Transition, 1965–1995* (Quezon City: Ateneo de Manila University Press, 2012) for an account of the Philippine social democratic movement from the Marcos period until the early years of redemocratization in the 1990s.

CHAPTER 3: CARLOS P. ROMULO AND THE ANTI-COMMUNIST THIRD WORLD

1 For a general history of Bandung, see Jamie Mackie, *Bandung 1955: Non-Alignment and Afro-Asian Solidarity* (Singapore: Editions Didier Millet, 2005). For a book that examines individuals who have been under-researched in Bandung, see Antonia Finnane and Derek McDougall, eds., *Bandung 1955: Little Histories* (Monash University Press, 2010).
2 Paul Johnson, *Modern Times: A History of the World from the 1920s to the Year 2000* (London: Phoenix Press, 2000), 489–90.
3 David Priestland, *The Red Flag: Communism and the Making of the Modern World* (London and New York: Allen Lane/Penguin Books, 2009), 374.
4 Christopher J. Lee, "Introduction: Between a Moment and an Era: The Origins and Afterlives of Bandung," in *Making a World after Empire: The Bandung Moment and Its Political Afterlives*, ed. Christopher J. Lee (Athens: Ohio University Press, 2010), 10.
5 Michael Adas, "Contested Hegemony: The Great War and the Afro-Asian Assault on the Civilizing Mission," in *Making a World after Empire: The Bandung Moment and Its Political Afterlives*, ed. Christopher J. Lee (Athens: Ohio University Press, 2010), 69–106.
6 Christopher J. Lee, "At the Rendezvous of Decolonization," *Interventions* 11, no. 1 (2009): 82.

7   Roland Burke, "'The Compelling Dialogue of Freedom': Human Rights at the Bandung Conference," *Human Rights Quarterly* 28, no. 4 (2006): 949.

8   The "postcolonial" reading of Bandung (common among American scholars), with its attendant focus on racial distinctions and the cultural matrices that inform these, can be traced to the beginning of Bandung historiography. The African American novelist Richard A. Wright's 1956 first-person account *The Color Curtain* is, indeed, fodder for trendy yet empirically barren courses on race and postcolonial studies (largely en vogue in American academia). For an analysis and critique of Wright, see Babacar M'Baye, "Richard Wright and the 1955 Bandung Conference: A Re-Evaluation of The Color Curtain," *Journeys* 10, no. 2 (2009): 31–44.

9   Pang Yang Huei, "The Four Faces of Bandung: Detainees, Soldiers, Revolutionaries and Statesmen," *Journal of Contemporary Asia* 39, no. 1 (2009): 200.

10 Anti-Communism, as such, refers to opposition to a specific political model that emerged in the aftermath of the 1917 Bolshevik revolution that split world socialism into the Social Democrats of the Second International and the Communists of Lenin's Comintern (Third International). Anti-Communism here should not be taken as a critique of philosophical "communism" or abstract Marxist theory, but of the historical Leninist Communism, premised on the creation of vanguard parties composed of professional revolutionaries— a model implemented on vast swathes of the earth until the collapse of the USSR. (It has become common, in studies of Communism, to refer to "Big C" Communism).

11 Walden Bello et al., *The Anti-Development State: The Political Economy of Permanent Crisis in the Philippines* (London and New York: Zed Books, 2006).

12 Armando Liwanag, "The Record of Stalin," 15 January 1992, http://www.bannedthought.net/Philippines/CPP/1992/SSAMR/SSAMR-06-RecordOfStalin.pdf, accessed 11 March 2013. This article presents Stalin as genuine leader of the proletariat. It is part of a larger work called "Stand for Socialism against Modern Revisionism," which Communist Party of the Philippines (CPP) Chairman Armando Liwanag (*nom de guerre* of CPP founding Chairman Jose Maria Sison) published during the "great rectification campaign" that purged the Party of all those who deviated from the Party's original doctrines.

13 See Patricio N. Abinales, "Kahos Revisited: The Mindanao Commission and its Narrative of a Tragedy," in *Brokering a Revolution: Cadres in a Philippine Insurgency*, ed. Rosanne Rutten (Quezon City: Ateneo de Manila University Press, 2008), 144–87; Robert Francis B. Garcia, *To Suffer Thy Comrades: How the Revolution Decimated Its Own* (Pasig: Anvil, 2001). Naturally, scholars and activists in the Philippines have placed more emphasis on the power of international forces, as these are, indeed, more powerful than a fledgling Communist movement. However, the Communist Party itself reproduces this

binary by claiming to be the vanguard against imperialism. In Romulo's writings on anti-Communism, it is clear that criticizing the problem must come in tandem with criticizing so-called solutions. I have presented this dual rejection of Communism and elitism in the Philippines in a previous work. See Lisandro E. Claudio, *Taming People's Power: The EDSA Revolutions and Their Contradictions* (Quezon City: Ateneo de Manila University Press, 2013).

14   Augusto Espiritu, "'To Carry Water on Both Shoulders': Carlos P. Romulo, American Empire, and the Meanings of Bandung," *Radical History Review* 2006, no. 95 (2006): 177.

15   Ibid., 179.

16   The history of European anti-Communism here is far from exhaustive. It does not, for example, include the diverse history of anarchist anti-Communism, which would include leaders such as Emma Goldman. These forms of anti-Communism do not resonate as clearly with Romulo's work. What I have done, instead, is to summarize the history of liberal anti-Communism based on a pantheon of anti-Communist thinkers discussed by contemporary anti-Communist historians such as Tony Judt and François Furet. Tony Judt, *Past Imperfect: French Intellectuals, 1944–1956* (New York and London: New York University Press, 2011); Tony Judt, *The Burden of Responsibility: Blum, Camus, Aron, and the French Twentieth Century* (London: University of Chicago Press, 1998); Francois Furet, *The Passing of an Illusion: The Idea of Communism in the Twentieth Century*, trans. Deborah Furet (Chicago and London: University Of Chicago Press, 2000).

17   By non-fascist anti-Communism, I simply refer to the anti-Communism outside the ambit of Hitler and Mussolini.

18   Quoted in Judt, *The Burden of Responsibility*, 67.

19   Ibid.

20   A typical example of this is Ernest Mandel's biography of Trotsky. Ernest Mandel, *Trotsky as Alternative* (Verso, 1995).

21   Anne Applebaum, *Gulag: A History* (New York: Anchor Books, 2003), 14.

22   Leszek Kolakowski, *Main Currents of Marxism: The Founders—The Golden Age—The Breakdown*, trans. P. S. Falla (New York and London: W. W. Norton & Company, 2005), 762.

23   George Orwell, "Review of Russia under Soviet Rule by N. de Basily," in *George Orwell: Essays*, ed. John Carey (New York, London, and Toronto: Alfred A. Knopf, 2002), 111.

24   For an analysis of how Communism's association with the anti-fascists blunted critiques of the Soviet Union and its allies, see Furet, *The Passing of an Illusion*.

25   Judt, *Past Imperfect*, 102.

26   Rubashov's "manner of thinking," notes Koestler, "was modeled on Nikolai Bukharin," and "his personality and physical appearance a synthesis of Leon Trotsky and Karl Radek." Arthur Koestler, *The Invisible Writing* (London: Vintage, 2005), 479. For Koestler's own comparison of the fictional account of *Darkness at Noon* with the firsthand account of former head of Soviet

intelligence General Walter Krivitsky, see 483–88 of the same book, which is the second volume of his autobiography.

27 Christopher Hitchens, *Why Orwell Matters* (New York: Basic Books, 2003), 27.
28 Michael Scammell, *Koestler: The Literary and Political Odyssey of a Twentieth-Century Skeptic*, Kindle Edition (New York: Random House, 2009), chap. 22, sec. 5, para. 7.
29 See chapter 24 of Ibid.
30 Judt, *The Burden of Responsibility*, 94–95.
31 Tony Judt, *Postwar: A History of Europe Since 1945*, Kindle Edition (London: Vintage, 2005), chap. 7, sec.4, para. 7.
32 Ibid., chap. 7, sec. 4, para. 22. The CCF, as it is now widely known, was funded by the CIA, though its members did not know of this when they joined the congress. According to Judt, this fact is not as serious in retrospect, because writers such as Koestler, Aron, and Silone "did not need official American encouragement to take a hard line against Communism, and there is no evidence that their own critical views about the US itself were ever toned down or censored to suit the paymasters in Washington." The same can be said of Filipino CCF member F. Sionil Jose, who is routinely accused in the Philippines of being a former CIA agent. Ibid., chap. 7, sec. 4, para. 6.
33 Office for Asian Affairs, Congress for Cultural Freedom, *Freedom and Economic Planning: Proceedings of a Session of the Conference on Cultural Freedom in Asia, Rangoon, February 1955*. (New Delhi: Office for Asian Affairs, Congress for Cultural Freedom, 1955), 2.
34 Ibid., 56.
35 Ibid., 3.
36 The proceedings for the conference do not state whether there were participants from the Philippines. This was, however, unlikely, because, as I show below, the first interaction of the CCF with Filipino intellectuals was in 1960.
37 F. Sionil Jose, interview with author, Manila, 1 March 2013.
38 Manglapus is a minor, but important, character in our story. He wrote the final communiqué's section on cultural relations and was a close associate of Carlos P. Romulo. See Helen M. Thompson, "The Asian-African Conference at Bandung, Indonesia" (M.A. thesis, University of the Philippines, 1956), 226–27.
39 Interview with F. Sionil Jose, Manila, 1 March 2013.
40 Naturally, because formal relations between Filipino intellectuals and the CCF began after Bandung, one cannot argue that the CCF directly influenced the anti-Communism of Filipinos in the conference. Nonetheless, the later association of these intellectuals with the CCF points to the resonance between their thinking and that of liberal anti-Communists in Europe. People such as Manglapus and Jose would not have been recruited by the CCF had they been ideological opponents of the Congress. Moreover, as noted earlier, my concern here is not just Bandung itself but the anti-Communist Third World that Romulo articulated before and after it.
41 Jose, interview with author.

42 Gregorio C. Brillantes, *Chronicles of Interesting Times: Essays, Discourses, Gems of Wisdom, Some Laughs and Other Non-Biodegradable Articles* (Pasig: Anvil, 2005), 94–95.
43 Resil B. Mojares, *Waiting for Mariang Makiling: Essays on Philippine Cultural History* (Quezon City: Ateneo de Manila University Press, 2002), 288–99.
44 Quoted in ibid. 289.
45 Ibid., 289.
46 Ibid., 290.
47 University of the Philippines—Reserve Officers' Training Corps, "General Carlos P. Romulo: Class of 1918," n.d., accessed 19 March 2013, http://www.uprotc.org/alumni/general-carlos-romulo.html. Numerous sources and interviews state that Romulo, until his death, insisted on being addressed as "general."
48 Augusto Fauni Espiritu, *Five Faces of Exile: The Nation and Filipino American Intellectuals* (Stanford, California: Stanford University Press, 2005), 10.
49 See Espiritu, *Five Faces of Exile*, 9–45, for an overview of Romulo's career and intellectual history. For an account of Romulo's retirement, see Brillantes's intimate and eloquent portrait of an old, sickly Romulo, disgraced after his association with Marcos. Brillantes, *Chronicles of Interesting Times*, 89–98.
50 Lee Kuan Yew, *From Third World to First: The Singapore Story: 1965–2000* (Singapore: Times Media Private Limited and The Straits Times Press, 2000), 336. One of his most common jokes after marrying his younger second wife, Beth Day: "I have committed the crime of attacking Beth Day with a blunt instrument!" Jose, interview with author.
51 See Lisandro E. Claudio, "Postcolonial Fissures and the Contingent Nation: An Antinationalist Critique of Philippine Historiography," *Philippine Studies: Historical and Ethnographic Viewpoints* 61, no. 1 (2013): 45–75 for an analysis of the Philippine Left's relationship with nationalism.
52 Jose Maria Sison and Juliet de Lima, "Historical Essay: Foundation for Sustained Development of the National Democratic Movement in the University of the Philippines," in *Serve the People: Ang Kasaysayan ng Radikal na Kilusan sa Unibersidad ng Pilipinas*, ed. Bienvenido Lumbera et al. (Quezon City: IBON Foundation Inc., 2008), 54.
53 Nemenzo, interview with author.
54 Four anonymous sources who knew Romulo confirm that much of the diplomat's writings in the mid-1960s were penned by the Marxist intellectual Petronilo Bn. Daroy—a close friend of Jose Maria Sison's. Other ghostwriters mentioned by my sources include the nationalist historian Renato Constantino, Romulo's protégé Salvador P. Lopez (who allegedly wrote Romulo's Pulitzer-Prize winning book), and the historian Cesar Majul. Despite this, one source close to Daroy notes that Romulo's ghostwriters wrote some of the material but many times also took dictation directly from Romulo. Moreover, the same source emphasizes, Romulo, a former journalist and literature instructor, edited all the works himself. Romulo's books can thus be seen as reflecting his own views.

55 Patricio N. Abinales, *Fellow Traveler: Essays on Filipino Communism* (Quezon City: University of the Philippines Press, 2001), 192–228.
56 Francisco Nemenzo, interview with author, Quezon City, 18 January 2013. Nemenzo was part of an independent review panel (the Committee to Review External Programs) on Romulo's projects with U.S. agencies and discovered that the University of the Philippines' Institute of Hygiene had a U.S. Navy-funded project studying mosquitoes that caused inflammation of the male genitals. This breed of mosquitoes could distinguish between Asians and Caucasians and infected only the latter. Nemenzo's expose came after the coalition Movement for the Advancement of Nationalism (MAN) revealed that research on napalm had been conducted at the UP's Los Baños campus.
57 Andrade, Jr., Pio. *The Fooling of America: The Untold Story of Carlos P. Romulo* (Manila: Pio Andrade, Jr., 1985).
58 Ibid., 77.
59 Ibid., 78.
60 Carlos P. Romulo (with Beth Day Romulo), *Romulo: A Third World Soldier at the UN* (New York: Praeger, 1986), 38–44.
61 Ibid., 67.
62 Ibid.
63 Ibid., 53.
64 Carlos P. Romulo, United Nations Oral History Project: General Carlos P. Romulo, interview by William Powell and Rebecca Akao, Transcription, 30 October 1984, Dag Hammarskjold Library, http://www.unmultimedia.org/oralhistory/2011/06/romulo-carlos/, 6, accessed 11 March 2013.
65 Central Intelligence Agency, "The Current Situation in the Philippines: CIA Historical Review Program Release in Full," 30 March 1949, 13, CIA Freedom of Information Act Electronic Reading Room, http://www.foia.ucia.gov/docs/DOC_0000258577/DOC_0000258577.pdf, 13, accessed 23 March 2013.
66 Ibid.
67 Robert Trumbull, "Voice of Asia Grows Stronger in World: Conference at New Delhi Foreshadows New Role in International Affairs," *The New York Times*, 30 January 1949, E5.
68 "At Conference on Indonesia: Nehru Asserts Asia Intends to Play Part in Global Affairs," *The Washington Post*, 24 January 1949, 1.
69 Trumbull, "Voice of Asia Grows Stronger in World."
70 Ibid.
71 "US Is Called Pact Violator on Jap Reparations," *The Washington Post*, 20 May 1949, 4.
72 "Romulo Protests Reparations Halt: Philippine Envoy Says U.S. Act Help Japan to Revive Her Ability to Wage War," *The New York Times*, 20 May 1949, 2.
73 Carlos P. Romulo to Dean Acheson, "Letter from Carlos P. Romulo to Dean Acheson, 2 March 1950. Secretary of State File. Acheson Papers," 2, Harry S. Truman Library & Museum, http://www.trumanlibrary.org/whistlestop/

74. Ibid., 3–4.
75. Ibid., 4.
76. Ibid., 5.
77. Dean Acheson, "Memorandum of Conversation with General Carlos P. Romulo, 10 March 1950. Secretary of State File. Acheson Papers," 1, Harry S. Truman Library & Museum, http://www.trumanlibrary.org/whistlestop/study_collections/achesonmemos/view.php?documentid=66-6_26&documentYear=1950&documentVersion=both, accessed 12 March 2013.
78. Ibid., 2.
79. Romulo, *Third World Solider*, 114.
80. Ibid., 124. Ho Chi Minh's attraction to Communism was obviously more complex than this. It is, however, true that he did not start out as an enemy of the United States and that he was a nationalist before a Communist. For an introduction to Ho Chi Minh's thinking, see Walden F. Bello, "Introduction," in *Walden Bello Introduces Down with Colonialism!* (London: Verso, 2007).
81. "Rethinking the 'Third World': Seeing the World Differently," *The Economist*, 10 June 2010, http://www.economist.com/node/16329442.
82. "Asia Held '3d Force' Between U.S., Soviet," *The New York Times*, 29 May 1949, 16.
83. Carlos P. Romulo, "The Crucial Battle for Asia," *The New York Times*, 11 September 1949, 13.
84. Ibid., 68.
85. Carlos P. Romulo, "The Position of Southeast Asia in the World Community," in *Southeast Asia in the Coming World*, ed. Philip W. Thayer, Essay Index Reprint Series (Baltimore: John Hopkins Press, 1953), 149.
86. Ibid.
87. Ibid., 250.
88. Alexander V. Pantsov and Steven I. Levine, *Mao: The Real Story*, Reprint (New York, London, Toronto, Sydney, New Delhi: Simon & Schuster, 2012), 383.
89. Antonio Molina, *The Philippines: Through the Centuries* (Manila: University of Santo Tomas Cooperative, 1961), 408.
90. Carlos P. Romulo, *The Meaning of Bandung* (Chapel Hill: University of North Carolina Press, 1956).
91. Ibid., 5.
92. Ibid., 6.
93. Ibid.
94. Burke, "The Compelling Dialogue of Freedom," 949–50.
95. Ibid., 950–57.
96. Ibid., 958.
97. Judt, *Postwar*, chap. 18, sec. 1.
98. John Kotelawala, *An Asian Prime Minister's Story* (London: Harrap, 1956), 181.

(continued from previous page): study_collections/achesonmemos/view.php?documentid=66-6_06&documentYear=1950&documentVersion=both, accessed 12 March 2013.

99   C. P. Fitzgerald, "East Asia after Bandung," *Far Eastern Survey* 24, no. 8 (August 1955): 113, doi:10.2307/3024146.
100 Kotelawala, *An Asian Prime Minister's Story*, 181.
101 See, for example, A. Appadorai, *The Bandung Conference* (New Delhi: Council of World Affairs, 1955), which makes no mention of Zhou's reaction to anti-Communist speeches.
102 "Bandung Conference," *Philippines Free Press*, 30 April 1955, sec. World in Brief, 69.
103 Ibid.
104 Ibid.
105 Ibid.
106 Romulo, *The Meaning of Bandung*, 11.
107 Carlos P. Romulo, "The Bandung Story," *The Fookien Times Yearbook*, September 1955, 34.
108 The Asian-African Conference, "The Text of the Final Communique of the Conference," in *The Meaning of Bandung*, by Carlos P. Romulo (Chapel Hill: The University of North Carolina Press, 1956), Section D, Article 1.
109 Romulo, "The Bandung Story," 34.
110 Romulo singles out these two in *The Meaning of Bandung*, 10.
111 Romulo, "The Bandung Story," 34.
112 Ibid.
113 Ibid.
114 Kotelawala, *An Asian Prime Minister's Story*, 187.
115 Ibid., 188. The latest account of the crushing of Eastern Europe is Anne Applebaum's *Iron Curtain: The Crushing of Eastern Europe, 1945–1956* (New York, London, Toronto, Sydney, and Auckland: Doubleday, 2012).
116 The comparison is prescient, especially since, like Third World countries, the states of Eastern Europe would also launch resistance movements against a foreign occupier. It is thus apt to trace continuities between the struggles of Asian anticolonialists in Bandung and those of Vaclav Havel and Lech Walesa. The latter too were "postcolonial" leaders.
117 There was a brief confrontation between Nehru and Kotelawala after the latter's speech. Despite this, Kotelawala says he and Nehru remained "best friends." Kotelawala, *An Asian Prime Minister's Story*, 187.
118 Romulo, *The Meaning of Bandung*, 31.
119 Ibid., 33.
120 Ibid., 188.
121 Ibid., 82.
122 Ibid. The similarity here with Blum is crucial. Romulo did not condemn socialism as a whole and was cognizant of the broader history of socialism, whereby the issue of using terror as a political strategy became a demarcation line between the socialists of the Second International and the Communists of the Third.

123 Ibid., 83.
124 Ibid., 84–88.
125 Ibid.
126 Jawaharlal Nehru, "Jawaharlal Nehru on Communism, War and Peace," interview by Blair Frasser, Television Broadcast, 21 April 1960, CBC Television Digital Archives, http://www.cbc.ca/player/Digital+Archives/Politics/International+Politics/ID/1694612491/?sort=MostPopular, accessed 10 March 2013.
127 Romulo, *Romulo: A Third World Soldier*, 139.
128 Orest Martyshin, *Jawaharlal Nehru and His Political Views*, trans. Oleg Grebenyuk (Moscow: Progress Publishers, 1989), 131–33.
129 Ibid., 121.
130 Romulo, "The Bandung Story," 35.
131 Carlos P. Romulo, *Identity and Change: Towards a National Definition* (Manila: Solidaridad Publishing House, 1965), 69.
132 Carlos P. Romulo, *The Asian Mystique: A Clarification of Asia's New Image* (Manila: Solidaridad Publishing House, 1970), 11.
133 Ibid.
134 Carlos P. Romulo, "The Meaning of La Solidaridad," *Solidarity* 2, no. 6 (April 1967): 36.
135 Romulo, *The Asian Mystique*, 10.
136 This would explain, for instance, why the latest research on Red Army terror reveals that in 1920 alone, Lenin's forces executed 50,000 White soldiers and their allies. Michael Scammell, "The Russian Nobility Under Red Terror," *The New York Review of Books* 60, no. 4 (7 March 2013): 12. As for Mao's China, to belong to the "wrong class," of course, was life-threatening during the period of the red guards. The latest biography of Mao, which is the first to examine Soviet sources on the Great Helmsman, establishes that he rose to power within the Comintern as a firm supporter of Stalinism. See Pantsov and Levine, *Mao: The Real Story*.
137 Romulo, *The Asian Mystique*, 10.
138 Romulo, *Identity and Change*, 78.
139 Pankaj Mishra, *From the Ruins of Empire: The Intellectuals Who Remade Asia* (New York: Farrar, Straus, and Giroux, 2012), 246.
140 Ibid., 254.
141 One of his top priorities when he became president of the UP was to promote secularism on campus. Silvino V. Epistola, "Romulo's Design for the Filipino University," in *University of the Philippines: The First 75 Years (1908–1983)* (Quezon City: University of the Philippines Press, 1985), 395.
142 See Carlos P. Romulo, *Contemporary Nationalism and the World Order* (Bombay, Calcutta, New Delhi, Madras, Lucknow, London, New York: Asia Publishing House, 1964), which is a compilation of his 1964 Maulana Azad lectures in New Delhi. Interestingly, it was his interlocutor at Bandung, Nehru, who invited Romulo to deliver these lectures.

143 Romulo, *Identity and Change*, 83.
144 Ibid., 76.
145 Romulo, *Romulo: A Third World Solider*, 141–42.
146 Ibid., 58.
147 Ibid., 59.
148 Epistola, "Romulo's Design for the Filipino University," 395.
149 Ibid., 394.
150 Nemenzo, interview with author.
151 Benjamin Muego, interview with author, Quezon City, 10 June 2013.
152 Ibid.
153 Ibid.
154 Ibid. It was under Romulo's term, for instance, that the UP established its Department of Filipino. During his term, Romulo also attempted to raise funds that would allow more local intellectuals to go to the United States for further education. Romulo's intellectual contributions as university president cannot be tackled at length in this paper, but it is important to note that the "America's Boy" in the country's national university was able to distance himself from this caricature.
155 Ibid.
156 For an analysis of the connections between nationalist liberalism and the radical politics of the 1970s, see Abinales (2001), particularly the chapter "Filipino Marxism and the 'National Question.'"
157 Romulo, United Nations Oral History Project, 28.
158 See Walden Bello, Severina Rivera, and D. B. Schirmer, *The Logistics of Repression and Other Essays: The Role of U.S. Assistance in Consolidating the Martial Law Regime in the Phil.* (Friends of the Filipino People, 1977); Raymond Bonner, *Waltzing with a Dictator: The Marcoses and the Making of American Policy* (New York: Times Books, 1987).
159 Muego, interview with author.
160 Quoted in Brillantes, *Chronicles of Interesting Times*, 95. It was his main preoccupation, but he was not completely detached from partisan politics. He attempted to become the presidential nominee of the Liberal Party in the early 1950s.
161 Espiritu, *Five Faces of Exile*, 41.
162 Romulo, *Romulo: A Third World Solider*, 139.
163 Carlos P. Romulo (with Beth Day Romulo), *The Philippine Presidents: Memoirs of Carlos P. Romulo* (Quezon City: New Day Publishers, 1988), 137.
164 Ibid., 137.
165 Romulo, *Romulo: A Third World Solider*, 155. The claim is difficult to verify. I cannot find evidence of Nixon either affirming or negating it. It is probably false.
166 Carlos P. Romulo, "Our Best Weapon for Survival," *Significant Speeches* 1, no. 2 (July 1969): 51.
167 Ibid.

168 "Romulo for Asian Conference," *The Indian Express*, 6 September 1969, excerpted in full in *Rejoining Our Asian Family* by Carlos P. Romulo, published by the Republic of the Philippines.

169 For a discussion of dependency theory, the Third World, and the legacy of Prebisch's UNCTAD, see Walden F. Bello, *Deglobalization: Ideas for a New World Economy*, Philippine Edition (Quezon City: Ateneo de Manila University Press, 2006), 32–58 and Raewyn Connell, *Southern Theory: The Global Dynamics of Knowledge in Social Science* (Cambridge, UK: Polity Press, 2007), 139–64.

170 "Romulo for Asian Conference," *Indian Express*.

171 "Romulo Plea for Asian Identity," *The Hindustan Times*, 6 September 1969, excerpted in full in *Rejoining Our Asian Family* by Carlos P. Romulo, published by the Republic of the Philippines.

172 Romulo, *The Philippine Presidents*, 153.

173 Romulo, "Towards a New Era in Asia," 9.

174 Romulo, *The Philippine Presidents*, 153.

175 Quoted in Brillantes, *Chronicles of Interesting Times*, 89.

176 Alegre, Edilberto N., and Doreen G. Fernandez. "Interview with Salvador P. Lopez." In *The Writer and His Milieu: An Oral History of First Generation Writers in English*, 155–79. (Manila: De La Salle University Press, 1984), 177.

177 According to Francois Furet, the ability of Communists to pass off their critics as fascists, or abetting fascism, was the legacy of Stalin's united front policy during World War II. Communist propaganda, especially under the supervision of Willi Munzenberg (Communism's Goebbels and one of the first mentors of future anti-Communist Arthur Koestler), turned the followers of Stalin into the ultimate symbols of anti-fascist resistance. Under this rubric, it became easy for Munzenberg to dismiss the Soviet Union's critics as abettors of German and Italian fascism. Furet, *The Passing of an Illusion*, 209–65.

178 The 1965 mass murder of members of the Communist Party of Indonesia is the most egregious example. For the latest scholarship on this tragedy, see Douglas Kammen and Katharine E. McGregor, eds., *The Countours of Mass Violence in Indonesia: 1965–1968* (Singapore: NUS Press, 2012).

179 See, Nathan Gilbert Quimpo, "The Left, Elections, and the Political Party System in the Philippines," *Critical Asian Studies* 37, no. 1 (March 2005): 3–28 and James Putzel, "Managing the 'Main Force': The Communist Party and the Peasantry in the Philippines," *Kasarinlan: Philippine Journal of Third World Studies* 11, no. 3 (1996): 135–66.

CHAPTER 4: SALVADOR P. LOPEZ AND THE SPACE OF LIBERTY

1 Petronilo Bn. Daroy, *Against the National Grain* (Manila: Rem Printing Press, 1966), 83.

2 Ibid., 81.

3 Ibid., 82.

4 Ibid., 83.

5 Ibid., 84.

6 See footnote 50 of the previous chapter for an explanation of Romulo's ghostwriters.
7 Benjamin Muego, interview with author, Quezon City, 10 June 2013.
8 Luis Teodoro, interview with author, Diliman, 27 March 2015.
9 Petronilo Bn. Daroy, *The Politics of Imagination: Essays on Contemporary Philippine Literature* (Diliman, Quezon City: Philippine Collegian, 1960), 10–11.
10 Quoted in P. N. Abinales, "Jose Maria Sison and the Philippine Revolution: A Critique of an Interface," *Kasarinlan: Philippine Journal of Third World Studies* 8, no. 1 (1992): 12.
11 Ibid., 14.
12 The Maoists at the time, however, were barely a threat. They were young students, reliant on largesse from elite politicians, using them for political gain. See Lisandro E. Claudio, *Taming People's Power: The EDSA Revolutions and Their Contradictions* (Quezon City: Ateneo de Manila University Press, 2013), 124–29.
13 Eric J. Hobsbawm, *The Age of Extremes: A History of the World, 1914–1991*, 1st Vintage Books (New York: Vintage Books, 1996).
14 The upsurge of political protest in the Philippines mirrored the radicalism of France and, to a lesser extent, the U.S. By 1968, many French and American radicals had discovered Maoism as an alternative to the ossified, gerontocratic Soviet Communism of the Brezhnev years (1964–1982). In the Philippines, the Maoist repudiation came after the student wing of the original Soviet-aligned Communist Party broke away and re-established a Maoist Communist Party in 1968. The most informative work on French Maoism is Richard Wolin's while Paul Berman's work partially documents the influence of Maoists on the American "New Left." See Richard Wolin, *The Wind from the East: French Intellectuals, the Cultural Revolution, and the Legacy of the 1960s* (Princeton: Princeton University Press, 2010); Paul Berman, *A Tale of Two Utopias: The Political Journey of the Generation of 1968* (New York: W.W. Norton & Company, 1997).
15 Edilberto N. Alegre and Doreen G. Fernandez, "Interview with Salvador P. Lopez," in *The Writer and His Milieu: An Oral History of First Generation Writers in English*, 155–79 (Manila: De La Salle University Press, 1984), 158.
16 Ibid., 162.
17 Aurora Roxas Lim, "Salvador P. Lopez: A Biographical Sketch," in *Parangal Kay Salvador P. Lopez*, ed. Belinda A. Aquino (Quezon City: Office of the Vice President of Public Affairs, University of the Philippines, 1990), 1.
18 Alegre and Fernandez, "Interview with Salvador P. Lopez," 162.
19 Salvador P. Lopez, *Literature and Society: Essays on Life and Letters* (Manila: University Publishing Company, 1941), 218.
20 For an analysis of SP as literary critic, see Rafael A. Acuña, "The World, the Text, and S.P. Lopez," *Kritika Kultura* 13 (2009): 23–63.
21 Roland Burke, *Decolonization and the Evolution of International Human Rights* (Philadelphia: University of Pennsylvania Press, 2010), 82–88.

22 Alegre and Fernandez, "Interview with Salvador P. Lopez," 162.
23 Ibid., 174.
24 Adelaida Lopez, interview by author, Alabang, 23 March 2015.
25 F. Sionil Jose, interview by author, Ermita, Manila, 28 March 2015.
26 Petronilo Bn. Daroy, "Not Just Another Death," *The Manila Standard*, 22 October 1993. Daroy adds that SP never thought publishers would be interested in his work. "He had always assumed that he would be financing the publications of his own books."
27 Quoted in Acuña, "The World, the Text, and S.P. Lopez," 29.
28 E. San Juan, Jr., *After Postcolonialism: Remapping Philippines-United States Confrontations* (Lanham: Rowman & Littlefield, 2000), 106–7.
29 Acuña, "The World, the Text, and S.P. Lopez," 29.
30 Alegre and Fernandez, "Interview with Salvador P. Lopez," 173.
31 Resil B. Mojares, "The Formation of Filipino Nationality under U.S. Colonial Rule," *Philippine Quarterly of Culture & Society* 34 (2006): 25.
32 Salvador P. Lopez, "The Social Philosophy of Dr. T. H. Pardo de Tavera: An Exposition and a Criticism" (M.A. thesis, University of the Philippines, 1933).
33 Salvador P. Lopez, *Literature and Society: Essays on Life and Letters* (Manila: University Publishing Company, 1940), 70.
34 Michael Sandel, *Democracy's Discontent: America in Search of a Public Philosophy* (Cambridge and London: The Belknap Press of Harvard University, 1996), 26.
35 Lopez, *Literature and Society*, 72.
36 Ibid., 232.
37 Ricaredo Demetillo, *The Authentic Voice of Poetry* (Quezon City: University of the Philippines Press, 1962), 307.
38 Ibid., 231–32.
39 Burke, *Decolonization and the Evolution of International Human Rights*, 82–88.
40 Alegre and Fernandez, "Interview with Salvador P. Lopez," 169.
41 Salvador P. Lopez, Handwritten note mistakenly dated 23 December 1968 (more likely to be 23 December 1969, as it says that SP became president almost a year before this speech), Box 3, Folder 15, Salvador P. Lopez Papers, University of the Philippines Archives. These papers are hitherto referred to as *SPLP*.
42 Statement of President Salvador P. Lopez upon taking his oath of office in Malacañang as president of the University of the Philippines, 23 January 1969, excerpted from *The Philippine Collegian* p. 1, 30 January 1969, SPLP, Box 3, Folder 15.
43 Salvador P. Lopez, Remarks during the meeting of the University Council, Wednesday, 29 January at the Abelardo Hall, *SPLP*, Box 13, Folder 15, p. 1.
44 Salvador P. Lopez, Speech at the U.P. in Baguio" n.d. (but probably November 1969 since SP mentions that he was ten months into his presidency), *SPLP*, Box 3, Folder 19, pp. 7–8.
45 Ibid., 9.

46 Salvador P. Lopez, Remarks at the University of the Philippines Faculty Alumni Dinner, University Gymnasium, Saturday, 19 April 1969 at 6:30 p.m. *SPLP*, Box 31, Folder 16, 2.
47 Ibid., 2.
48 Ibid., pp. 3–4.
49 Eduardo Araullo, Fernando Barican, and Reuben Seguritan, "SP Non-Commital," *The Philippine Collegian*, 30 January 1969, sec. Letters to the Editor, 3.
50 "Council of Leaders: Report to Students," *The Philippine Collegian*, 4 February 1969, 3.
51 "The University of the Philippines Gazette," 31 January 1970, Executive Order (E.O) no. 1, Website of the University of the Philippines Office of the Secretary of the University, http://osu.up.edu.ph/wp-content/uploads/gazette/1970.pdf.
52 Ibid., E.O. no. 6.
53 Ibid., E.O. no. 7.
54 Ibid., E.O. no. 5.
55 Ibid., E.O. no. 8.
56 Lopez, Handwritten note.
57 Burke, *Decolonization and the Evolution of International Human Rights*, 46.
58 Salvador P. Lopez, "Human Values and the Cold War," First of a series of speeches on "Education and Filipino Nationhood, sponsored by the Graduate College of Education, University of the Philippines, 1959. *SPLP*, Box 3 Folder, 13, p. 11.
59 Ibid., 12.
60 Lopez, Speech at the U.P. in Baguio, 15.
61 Salvador P. Lopez, "A Year of Testing and Trial," Remarks at the 791st Meeting of the Board of Regents, 21 January 1970, *SPLP*, Box 31, Folder 20, 2.
62 Salvador P. Lopez, Remarks during the 1969 National Conference on Higher Education, sponsored by the Phi Delta Kappa (Int.) St. Louis University, Baguio City, 26 May 1969, *SPLP*, Box 31, Folder 18, p. 6.
63 There is a nasty tradition in the University of the Philippines (one that continues until today) of radical and Communist-aligned professors mandating that their students attend political rallies. Others induce their students to attend by giving them bonus points. Members of organizations are also, at times, compelled by officers to attend protests.
64 Oscar L. Evangelista, "Lopez's Beleaguered Tenure (1969–1985): Barricades on Campus at the Peak of Student Discontent," in *University of the Philippines: The First 75 Years (1908–1983)*, ed. Oscar M. Alfonso (Quezon City: The University of the Philippines, 1985), 453.
65 Nick Joaquin, "Foreword: The Hurrying of History," in *Days of Disquiet, Nights of Rage: The First Quarter Storm & Related Events*, by Jose F. Lacaba, New Edition (Pasig City: Anvil Publishing, Inc., 2003), xii.
66 Ibid.

67 Jose F. Lacaba, *Days of Disquiet, Nights of Rage: The First Quarter Storm & Related Events*, New Edition (Pasig City: Anvil Publishing Inc., 2003), 47.
68 Ibid.
69 Ibid., 52–54.
70 Ibid., 57.
71 Salvador, P. Lopez, Memorandum for the Members of the Faculty on the U.P. Faculty Demonstration on 29 January 1970; 10 March 1970, *SPLP*, Box 31, Folder 4, p. 1.
72 Ibid., 2.
73 Ibid.
74 Ibid.
75 Kerima Polotan, "The Long Week: Bombs, Stones-Violence, Hate, Death," *The Philippines Free Press*, 7 February 1970, Online edition, https://philippinesfreepress.wordpress.com/1970/02/07/the-long-week-february-7-1970/, accessed 21 August 2015.
76 Ibid.
77 Ibid.
78 Lopez, Memorandum for the Members of the Faculty on the U.P. Faculty Demonstration, 3.
79 Ibid.
80 Ibid., 5.
81 His account of Majul's comment about he who heads the house being responsible for what is happening in it is consistent with SP's.
82 Ferdinand E. Marcos, Diary, 29 January 1970, p. 58, *The Philippine Diary Project*, http://philippinediaryproject.com/1970/01/29/january-29-1970/, accessed 12 February 2015.
83 Given the arrogant and intransigent tone of Marcos's diary entry, he would have likely mentioned an apology.
84 Lopez, Memorandum for the Members of the Faculty on the U.P. Faculty Demonstration, 5.
85 Evangelista, "Lopez's Beleaguered Tenure," 461.
86 Ibid., 462.
87 Ibid.
88 Salvador P. Lopez, "Home of the Free Mind," in *Parangal Kay Salvador P. Lopez*, ed. Belinda A Aquino (Quezon City: Office of the Vice President of Public Affairs, University of the Philippines, 1990), 37.
89 Evangelista, "Lopez's Beleaguered Tenure," 462–63.
90 Lopez, "Home of the Free Mind," 37.
91 Salvador P. Lopez, Remarks at the Eighth Annual Ball of the Alpha Sigma Fraternity, Saturday, 28 February 1970 held at Nile Restaurant, *SPLP*, Box 31, Folder 20, p. 2.
92 Ibid., 3.
93 Ibid., 4.
94 Ibid., 5–6.

95 Ibid., 6.
96 Armando J. Malay, "Diary of a Decrepit Dean," 14 December 1971.
97 Patricio N. Abinales, "Fragments of History, Silhouettes of Resurgence: Student Radicalism in the Early Years of the Marcos Dictatorship," *Southeast Asian Studies* 46, no. 2 (2008): 178.
98 Salvador P. Lopez, "The University under Martial Law," Transcript of the verbal report made to the meeting of U.P. Deans and Directors on 17 October 1972, *SPLP*, Box 31, Folder 12.
99 Ibid.
100 Salvador P. Lopez, Memorandum Circular on the Resumption of Classes, *UP Gazette* III, no. 9 (September–October 1972): 116.
101 Salvador P. Lopez, Memorandum Circular on the Guidelines for University of the Philippines Under Martial Law, *UP Gazette* III, no. 9 (September–October 1972): 116
102 Salvador P. Lopez, "Freedom with Responsibility," Address delivered at the Commencement Exercises, University of the Philippines, 27 May 1973, *UP Gazette* IV, no. 5 (May 1973): 54.
103 Ibid., 55.
104 Ibid.
105 Roberto E. Reyes, "When Martial Law Was Declared: University of the Philippines (UP)," *Beto Reyes Blog: Recollections of a Former Anti-Martial Law Activist in the Philippines*, 19 September 2012, http://beto-reyes.blogspot.jp/2012/09/september-morn-student-council-concomsa.html.
106 Salvador P. Lopez, "Freedom and National Development," Paper read at the Symposium of the Philippine Political Science Association, U.P. Faculty Center, 26 June 1976, Mimeographed and bound speeches of S.P. Lopez found in the Filipiniana section, Rizal Library, Ateneo de Manila University, 1.
107 Ibid.
108 Oscar L. Evangelista, *Icons and Institutions: Essays on the History of the University of the Philippines, 1952–2000* (Quezon City: University of the Philippines Press, 2008), 123.
109 Earl G. Parreño, *Boss Danding* (Quezon City: Earl G. Parreño and the First Quarter Storm Foundation, Inc., 2003), 85–86. I thank Carlo Hau for finding this anecdote.
110 Reyes, "When Martial Law Was Declared." Reyes speculates that the *Collegian* was treated with "kid gloves" because its editor, Oscar Yabes, was not closely identified with student radicals. Moreover, Yabes belonged to the same fraternity as Defense Minister Juan Ponce Enrile, who may have interceded on behalf of the *Collegian*.
111 Elizabeth Protacio-de Castro, interview by author, Online through Skype, 30 April 2015. Protacio-de Castro was the president of the Psychology Society. She would eventually be recruited by the Communist underground and would realize the extent to which the Party had influenced their aboveground activities.

112 Protacio-de Castro, interview by author. Protacio herself was the daughter of a Navy Commodore. Another one of her CONCOMSA colleagues, Roberto Crisol, was the son of Deputy Defense Minister Jose Crisol. Their relationships with their pro-Marcos parents were tempestuous. Protacio-de Castro recalls that she and Crisol would call arguments with their parents "World War 3."
113 Reyes, "When Martial Law was Declared."
114 Protacio-de Castro, interview by author.
115 Ibid.
116 Malay, *Diary of a Decrepit Dean*, 13 May 1974.
117 Malay, *Diary of a Decrepit Dean*, 20 December 1972.
118 Salvador P. Lopez, "A Layman Looks at the Constitution," Keynote Address at the Lecture Series on the 1973 Constitution of the Philippines, U.P. Law Center, 3 December 1973, *SPLP*, Box 32, Folder 15, p. 1.
119 Ibid., 2.
120 Ibid., 5.
121 Ibid., 6.
122 Ibid., 7.
123 Ibid.
124 Malay, *Diary of a Decrepit Dean*, 24 October 1974.
125 Belinda Aquino, interview by author, Manoa, 14 April 2015. Aquino, who would eventually become the first director of the University of Hawaii's Center for Philippine Studies, chanced upon SP on campus, and invited him to speak to the Filipino community. SP obliged and shared with them the contents of his East-West Center speech. Prior to her exile in Hawaii, Aquino was a member of the UP faculty.
126 Teodoro is quick to emphasize that SP wrote many of his speeches, but that he required speechwriters simply because there were too many speeches to deliver. As with Romulo, however, SP gave clear instructions of what he wanted written and edited his speeches.
127 Teodoro, interview with author.
128 Ibid.
129 Malay, *Diary of a Decrepit Dean*, 31 October 1974. SP delivered the speech on 30 October in Hawaii. Since Honolulu is 18 hours behind Manila, Malay's 31 October entry corresponds with the date of the speech.
130 Salvador P. Lopez, *The Dillingham Lecture Series: The Philippines Under Martial Law* (Quezon City: University of the Philippines Press, 1974), 1.
131 Ibid., 2.
132 Ibid., 3. He also discussed the increasing Communist threat from the countryside and the country's economic woes.
133 Ibid., 6.
134 Ibid., 7.
135 Ibid., 8. As noted in the previous chapter, this foreign policy shift was largely facilitated by Romulo as Marcos's chief diplomat. It is no wonder that SP

viewed this shift with approval. Compared to Romulo, SP was a less vocal anti-Communist.
136 Ibid., 8-9.
137 Ibid., 10.
138 Ibid., 11.
139 Ibid., 12.
140 Ibid., 13.
141 Ibid., 14.
142 Ibid., 16. It may not have been codified as public policy, but torture was systematically practiced by the Marcos military. The best account of torture, disappearances, and illegal detention under the Marcos military is Alfred W. McCoy, *Closer than Brothers: Manhood at the Philippine Military Academy* (New Haven, Connecticut: Yale University Press, 1999).
143 Ibid.
144 Ibid. 18.
145 Ibid., 18-19.
146 Ibid., 20.
147 Ibid., 21.
148 Malay, *Diary of a Decrepit Dean*, 23 November 1974.
149 Ibid., 6 November 1974. In this entry, Malay details a funny story concerning the publication of the speech: "Seems 5,000 copies were destroyed because title of SP's speech before East-West Center 'The Philippines Under Martial Law' became 'The Philippines Law Under Martial,' obviously a transposition of slugs during the 'clean up.'"
150 Ibid., 11 November 1974.
151 Ibid., 2 December 1974.
152 Teodoro, personal interview.
153 Malay, *Diary of a Decrepit Dean*, 3 December 1974.
154 Ibid., 6 December 1974.
155 Ibid., 13 December 1974.
156 Ibid., 18 December 1974.
157 Ibid., 19 December 1974.
158 Ibid., 20 December 1974.
159 Ibid., 21 December 1974.
160 Ibid.
161 Ibid.
162 Ibid.
163 Quoted in ibid, 23 December 1974.
164 Ibid., 6 January 1975.
165 Ibid., 13 January and 14 January 1975.
166 Ibid., 17 January 1975.
167 Ibid.
168 Teodoro, personal interview.

169   Malay, "Diary of a Decrepit Dean," 20 January 1975.
170   Teodoro, personal interview.
171   Ibid., 18 February 1975. It is unclear how Malay got wind of Romulo's version of the story. It is most likely second hand.
172   Salvador P. Lopez, "The Pleasures of Reading," Keynote address at the Fifth National Convention of the Reading Association of the Philippines, 17 May 1975, Mimeographed and bound speeches of S.P. Lopez found in the Filipiniana section, Rizal Library, Ateneo de Manila University: 4.
173   Ibid.
174   Ibid., 5.
175   Alegre and Fernandez, "Interview with Salvador P. Lopez," in *The Writer and His Milieu*, 171.
176   Jose, personal interview.
177   Butch Dalisay, "The Literary Lopez," *The Philippine Star*, sec. Lifestyle, http://www.philstar.com/arts-and-culture/772126/literary-lopez, accessed 19 June 2015.
178   Ibid.
179   Ibid.
180   Ibid.
181   A similar story to what Paul Berman eloquently tells in *Power and the Idealists: Or, the Passion of Joschka Fischer and Its Aftermath* (New York: W.W. Norton & Company, 2007).
182   Lisandro E. Claudio, *Taming People's Power: The EDSA Revolutions and Their Contradictions* (Quezon City: Ateneo de Manila University Press, 2013), vii–xiii, 153–64.
183   Apart from Dalisay, Patricio Abinales has grappled with the disillusionment of his generation. See "Between State and Revolution: Autobiographical Notes on Radical Scholarship during the Marcos Period," in *Decentring and Diversifying Southeast Asian Studies: Perspectives from the Region*, ed. Goh Beng Lan (Singapore: Institute of Southeast Asian Studies, 2011), 207–38.

CONCLUSION: POSTCOLONIAL LIBERALISM, A GLOBAL IDEA

1   Zeus A. Salazar, *The Malayan Connection: Ang Pilipinas sa Dunia Melayu* (Quezon City: Palimbagan ng Lahi, 1998).
2   Megan C. Thomas, *Orientalists, Propagandists, and Ilustrados: Filipino Scholarship and the End of Spanish Colonialism* (Minneapolis and London: University of Minnesota Press, 2012), 4.
3   Richard Rorty, *Achieving Our Country: Leftist Thought in Twentieth Century America* (Cambridge: Harvard University Press, 1998), 8.
4   Pascal Bruckner, *The Tears of the White Man: Compassion as Contempt*, trans. William R. Beer (New York: The Free Press, 1986), 138.
5   Tony Judt, *Ill Fares the Land* (London: Penguin Books, 2010), 52.
6   "IN NUMBERS: The Philippnes' 'War on Drugs,'" *Rappler*, 28 January 2017, http://www.rappler.com/newsbreak/iq/145814-numbers-statistics-philippines-war-drugs.

7   Nicole Curato, "Deliberative Capacity as an Indicator of Democratic Quality: The Case of the Philippines," *International Political Science Review* 36, no. 1 (January 2015): 112. The solution for creating this empowered space is a renewed focus on local politics. Indeed, more work in political science requires focus on the democratization of Philippine local politics. See Patricio N. Abinales, "National Advocacy and Local Power in the Philippines," in *The Politics of Change in the Philippines*, ed. Nathan Gilbert Quimpo and Yuko Kasuya (Pasig City: Anvil Publishing, Inc., 2010), 390–417.
8   Nathan Gilbert Quimpo, *Contested Democracy and the Left in the Philippines after Marcos: Governance and Political Change* (Quezon City: Ateneo de Manila University Press, 2008).

AFTERWORD: A FIFTH LIBERAL
1   Incidentally, this is also my mother's teaching style, which I try to mimic in my own classroom.
2   Rita D. Estrada, "An Inquiry into the Sexism in the Tagalog Language" (M.A. thesis, University of the Philippines, 1981), vii.
3   Ibid., 19.
4   Ibid., 18–19.
5   Ibid., 63.
6   Ibid., 1.
7   Ibid., 59.
8   Ibid., xi.
9   Ibid., 60.
10 Ibid., 64.

Bibliography

ARCHIVE COLLECTIONS

Ambeth Ocampo Collection, Center for Southeast Asian Studies, Kyoto University
Diary of a Decrepit Dean, Diary of Armando J. Malay, University of the Philippines Archives
CIA Freedom of Information Act Reading Room (Online)
Filipiniana Section, Rizal Library, Ateneo de Manila University
Harry S. Truman Library and Museum Online Archive
Lopez Museum and Library
Manila Times Photo Collection, Rizal Library, Ateneo de Manila University
Salvador P. Lopez Papers, Main Library, University of the Philippines, Diliman
The Philippine Diary Project
Website of the University of the Philippines Office of the University Secretary

NEWSPAPERS AND ONLINE NEWS SITES

Daily Mirror
GMA News Online
Philippines Free Press
Pinoy Weekly
The Economist
The Fookien Times Yearbook
The Hindustan Times
The Indian Express
The Manila Chronicle
The Manila Times
The Manila Standard
The New York Times
The Philippine Collegian
The Philippine Star
The Washington Post
University of the Philippines Gazette
Rappler.com

INTERVIEWS

Alegre, Edilberto N., and Doreen G. Fernandez. "Interview with Salvador P. Lopez." In *The Writer and His Milieu: An Oral History of First Generation Writers in English*, 155–79. Manila: De La Salle University Press, 1984.

Aquino, Belinda. Personal Interview. Manoa, 14 April 2015.

Jose, F. Sionil. Personal Interview. Manila City, 1 March 2013.

———. Personal Interview. Manila City, 28 March 2015.

Lopez, Adelaida. Personal Interview. Alabang, 23 March 2015.

Muego, Benjamin. Personal Interview. Quezon City, 10 June 2013.

Nehru, Jawaharlal. Jawaharlal Nehru on Communism, War and Peace. Interview by Blair Frasser. Television Broadcast, 21 April 1960. CBC Television Digital Archives. http://www.cbc.ca/player/Digital+Archives/Politics/International+Politics/ID/1694612491/?sort=MostPopular, Accessed: 10 March 2013.

Nemenzo, Francisco. Personal Interview. Quezon City, 18 January 2013.

Protacio-de Castro, Elizabeth. Personal Interview. Via Skype, 30 April 2015.

Romulo, Carlos P. United Nations Oral History Project: General Carlos P. Romulo. Interview by William Powell and Rebecca Akao. Transcription, 30 October 1984. Dag Hammarskjold Library. http://www.unmultimedia.org/oralhistory/2011/06/romulo-carlos/. Accessed 11 March 2013.

Teodoro, Luis. Personal Interview. Diliman, 27 March 2015.

WEB SOURCES

Alba, Reinerio A. "Nurturing Children's Literature in the Philippines." National Commission for Culture and the Arts, 28 July 2003. http://www.ncca.gov.ph/about-culture-and-arts/articles-on-c-n-a/article.php?i=63&subcat=13. Accessed 29 August 2014.

Department of Economics, Ateneo de Manila University. "About." http://www.ateneo.edu/ls/soss/economics/about-us. Accessed 6 November 2015.

Liwanag, Armando. "The Record of Stalin," 15 January 1992. http://www.bannedthought.net/Philippines/CPP/1992/SSAMR/SSAMR-06-RecordOfStalin.pdf. Accessed 11 March 2013.

"MW Camilo Osias." *The Most Worshipful Grand Lodge of Free and Accepted Masons of the Philippines*, n.d. https://grandlodge.ph/about/past-grand-masters/mw-camilo-osias. Accessed 4 November 2015.

Reyes, Roberto E. "When Martial Law Was Declared: University of the Philippines (UP)." *Beto Reyes Blog: Recollections of a Former Anti-Martial Law Activist in the Philippines*, 19 September 2012. http://beto-reyes.blogspot.jp/2012/09/

september-morn-student-council-concomsa.html. Accessed 20 January 2015.

University of the Philippines – Reserve Officers' Training Corps. "General Carlos P. Romulo: Class of 1918." http://www.uprotc.org/alumni/general-carlos-romulo.html. Accessed 19 March 2013.

BOOKS, ARTICLES, UNPUBLISHED MATERIALS

Abinales, Patricio N. "Jose Maria Sison and the Philippine Revolution: A Critique of an Interface." *Kasarinlan: Philippine Journal of Third World Studies* 8, no. 1 (1992): 7–95.

———. *Fellow Traveler: Essays on Filipino Communism*. Quezon City: University of the Philippines Press, 2001.

———. "Fragments of History, Silhouettes of Resurgence: Student Radicalism in the Early Years of the Marcos Dictatorship." *Southeast Asian Studies* 46, no. 2 (2008): 175–99.

———. "Kahos Revisited: The Mindanao Commission and Its Narrative of a Tragedy." In *Brokering a Revolution: Cadres in a Philippine Insurgency*, ed. Rosanne Rutten, 144–87. Quezon City: Ateneo de Manila University Press, 2008.

———. "National Advocacy and Local Power in the Philippines." In *The Politics of Change in the Philippines*, ed. Nathan Gilbert Quimpo and Yuko Kasuya, 390–417. Pasig City: Anvil Publishing Inc., 2010.

———. "Between State and Revolution: Autobiographical Notes on Radical Scholarship during the Marcos Period." In *Decentring and Diversifying Southeast Asian Studies: Perspectives from the Region*, ed. Goh Beng Lan, 207–38. Singapore: Institute of Southeast Asian Studies, 2011.

———. "Absent Characters in the National Story." *The Manila Review*, September 2014. http://themanilareview.com/issues/view/absent-characters-in-the-national-story. Accessed 4 April 2015.

Abinales, Patricio N., and Donna J. Amoroso. *State and Society in the Philippines*. Lanham, MD: Rowman & Littlefield, 2005.

Abueva, Jose V. *Eugenio H. Lopez, Sr.: Pioneering Entrepreneur and Business Leader*. Quezon City: Leadership, Citizenship and Democracy Program, College of Public Administration, University of the Philippines, 1998.

Acierto, Maria Guillen. "American Influence in Shaping Philippine Secondary Education: An Historical Perspective, 1898–1978." Ph.D Dissertation, Loyola University of Chicago, 1980.

Acuña, Rafael A. "The World, the Text, and S.P. Lopez." *Kritika Kultura* 13 (2009): 23–63.

Adas, Michael. "Contested Hegemony: The Great War and the Afro-Asian Assault on the Civilizing Mission." In *Making a World after Empire: The Bandung Moment and Its Political Afterlives*, ed. Christopher J. Lee, 69–106. Athens: Ohio University Press, 2010.

Agoncillo, Teodoro A. *The Revolt of the Masses*. Quezon City: University of the Philippines, 1956.

Aguilar, Filomeno V. "Tracing Origins: Ilustrado Nationalism and the Racial Science of Migration Waves." *The Journal of Asian Studies* 64, no. 3 (2005): 605–37.

———. "Filibustero, Rizal, and the Manilamen of the Nineteenth Century." *Philippine Studies* 59, no. 4 (2011): 429–69.

———. "Church-State Relations in the 1899 Malolos Constitution: Filipinization and Visions of National Community." *Southeast Asian Studies* 4, no. 2 (August 2015): 279–311.

Aldana, Benigno. *The Educational System of the Philippines*. Manila: University Publishing Company, 1949.

Anderson, Benedict. *Imagined Communities : Reflections on the Origin and Spread of Nationalism*. London and New York: Verso, 1983.

———. "Cacique Democracy in the Philippines: Origins and Dreams." *New Left Review* 169, no. 3 (1988): 3–31.

———. *The Spectre of Comparisons: Nationalism, Southeast Asia, and the World*. New York: Verso, 1998.

———. *Under Three Flags: Anarchism and the Anti-Colonial Imagination*. London: Verso, 2007.

Andrade, Jr., Pio. *The Fooling of America: The Untold Story of Carlos P. Romulo*. Manila: Pio Andrade, Jr., 1985.

Appadorai, Angadipuram. *The Bandung Conference*. New Delhi: Council of World Affairs, 1955.

Appadurai, Arjun. "Diversity and Disciplinarity as Cultural Artifacts." In *Race, Identity and Representation in Education*, ed. Cameron McCarthy, Warren Crichlow, Greg Dimitriadis, and Nadine Dolby, 427–38. New York: Routledge, 2005.

Applebaum, Anne. *Gulag: A History*. New York: Anchor Books, 2003.

———. *Iron Curtain: The Crushing of Eastern Europe, 1945–1956*. New York, London, Toronto, Sydney, and Auckland: Doubleday, 2012.

Araneta, Salvador. *Christian Democracy for the Philippines: A Re-Examination of Attitudes and Views*. Malabon, Rizal: Araneta University Press, 1958.

———. "The Central Bank and Our Production Program." *Philippine Economy Review* (April 1958): 54.

―――. *Economic Nationalism & Capitalism for All in a Directed Economy.* Rizal: Araneta University Press, 1965.

―――. "Life with Father by His Son, Salvador." In *A Molave for His Country,* ed. Salvador Araneta, ix–x, 135–63. Malabon, Rizal: AIA Inc. Press, 1970.

―――. *Bayanikasan: The Effective Democracy for All.* Malabon, Metro Manila: The Bayanikasan Research Foundation, 1976.

―――. *Salvador Araneta: Reflections of a Filipino Exile.* Edited by Michael P. Onorato. Fullerton: The Oral History Program, California State University, 1979.

Araneta Santiago, Ma. Lina. *Salvador Araneta: A Man Ahead of His Time.* Malabon, Metro Manila: A.I.A. Inc. Press, 1986.

Bananal, Eduardo. *Camilo Osias, Educator and Statesman.* Quezon City: Manlapaz Publishing Company, 1974.

Bello, Walden F. "Introduction: Ho Chi Minh: The Communist as Nationalist." In *Walden Bello Presents Hò Chí Minh: Down with Colonialism!,* ix–xxviii. London: Verso, 2007.

Bello, Walden, Herbert Docena, Marissa de Guzman, and Mary Lou Malig. *The Anti-Development State: The Political Economy of Permanent Crisis in the Philippines.* London and New York: Zed Books, 2006.

Bello, Walden, Severina Rivera, and D. B. Schirmer. *The Logistics of Repression and Other Essays: The Role of U.S. Assistance in Consolidating the Martial Law Regime in the Phil.* Friends of the Filipino People, 1977.

Benitez, Francisco. "The Contributions of America to Filipino Life." *Philippine Journal of Education* X, no. 7 (December 1927): 4, 39.

Berman, Paul. *A Tale of Two Utopias: The Political Journey of the Generation of 1968.* New York: W.W. Norton & Company, 1997.

―――. *Power and the Idealists: Or, the Passion of Joschka Fischer and Its Aftermath.* New York: W.W. Norton & Company, 2007.

Blyth, Mark. *Austerity: The History of a Dangerous Idea.* New York: Oxford University Press, 2013.

Bonner, Raymond. *Waltzing with a Dictator: The Marcoses and the Making of American Policy.* New York: Times Books, 1987.

Brillantes, Gregorio C. *Chronicles of Interesting Times: Essays, Discourses, Gems of Wisdom, Some Laughs and Other Non-Biodegradable Articles.* Pasig: Anvil, 2005.

Brinkley, Alan. *The End of Reform: New Deal Liberalism in Recession and War.* Reprint edition. New York: Vintage, 2011.

Bruckner, Pascal. *The Tears of the White Man: Compassion as Contempt.* Translated by William R. Beer. New York: The Free Press, 1986.

Buhain, Dominador D. *A History of Publishing in the Philippines*. Quezon City: Rex Printing Company Inc., 1998.

Burdiel, Isabel. "Myths of Failure, Myths of Success: New Perspectives on Nineteenth-Century Spanish Liberalism." *The Journal of Modern History* 70, no. 4 (December 1998): 892–912.

Burke, Roland. "'The Compelling Dialogue of Freedom': Human Rights at the Bandung Conference." *Human Rights Quarterly* 28, no. 4 (2006): 947–65.

———. *Decolonization and the Evolution of International Human Rights*. Philadelphia: University of Pennsylvania Press, 2010.

Burnett, Joe R. "Preface." In *The School and Society*, by John Dewey, ed. Jo Ann Boydston. London and Amsterdam: Southern Illinois University Press, Carbondale and Edwardsville, 1980.

Cayco, Florentino. "The Role of Youth." In *The Magus of Progressive Education: The Writings of Florentino Cayco*, ed. Merlita Lorena Tariman, 77–79. Manila: Arellano University, 1938.

———. "Democracy and Nationalism." In *The Magus of Progressive Education: The Writings of Florentino Cayco*, ed. Merlita Lorena Tariman, 154–56. Manila: Arellano University, 1940.

Cayco, Francisco Paulino. "Introduction." In *The Magus of Progressive Education: The Writings of Florentino Cayco*, ed. Merlita Lorena Tariman, vii–ix. Manila: Arellano University, 2007.

Chakrabarty, Dipesh. "Notes toward a Conversation Between Area Studies and Diasporic Studies." In *Orientations: Mapping Studies in the Asian Diaspora*, ed. Kandice Chuh and Karen Shimakawa. Durham: Duke University Press, 2001.

Chibber, Vivek. *Postcolonial Theory and the Specter of Capital*. London and New York: Verso, 2013.

Claudio, Lisandro E. *Taming People's Power: The EDSA Revolutions and Their Contradictions*. Quezon City: Ateneo de Manila University Press, 2013.

———. "Postcolonial Fissures and the Contingent Nation An Antinationalist Critique of Philippine Historiography." *Philippine Studies: Historical and Ethnographic Viewpoints* 61, no. 1 (April 2013): 45–75.

———. "Locating the Global South." In *The Sage Handbook of Globalization*, ed. Manfred B. Steger, Paul Battersby, and Joe Siracusa, 185–99. Thousand Oaks: Sage, 2014.

Coloma, Roland Sintos. "Empire and Education: Filipino Schooling under United States Rule, 1900–1910." Ph.D Dissertation, The Ohio State University, 2004.

———. "Disidentifying Nationalism: Camilo Osias and Filipino Education in the Early 20th Century." In *Revolution and Pedagogy: Interdisciplinary and*

Transnational Perspectives on Educational Foundations, ed. E. Thomas Ewing, 19–37. New York: Palgrave Macmillan, 2005.

———. "Care of the Postcolonial Self: Cultivating Nationalism in the Philippine Readers." *Qualitative Research in Education* 2, no. 3 (October 2013): 302–27.

Comaroff, Jean, and John L. Comaroff. *Theory from the South: Or, How Euro-America Is Evolving Toward Africa*. Boulder and London: Paradigm Publishers, 2012.

Constantino, Renato. "The Mis-Education of the Filipino." *Journal of Contemporary Asia* 1, no. 1 (1970 1966): 20–36.

———. *A History of the Philippines: From Spanish Colonization to the Second World War*. New York: Monthly Review Press, 1975.

Cuaderno Sr., Miguel. "My Solution to the Present Economic Crisis." *Philippine Economy Review* (April 1958): 30.

———. *Guidelines to Economic Stability and Progress: A Selection of the Speeches and Articles of Miguel Cuaderno Sr. Governor of the Central Bank of the Philippines*. Manila: Central Bank of the Philippines, 1960.

Cullather, Nick. *Illusions of Influence: The Political Economy of United State-Philippines Relations, 1942, 1960*. Stanford, California: Stanford University Press, 1994.

Cullinane, Michael. *Ilustrado Politics: Filipino Elite Responses to American Rule, 1898–1908*. Quezon City: Ateneo de Manila University Press, 2003.

———. *Arenas of Conspiracy and Rebellion in Late Nineteenth-Century Philippines: The Case of the April 1898 Uprising in Cebu*. Quezon City: Ateneo de Manila University Press, 2014.

Curaming, Rommel. "When Clio Meets the Titans: Re-Thinking State-Historian Relations in Indonesia and the Philippines." Ph.D. Thesis, Australian National University, 2006.

Curato, Nicole. "Deliberative Capacity as an Indicator of Democratic Quality: The Case of the Philippines." *International Political Science Review* 36, no. 1 (January 2015): 99–116.

de Sousa Santos, Boaventura. *Epistemologies of the South: Justice Against Epistemicide*. Boulder and London: Paradigm Publishers, 2014.

Daroy, Petronilo Bn. *The Politics of Imagination: Essays on Contemporary Philippine Literature*. Quezon City: Philippine Collegian, 1960.

———. *Against the National Grain*. Manila: Rem Printing Press, 1966.

Demetillo, Ricaredo. *The Authentic Voice of Poetry*. Quezon City: University of the Philippines Press, 1962.

Dewey, John. *The School and Society*. Edited by Jo Ann Boydston. London and Amsterdam: Southern Illinois University Press, Carbondale and Edwardsville, 1980.

Doronila, Amando. *The State, Economic Transformation, and Political Change in the Philippines: 1946–1972*. Singapore, Oxford, and New York: Oxford University Press, 1992.

Dotsey, Michael, and Thomas Stark. "The Relationship Between Capacity Utilization and Inflation." *Business Review*, no. Q2 (2005): 8–17.

Epistola, Silvino V. "Romulo's Design for the Filipino University." In *University of the Philippines: The First 75 Years (1908–1983)*, 389–442. Quezon City: University of the Philippines Press, 1985.

Espiritu, Augusto Fauni. *Five Faces of Exile: The Nation and Filipino American Intellectuals*. Stanford, California: Stanford University Press, 2005.

———. "'To Carry Water on Both Shoulders': Carlos P. Romulo, American Empire, and the Meanings of Bandung." *Radical History Review* 2006, no. 95 (2006): 173–90.

Estrada, Rita D. "An Inquiry into the Sexism in the Tagalog Language." M.A. Thesis, University of the Philippines, 1981.

Evangelista, Oscar L. "Lopez's Beleaguered Tenure (1969–1985): Barricades on Campus at the Peak of Student Discontent." In *University of the Philippines: The First 75 Years (1908–1983)*, ed. Oscar M. Alfonso, 443–98. Quezon City: University of the Philippines, 1985.

———. *Icons and Institutions: Essays on the History of the University of the Philippines, 1952–2000*. Quezon City: University of the Philippines Press, 2008.

Fabella, Raul V., and Emmanuel de Dios. "Introduction." In *Choice, Growth and Development: Emerging and Enduring Issues: Essays in Honor of Jose Encarnacion*, ed. Emmanuel de Dios and Raul V. Fabella, xi–xxxvi. Quezon City: University of the Philippines Press and the School of Economics, University of the Philippines, 1996.

Fawcett, Edmund. *Liberalism: The Life of an Idea*. Princeton and Oxford: Princeton University Press, 2014.

Finnane, Antonia, and Derek McDougall, eds. *Bandung 1955: Little Histories*. Clayton: Monash University Press, 2010.

Fitzgerald, C. P. "East Asia after Bandung." *Far Eastern Survey* 24, no. 8 (August 1955): 113–19.

Fitzmaurice, Andrew. "Liberalism and Empire in Nineteenth-Century International Law." *The American Historical Review* 117, no. 1 (February 2012): 122–40.

Fresnoza, Florencio P. *Essentials of the Philippine Educational System*. Manila: Abiva Publishing, 1950.

Furuoka, Fumitaka, Qaiser Munir, and Hanafiah Harvey. "Does the Phillips Curve Exist in the Philippines?" *Economics Bulletin* 33, no. 3 (2013): 2001–16.

Furet, Francois. "The Terror." In *A Critical Dictionary of the French Revolution*, ed. Francois Furet and Mona Ozouf, translated by Arthur Goldhammer. Cambridge: Harvard University Press, 1989.

———. *The Passing of an Illusion: The Idea of Communism in the Twentieth Century.* Translated by Deborah Furet. Chicago and London: University of Chicago Press, 2000.

Garcia, Robert Francis B. *To Suffer Thy Comrades: How the Revolution Decimated Its Own*. Pasig: Anvil Publishing Inc., 2001.

Gilman, Nils. *Mandarins of the Future: Modernization Theory in Cold War America.* Baltimore and London: The Johns Hopkins University Press, 2003.

Golay, Frank H. "The Philippine Monetary Policy Debate." *Pacific Affairs* 29, no. 3 (September 1956): 253–64.

———. *The Philippines: Public Policy and National Economic Development*. Ithaca, New York: Cornell University Press, 1961.

———. *Face of Empire: United States-Philippine Relations, 1898–1946*. Quezon City: Ateneo de Manila University Press, 1997.

Goodenow, Ronald K. "To Build a New World: Toward Two Case Studies on Transfer in the Twentieth Century." *Compare: A Journal of Comparative and International Education* 13, no. 1 (January 1983): 43–59.

———. "The Progressive Educator and the Third World: A Look at John Dewey." *History of Education* 19, no. 1 (1990): 23–40.

Goodenow, Ronald K., and Robert Cowen. "The American School of Education and the Third World in the Twentieth Century: Teachers College and Africa, 1920–1950." *History of Education* 15, no. 4 (December 1986): 271–89.

Gray, John. *Two Faces of Liberalism*. New York: The New Press, 2000.

Guerrero, Milagros Camayon. *Luzon at War: Contradiction in Philippine Society, 1898-1902*. Pasig City: Anvil Publishing Inc., 2015.

Guha, Ramachandra. "The Absent Liberal: An Essay on Politics and Intellectual Life." *Economic and Political Weekly* 36, no. 50 (15 December 2001): 4663–70.

Hau, Caroline Sy. "'Patria e intereses': Reflections on the Origins and Changing Meanings of Ilustrado." *Philippine Studies: Historical and Ethnographic Viewpoints* 59, no. 1 (March 2011): 3–54.

———. "Sins of the Fathers: The Elite in Philippine Literature." *The Manila Review*, February 2014. http://themanilareview.com/issues/view/sins-of-the-fathers-the-elite-in-philippine-literature. Accessed 2 November 2015.

———. *Elites and Ilustrados*. Unpublished Manuscript (Forthcoming, Ateneo de Manila University Press).

Hildermeier, Manfred. *The Russian Socialist Revolutionary Party Before the First World War*. New York: St. Martin's Press, Inc., 2000.

Hitchens, Christopher. *Why Orwell Matters*. New York: Basic Books, 2003.

Hobsbawm, Eric J. "The Future of the State." *Development and Change* 27, no. 2 (April 1996): 267–78.

———. *The Age of Extremes: A History of the World, 1914–1991*. 1st Vintage Books. New York: Vintage Books, 1996.

Hutchcroft, Paul D. *Booty Capitalism: The Politics of Banking in the Philippines*. Ithaca and London: Cornell University Press, 1998.

Ileto, Reynaldo C. *Pasyon and Revolution: Popular Movements in the Philippines, 1840–1910*. Quezon City: Ateneo de Manila University Press, 1979.

———. *Filipinos and Their Revolution: Event, Discourse, and Historiography*. Quezon City: Ateneo de Manila University Press, 1998.

———. "Reflections on Agoncillo's *The Revolt of the Masses* and the Politics of History." *Southeast Asian Studies* 49, no. 3 (December 2011): 496–520.

Jamias, Cristino. *The University of the Philippines: The First Half-Century*. Quezon City: University of the Philippines, 1962.

Joaquin, Nick. "Foreword: The Hurrying of History." In *Days of Disquiet, Nights of Rage: The First Quarter Storm & Related Events*, by Jose F. Lacaba, vii–xxvi, New Edition. Pasig City: Anvil Publishing Inc., 2003.

———. *A Question of Heroes*. Pasig City: Anvil Publishing Inc., 2005.

Johnson, Chalmers. *MITI and the Japanese Miracle: The Growth of Industrial Policy: 1925–1975*. Stanford: Stanford University Press, 1982.

Johnson, Paul. *Modern Times: A History of the World from the 1920s to the Year 2000*. London: Phoenix Press, 2000.

Johnstone, Andrew E. *Dilemmas of Internationalism: The American Association for the United Nations and US Foreign Policy, 1941–1948*. Surrey: Ashgate, 2009.

Judt, Tony. *The Burden of Responsibility: Blum, Camus, Aron, and the French Twentieth Century*. London: University of Chicago Press, 1998.

———. *Ill Fares the Land*. New York: Penguin Press, 2010.

———. *Past Imperfect: French Intellectuals, 1944–1956*. New York and London: New York University Press, 2011.

———. *Postwar: A History of Europe Since 1945*. Kindle Edition. London: Vintage, 2005.

———. *When the Facts Change: Essays 1995–2010*. New York: Penguin Press, 2015.

Jurilla, Patricia May B. *Tagalog Bestsellers of the Twentieth Century: A History of the Book in the Philippines*. Quezon City: Ateneo de Manila University Press, 2008.

Kammen, Douglas, and Katharine E. McGregor, eds. *The Contours of Mass Violence in Indonesia: 1965–1968*. Singapore: NUS Press, 2012.

Keynes, John Maynard. *The Collected Writings of John Maynard Keynes*. Edited by Elizabeth S. Johnson and D. E. Moggridge. Vol. 4. London: Macmillan, 1971.

Kirsch, Adam. "Melancholy Liberalism." *City Journal*, Winter 2016. http://www.city-journal.org/2016/26_1_melancholy-liberalism.html. Accessed 26 January 2016.

Koestler, Arthur. *The Invisible Writing*. London: Vintage, 2005.

Kolakowski, Leszek. *Main Currents of Marxism: The Founders—The Golden Age— The Breakdown*. Translated by P. S. Falla. New York and London: W. W. Norton & Company, 2005.

Kotelawala, John. *An Asian Prime Minister's Story*. London: Harrap, 1956.

Lazarus, Neil. "The Fetish of 'the West' in Postcolonial Theory." In *Marxism, Modernity, and Postcolonial Studies*, ed. Crystal Bartolovich and Neil Lazarus, 43–64. Cambridge: Cambridge University Press, 2002.

Lee, Christopher J. "At the Rendezvous of Decolonization." *Interventions* 11, no. 1 (2009): 81–93.

———. "Introduction: Between a Moment and an Era: The Origins and Afterlives of Bandung." In *Making a World after Empire: The Bandung Moment and Its Political Afterlives*, ed. Christopher J. Lee, 1–44. Athens: Ohio University Press, 2010.

Lee Kuan Yew. *From Third World to First: The Singapore Story: 1965–2000*. Singapore: Times Media Private Limited and The Straits Times Press, 2000.

Lim, Aurora Roxas. "Salvador P. Lopez: A Biographical Sketch." In *Parangal Kay Salvador P. Lopez*, ed. Belinda A. Aquino, 1–7. Quezon City: Office of the Vice President of Public Affairs, University of the Philippines, 1990.

Lopez, Salvador P. "The Social Philosophy of Dr. T. H. Pardo de Tavera: An Exposition and a Criticism." University of the Philippines, 1933.

———. *Literature and Society: Essays on Life and Letters*. Manila: University Publishing Company, 1940.

———. *The Dillingham Lecture Series: The Philippines under Martial Law*. Quezon City: University of the Philippines Press, 1974.

———. "Home of the Free Mind." In *Parangal Kay Salvador P. Lopez*, ed. Belinda A. Aquino, 37–39. Quezon City: Office of the Vice President of Public Affairs, University of the Philippines, 1990.

Lumba, Allan E. S. "Materializing the Central Bank of the Philippines: The Uncanny Postwar History of Money and Modernity." International Studies Association Annual Convention, Hilton San Francisco, San Francisco, CA, 2008.

MacIsaac, Steven Dale. "Nationalists, Expansionists and Internationalists: American Interests and the Struggle for National Economic Development in the Philippines, 1937–1950." Ph.D. Dissertation, University of Washington, 1993.

Mackie, Jamie. *Bandung 1955: Non-Alignment and Afro-Asian Solidarity*. Singapore: Editions Didier Millet, 2005.

Manalang, Priscila S. "Francisco Benitez." *Philippine Journal of Education* XXX, no. 2 (August 1951): 81, 114.

Mandel, Ernest. *Trotsky as Alternative*. London: Verso, 1995.

Mantena, Karuna. *Alibis of Empire: Henry Maine and the Ends of Liberal Imperialism*. Princeton: Princeton University Press, 2010.

Martin, Isabel P. "Longfellow's Legacy: Education and the Shaping of Philippine Writing." *World Englishes* 23, no. 1 (2004): 129–39.

Martyshin, Orest. *Jawaharlal Nehru and His Political Views*. Translated by Oleg Grebenyuk. Moscow: Progress Publishers, 1989.

Mazower, Mark. *Governing the World: The History of an Idea*. New York: Penguin Press, 2012.

M'Baye, Babacar. "Richard Wright and the 1955 Bandung Conference: A Re-Evaluation of The Color Curtain." *Journeys* 10, no. 2 (2009): 31–44.

McCoy, Alfred W., ed. *An Anarchy of Families: State and Family in the Philippines*. Quezon City: Ateneo de Manila University Press, 1994.

———. "Rent-Seeking Families and the Philippine State: A History of the Lopez Family." In *An Anarchy of Families: State and Family in the Philippines*, ed. Alfred W. McCoy, 429–536. Quezon City: Ateneo de Manila University Press, 1994.

———. *Closer Than Brothers: Manhood at the Philippine Military Academy*. New Haven, Connecticut: Yale University Press, 1999.

Mehta, Uday Singh. *Liberalism and Empire*. Chicago and London: University of Chicago Press, 1999.

Menand, Louis. *The Metaphysical Club: A Story of Ideas in America*. New York: Farrar, Straus and Giroux, 2001.

Mishra, Pankaj. *From the Ruins of Empire: The Intellectuals Who Remade Asia*. New York: Farrar, Straus, and Giroux, 2012.

Mojares, Resil B. "Reinventing the Revolution: Sergio Osmeña and Post-Revolutionary Intellectuals in the Philippines." *Philippine Quarterly of Culture & Society* 24 (1996): 269–86.

———. *Waiting for Mariang Makiling: Essays on Philippine Cultural History*. Quezon City: Ateneo de Manila University Press, 2002.

_____. *Brains of the Nation: Pedro Paterno, T. H. Pardo de Tavera, Isabelo de Los Reyes and the Production of Modern Knowledge*. Quezon City: Ateneo de Manila University Press, 2006.

_____. "The Formation of Filipino Nationality under U.S. Colonial Rule." *Philippine Quarterly of Culture & Society* 34 (2006): 11–32.

_____. *Isabelo's Archive*. Pasig: Anvil Publishing Inc., 2013.

Nagano, Yoshiko. *State and Finance in the Philippines, 1898–1941: The Mismanagement of an American Colony*. Quezon City: Ateneo de Manila University Press, 2015.

Nagel, Thomas. *The View from Nowhere*. New York and Oxford: Oxford University Press, 1989.

National Historical Institute. *Filipinos in History*. Vol. 3. Manila: National Historical Institute, 1992.

Nakano, Satoshi. "Appeasement and Coercion." In *The Philippines under Japan: Occupation Policy and Reaction*, ed. Setsuho Ikehata and Ricardo Trota Jose, 21–58. Quezon City: Ateneo de Manila University Press, 1999.

Office for Asian Affairs, Congress for Cultural Freedom. *Freedom and Economic Planning: Proceedings of a Session of the Conference on Cultural Freedom in Asia, Rangoon, February 1955*. New Delhi: Office for Asian Affairs, Congress for Cultural Freedom, 1955.

Orwell, George. "Review of Russia under Soviet Rule by N. de Basily." In *George Orwell: Essays*, ed. John Carey, 108–11. New York, London, and Toronto: Alfred A. Knopf, 2002.

Osias, Camilo. *The Philippine Readers, Book 4*. Boston: Ginn and Company, 1922.

_____. "Private Schools in Philippine Education." *Philippine Journal of Education*, (November 1927): 1, 22.

_____. *The Philippine Readers, Book 7*. Boston: Ginn and Company, 1932.

_____. *Separation of Church and State*. Manila: S. N. (Probably self-published), 1934.

_____. *The Filipino Way of Life*. Boston: Ginn and Company, 1940.

_____. *Life-Centered Education*. Quezon City: Bustamante Press, 1954.

_____. "Education for New Japan." *Philippine Economy Review* 5, no. 6 (1959): 9.

_____. "Rizal: Pioneer Nationalist and Internationalist." *Historical Bulletin* IV, no. 2 (1960): 39–54.

_____. "Education: An Instrument of National Goals." Lecture presented at the Philippine Women's University, Ramona S. Tirona Memorial Lecture Series, Manila, 20 May 1967.

_____. *The Story of a Long Career of Varied Tasks*. Quezon City: Manlapaz Publishing Company, 1971.

———. "Appendix A: Inaugural Address of Camilo Osias as First President of National University Delivered at the Manila Grand Opera House." In *Camilo Osias: Educator and Statesman*, by Eduardo Bananal, 147–56. Quezon City: Manlapaz Publishing Company, 1974.

Packer, George. *Blood of the Liberals*. New York: Farrar, Straus and Giroux, 2000.

Paderanga, Cayetano. "The Macroeconomic Dimensions of Philippine Development." Philippine Studies Conference in Japan (PSCJ), Center for Southeast Asian Studies, Kyoto University, 2014.

Pang Yang Huei. "The Four Faces of Bandung: Detainees, Soldiers, Revolutionaries and Statesmen." *Journal of Contemporary Asia* 39, no. 1 (2009): 63–86.

Pantsov, Alexander V., and Steven I. Levine. *Mao: The Real Story*. New York, London, Toronto, Sydney, New Delhi: Simon & Schuster, 2012.

Parayno, Salud M. *Children's Literature*. Revised. Quezon City: Katha Publishing Co., Inc., 1997.

Paredes, Ruby Rivera. "The Partido Federal, 1900–1907: Political Collaboration in Colonial Manila." Doctoral Dissertation, University of Michigan, 1990.

Parreño, Earl G. *Boss Danding*. Quezon City: Earl G. Parreño and the First Quarter Storm Foundation, Inc., 2003.

Parekh, Bhikku. "Liberalism and Colonialism: A Critique of Locke and Mill." In *The Decolonization of Imagination: Culture, Knowledge and Power*, ed. Jan Nederveen Pieterse and Bhikku Parekh. London: Zed Books, 1995.

Phillips, A. W. "The Relation between Unemployment and the Rate of Change of Money Wage Rates in the United Kingdom, 1861–1957." *Economica* 25, no. 100 (1958): 283–99.

Polansky, Janet. *Revolutions Without Borders: The Call to Liberty in the Atlantic World*. New Haven: Yale University Press, 2015.

Power, John H., and Gerardo P. Sicat. *The Philippines: Industrialization and Trade Policies*. London, New York, and Kuala Lumpur: Oxford University Press, 1971.

Priestland, David. *The Red Flag: Communism and the Making of the Modern World*. London and New York: Allen Lane/Penguin Books, 2009.

Putzel, James. "Managing the 'Main Force': The Communist Party and the Peasantry in the Philippines." *Kasarinlan: Philippine Journal of Third World Studies* 11, no. 3 (1996): 135–66.

Quimpo, Nathan Gilbert. "The Left, Elections, and the Political Party System in the Philippines." *Critical Asian Studies* 37, no. 1 (March 2005): 3–28.

———. *Contested Democracy and the Left in the Philippines after Marcos*. Quezon City: Ateneo de Manila University Press, 2008.

Rafael, Vicente L. "Introduction: Revolutionary Contradictions." In *Luzon at War: Contradictions in Philippine Society, 1898–1902*, by Milagros Camayon Guerrero, 1–19. Pasig City: Anvil Publishing Inc., 2015.

Recto, Claro M. "Foreword." In *Christian Democracy for the Philippines: A Re-Examination of Attitudes and Views*, v–viii. Malabon, Rizal: Araneta University Press, 1958.

Richardson, Jim. *The Light of Liberty: Documents and Studies on the Katipunan, 1892–1897*. Quezon City: Ateneo de Manila University Press, 2013.

Romer, Christina D. "What Ended the Great Depression." *The Journal of Economic History* 52, no. 4 (December 1992): 757–84.

Romulo, Carlos P. "The Position of Southeast Asia in the World Community." In *Southeast Asia in the Coming World*, ed. Philip W. Thayer, 249–56. Essay Index Reprint Series. Baltimore: Johns Hopkins Press, 1953.

———. *The Meaning of Bandung*. Chapel Hill: University of North Carolina Press, 1956.

———. *Contemporary Nationalism and the World Order*. Bombay, Calcutta, New Delhi, Madras, Lucknow, London, New York: Asia Publishing House, 1964.

———. *Identity and Change: Towards a National Definition*. Manila: Solidaridad Publishing House, 1965.

———. "The Meaning of La Solidaridad." *Solidarity* 2, no. 6 (April 1967): 35–36.

———. "Our Best Weapon for Survival." *Significant Speeches* 1, no. 2 (July 1969): 49–51.

———. *The Asian Mystique: A Clarification of Asia's New Image*. Manila: Solidaridad Publishing House, 1970.

Romulo, Carlos P. (with Beth Day Romulo). *Romulo: A Third World Soldier at the UN*. New York: Praeger, 1986.

———. *The Philippine Presidents: Memoirs of Carlos P. Romulo*. Quezon City: New Day Publishers, 1988.

Rorty, Richard. *Achieving Our Country: Leftist Thought in Twentieth Century America*. Cambridge: Harvard University Press, 1998.

Ryan, Alan. *John Dewey and the High Tide of American Liberalism*. New York: W.W. Norton, 1995.

———. *The Making of Modern Liberalism*. Princeton and Oxford: Princeton University Press, 2012.

Salazar, Zeus A. *The Malayan Connection: Ang Pilipinas sa Dunia Melayu*. Quezon City: Palimbagan ng Lahi, 1998.

———. "Wika ng Himagsikan, Lengguwahe ng Rebolusyon: Mga Suliranin ng Pagpapakahulugan sa Pagbuo ng Bansa." In *Journal Launching of Bagong Kasaysayan*. DAPP-AVR, Bulwagang Palma Silid, U.P. Diliman, 1998.

Sandel, Michael. *Democracy's Discontent: America in Search of a Public Philosophy.* Cambridge and London: The Belknap Press of Harvard University, 1996.

San Juan, Jr., E. *After Postcolonialism: Remapping Philippines-United States Confrontations.* Lanham: Rowman & Littlefield, 2000.

Scammell, Michael. *Koestler: The Literary and Political Odyssey of a Twentieth-Century Skeptic.* Kindle Edition. New York: Random House, 2009.

———. "The Russian Nobility Under Red Terror." *The New York Review of Books* 60, no. 4 (7 March 2013): 11–13.

Schueller, Malini Johar. "Colonial Management, Collaborative Fissent: English Readers in the Philippines and Camilo Osias, 1905–1932." *Journal of Asian American Studies* 17, no. 2 (2014): 161–98.

Schumacher, John N. *The Propaganda Movement: 1880–1895: The Creation of a Filipino Consciousness, the Making of a Revolution.* Quezon City: Ateneo de Manila University Press, 1997.

Scott, James C. *Domination and the Arts of Resistance: Hidden Transcripts.* New Haven: Yale University Press, 1990.

Sen, Amartya. *The Idea of Justice.* London: Penguin Books, 2011.

Sibayan, Bonifacio P. "Becoming Bilingual in English in a Non-English Environment (Retrospective Essay in Honor of Joshua A. Fishman)." In *Focus on Bilingual Education: Essays in Honor of Joshua A. Fishman*, ed. Ofelia Garcia, 283–98. Amsterdam: John Benjamins Publishing Company, 1991.

Sicat, Gerardo P. "A Historical and Current Perspective of Philippine Economic Problems." Philippine Institute for Development Studies, 1986. http://opendocs.ids.ac.uk/opendocs/handle/123456789/3476 Accessed 20 September 2015.

Sison, Jose Maria, and Juliet de Lima. "Historical Essay: Foundation for Sustained Development of the National Democratic Movement in the University of the Philippines." In *Serve the People: Ang Kasaysayan ng Radikal na Kilusan sa Unibersidad ng Pilipinas*, ed. Bienvenido Lumbera, Judy Taguiwalo, Rolando Tolentino, Arnold Alamon, and Ramon Guillermo, 43–62. Quezon City: IBON Foundation Inc., 2008.

Smith, Jason Scott. *Building New Deal Liberalism: The Political Economy of Public Works, 1933–1956.* New York: Cambridge University Press, 2009.

Smith, Warren D. "Book Review: The Filipino Way of Life by Camilo Osias." *Pacific Affairs* 13, no. 4 (December 1940): 494–96.

Steil, Benn. *The Battle of Bretton Woods: John Maynard Keynes, Harry Dexter White, and the Making of a New World Order.* Princeton and Oxford: Princeton University Press, 2013.

Tadem, Teresa. "Social Capital and the Martial Law Technocracy: The Making Unmaking of a Power Elite." *Kritika Kultura*, no. 20 (April 2013): 69–94.

Tadiar, Neferti Xina M. *Fantasy-Production: Sexual Economies and Other Philip_ Consequences for the New World Order*. Quezon City: Ateneo de Ma University Press, 2004.

Takagi, Yusuke. "Politics of the Great Debate in the 1950s: Revisiting Econo Decolonization in the Philippines." *Kasarinlan: Philippine Journal of T World Studies* 23, no. 1 (2008): 91–114.

———. "Nationalism in Philippine State Building: The Politics of the Central Bank, 1933–1964." Doctoral Dissertation, Keio University, 2014.

———. "Beyond the Colonial State: Central Bank Making as State Building in the 1930s." *Southeast Asian Studies* 3, no. 1 (April 2014): 85–117.

Terami-Wada, Motoe. *Sakdalistas' Struggle for Philippine Independence 1930–1945*. Quezon City: Ateneo de Manila University Press, 2014.

The Asian-African Conference. "The Text of the Final Communique of the Conference." In *The Meaning of Bandung*, by Carlos P. Romulo, 92–102. Chapel Hill: The University of North Carolina Press, 1956.

Thomas, Megan C. *Orientalists, Propagandists, and Ilustrados: Filipino Scholarship and the End of Spanish Colonialism*. Minneapolis and London: University of Minnesota Press, 2012.

Tolosa Jr., Benjamin T., ed. *Socdem: Filipino Social Democracy in a Time of Turmoil and Transition, 1965–1995*. Quezon City: Ateneo de Manila University Press, 2012.

Totanes, Vernon R. "'History of the Filipino People' and Martial Law: A Forgotten Chapter in the History of a History Book, 1960–2010." *Philippine Studies* 58, no. 3 (2010): 313–48.

———. "History of the Filipino History Book." Ph.D Dissertation, University of Toronto, 2012.

Turner, Bryan. "Democracy in One Country? Reflections on Patriotism, Politics and Pragmatism." *European Journal of Social Theory* 7, no. 3 (August 2004): 275–89.

Valdepeñas, Jr., Vicente B., and Germelino M. Bautista. *The Emergence of the Philippine Economy*. Manila: Papyrus Press, 1977.

Viswanathan, Gauri. *Masks of Conquest: Literary Study and British Rule in India*. New York: Columbia University Press, 1989.

Wolin, Richard. *The Wind from the East: French Intellectuals, the Cultural Revolution, and the Legacy of the 1960s*. Princeton: Princeton University Press, 2010.

Wright, Richard. *The Color Curtain: A Report on the Bandung Conference*. New York: World Publishing Company, 1956.

Index

A

Abinales, Patricio, 90
Acheson, Dean, 93, 94
Acuña, Rafael, 117
Adas, Michael, 82
Afro-Asia solidarity, 82. *See also* Bandung Conference
Age of Revolution, 18
Agoncillo, Teodoro, 13–14, 116
Aguilar, Filomeno, 11
Aguinaldo, Emilio, 11, 168n67
Alba, Reinerio, 39
Aldana, Benigno, 37–38
Alejandro, Lean, 160
Alfonso, Oscar, 140
americanization (Philippines), 12
Andrade, Pio R., 91;
anti-communism, 84, 86–87; in Bandung Conference, 95–100; Romulo's 93, 94–95, 101–3, 122
antitotalitarian thought, 85
Appadurai, Arjun, 2
Aquino, Belinda, 200n125
Aquino, Jr., Benigno, 108
Aquino III, Benigno, 154
Araneta, Salvador, 47; biography, 48–51; on inflation, 64–65; on Marcos, 68
Aristotle, 118

Aron, Raymond, 114
Association of Southeast Asian Nations (ASEAN), 106, 107
austerity, 58–59

B

Bandung Conference 81–82, 90–91, 95–100
Bao Dai, Emperor, 93
Bautista, Germelino, 65
Bell Trade Act, 52
Benitez, Francisco, 37
Blum, Leon, 84–85
Blyth, Mark, 46
Bolshevism, 85, 86
Bonifacio, Andres, 13
Bretton Woods, 69–70
Brillantes, Gregorio, 88
bureaucratic liberalism, 7
Burgos, Jose, 10
Burke, Roland, 82, 96, 115

C

Camus, Albert, 87
capacity utilization, 64

Cavite mutiny (1872), 10
Cayco, Florentino, 38
Central Bank of the Philippines, 52–53, 61
chauvinistic nationalism, 38
Cheka, 85
Chibber, Vivek, 5, 17
Cold War, 104–5, 149
Coloma, Roland S., 28, 30, 34–35
colonialism, 3, 98
Columbia Teachers College, 32
Comaroff, John, 3
communism, 84–93, 94, 122
Communist Party of the Philippines (CPP), 113
Congress for Cultural Freedom (CCF), 87
Constantino, Renato, 14, 23, 38, 116
Coordinating Committee on Student Affairs (CONCOMSA), 133, 141
Corpuz, Onofre D., 142
cosmopolitanism, 37
Creole libertarian movement, 10
Cuaderno, Miguel, 47, 50–51, 54, 58–59, 61
Cullather, Nick, 50

D

Dalisay, Jose "Butch," 145
Darkness at Noon, 86
Daroy, Petronilo Bn, 104, 111
de la Torre, Carlos Maria, 10
de Lima, Juliet, 90
de los Reyes, Isabelo, 33
deficit spending, 54–55
deflation, 60
deliberate decision, 61
devaluation, 60
devalued peso, 55

Dewey, John, 26, 31, 32, 148
Diliman Commune, 127–28
Diliman Consensus, 13, 14, 117
dollar allocations, 55
Doronila, Amando, 50
Duterte, Rodrigo R., 154–56
DZUP, 133

E

East-West Center, 136
economic planning, 52, 70
economics, 52
education, 33; American-era, 23, 24; Meiji-era, 32–33; nationalist, 24, 32
elite vs. masses demonology, 14–15
empire, 3
Enriquez, Virgilio, 161
Espiritu, Augusto, 84
Estrada, Horacio, 158
Estrada, Rita, 158, 159–63
Eurocentrism, 148
exchange control, 55
exchange rate, 66–67
exports, 55–56

F

fascism, 113
Fawcett, Edmund, 7
FEATI University, 49
Fernandez, Leandro, 26
Filipinismo, 27–30
Filipino, 10–11, 14
first quarter storm, 113, 123–28

Fitzgerald, C.P., 96
folktales, 41
French revolution, 18
full employment, 56–57
Furet, Francois, 4

G

Gilman, Nils, 47
Gomez, Mariano, 10
gradualism, 12
Gray, John, 4, 5
Great Debate, 47–48, 50–51, 52, 54
Great Depression, 46
Guha, Ramachandra, 7
Guha, Ranajit, 17

H

Hau, Caroline, 9, 14, 67
hidden transcript, 29
Hildermeir, Manfred, 16
Hitchens, Christopher, 87
Ho, Chi Minh, 93–94
Hobsbawm, Eric, 3, 46, 86, 113
Hukbong Mapagpalaya ng Bayan, 13, 112
human rights, 96
Humphrey, John, 115
Hutchcroft, Paul, 50

I

Ileto, Reynaldo, 13
ilustrados, 8–9

India, 105–6, 107
indifference, 3
industrialization, 57–58
inflation, 58, 59–61, 65–66
Institute of Pacific Relations, 34
International Monetary Fund (IMF), 69–70
internationalism, 36–38, 40, 148

J

James, William, 31
Japan, 58
jingoism, 40
Joaquin, Nick, 9
Johnson, Paul, 81
Jose, F. Sionil, 88
Judt, Tony, 18, 46, 96, 153

K

Kabataang Makabayan, 124
Kalaw, Teodoro, 28
Katipunan, 11, 15
Kelso, Louis O., 49
Keynes, John Maynard, 46, 60, 61
Keynesianism, 46, 69
Kirsch, Adam, 2
Koestler, Arthur, 86
Korean War, 95
Kotelawala, John, 96, 98

L

Lacaba, Jose F., 124

Laurel-Langley agreement, 52
Lazarus, Neil, 4
League of Nations, 36
Lee, Christopher J., 82
Lee, Wei-kuo, 93
Lenin, Vladimir, 85
liberal constitution (Spain), 9
liberal modernism, 3
liberal revolution, 18
liberalism: definition, 2, 6–7; current state, 1; in crisis. 1; faces of, 5–6; in the 1950s, 111–12; Indian, 7–8; Philippine, 8–13, 149, 154–56; postcolonial, 3–4, 6, 150–54; reinventing, 2
liberals, 146
liberty, 7
Lie, Trygve, 102
Literature and Society, 34, 115, 116
Lopez Sugar Central, 49
Lopez, Salvador P., 34; after UP presidency, 144; biography, 114–16; dismissal, 139–44; liberalism, 116–18, 128–30; during first quarter storm, 123–28; on martial law, 130–39; relationship with CPR, 114, 119, 143; as UP President, 113–14, 119–23
Lopez, Victoria, 48

M

MacArthur, Douglas, 89
MacIsaac, Steve Dale, 52
Magsaysay, Ramon, 95
Majul, Cesar, 104, 126
Malay, Armando J., 130, 140
Manglapus, Raul, 88
Maoism, 113
Marcos, Ferdinand; economic policy, 67–68; on first quarter storm, 125–26, 127; martial law years, 105–6, 133
martial law, 131–39
Martin, Isabel Pefianco, 39
Masonry, 11, 27
Mazzini, Giuseppe, 31, 37
McCarthy, Joseph, 103
McCarthyism, 102
Medina, Pastor, 127
Mehta, Uday Singh, 3
Meiji-era education, 32–33
middle class, 16
modus vivendi, 4, 6
Mojares, Resil B., 12, 27–28, 117
Morgenthau, Henry, 63
Movement for the Advancement of Nationalism, 103
Muego, Benjamin, 103

N

Nagel, Thomas, 5
National Economic Council (NEC), 49, 53
National Economic Protection Association (NEPA), 50
National Federation of Teachers, 37
National Union of Students of the Philippines (NUSP), 124
National University, 26
nationalism, 30–31, 150
nationalist education, 32
nationalist internationalism, 31–38

Nehru, Jawaharlal, 92, 99–100, 106
Nemenzo, Francisco, 90
New Deal, 46, 54, 62–63
New Delhi conference, 92
"New Left," 114
19th-century, 18
Non-Aligned Movement (NAM), 105

O

Orwell, George, 85–86, 87
Osias Readers. *See* The Philippine Readers,
Osias, Camilo: biography, 25–27; contribution, 38–42; Filipinismo, 27–30, 35; nationalist internationalism, 31–38; thoughts, 24–25, 148

P

Pacific Affairs, 34
Paderanga, Cayetano, 66
Padhye, Prabhakar, 87–88
Palma, Rafael, 28, 136
Pang, Yang Huei, 82
Pardo de Tavera, Trinidad, 12, 117
parity rights, 52
Partido Federal, 48
pedagogy, 34
pensionados, 19, 26
People's Liberation Army, 13
peso, 66–67, 69–70
Philippine Sugar Association, 49
Philippines: economy, 52–70; revolution, 15–17, 18

Phillips curve, 65, 66
Phillips, William, 65
Pierce, Charles Sanders, 31
pluralization, 41
police brutalities, 124
Polotan, Kerima, 124–26
postcolonial liberalism, 150–54
postcolonial theory, 4–5
pragmatism, 31
Prebisch, Raul, 106
Priestland, David, 81
progressive educators, 36
Propaganda Movement, 9, 11
Protacio-de Castro, Elizabeth, 133–34
proletarian intelligentsia, 16

R

radicalism, 114
Rafael, Vicente, 15–17
Recto, Claro M., 57, 90, 111
retail trade, 49
Reyes, Roberto E., 132
Rizal, Jose, 8, 27
Romer, Christina, 63
Romualdez, Benjamin "Kokoy," 140
Romulo, Carlos P., 50; anti-communism, 93, 94–95, 101–3; Asianist view, 106–8; in Bandung Conference, 95–100; biography, 88–90; president of UP, 103–4; politics of, 90–95, 106; relationship with SP, 114, 119, 143; support for Marcos, 105–6; on Third Worldism, 83–84, 98, 104–5 writings, 88, 100–3, 106

Roosevelt, Franklin Delano, 46
Rorty, Richard, 150
Russell, Bertrand, 87

S

"'68 generation," 145
Saenz, Moises, 32
Sakdal revolutionaries, 39
San Juan Jr., E., 116
Sandel, Michael, 5–6, 117–18
Santiago, Lina Araneta, 50
Santos, Boaventura de Sousa, 3
Sauvy, Alfred, 94
Schueller, Malini Johar, 29, 30
Schumacher, John N., 10
Sen, Amartya, 5
Sibayan, Bonifacio P., 39–40
Sicat, Gerardo P., 65
Sikolohiyang Pilipino, 161
Sison, Jose Maria, 90, 112–13
Smith, Warren D., 34
socialists, 85
Solidaridad (Publishing), 88
Solidarity, 88
Southeast Asian Treaty Organization (SEATO), 106
Stalin, Joseph, 85–86

T

Tadem, Teresa, 52
Tagalog language, 162–63
Takagi, Yusuke, 14, 50
Tan, Jaime Galvez, 132
Tañada, Lorenzo, 103
tayo, 35
technocracy, 52
Teodoro, Luis, 136, 142
textbooks, 28
The Asian Mystique, 101
The Filipino Way of Life, 34, 35, 36
The Filipino Way of Life: The Pluralized Philosophy, 33, 41
The General Theory of Employment, Interest and Money, 60
The Mis-Education of the Filipino, 23
The Philippine Collegian, 126, 133, 141
The Philippine Readers, 26, 29, 38–42
Third Worldism, 81, 82–83, 98, 149
Thomas, Megan, 10, 147
toleration, 5
totalitarianism, 85
Trumbull, Robert, 92
Turner, Bryan, 37
20th century, 3, 19

U

UN Charter, 91, 92
United Nations Conference on Trade and Development (UNCTAD), 106

V

Valdepeñas, Vicente B., 65
Varela, Luis Rodriguez, 9
veto power, 92
Vietnam, 93

W

Wilson, Woodrow, 31, 36

Z

Zamora, Jacinto, 10
Zhou, Enlai, 96–97

KYOTO-CSEAS SERIES ON ASIAN STUDIES
Center for Southeast Asian Studies, Kyoto University

LIST OF PUBLISHED TITLES

The Economic Transition in Myanmar after 1988: Market Economy versus State Control, edited by Koichi Fujita, Fumiharu Mieno and Ikuko Okamoto, 2009

Populism in Asia, edited by Kosuke Mizuno and Pasuk Phongpaichit, 2009

Traveling Nation-Makers: Transnational Flows and Movements in the Making of Modern Southeast Asia, edited by Caroline S. Hau and Kasian Tejapira, 2011

China and the Shaping of Indonesia, 1949–1965, by Hong Liu, 2011

Questioning Modernity in Indonesia and Malaysia, edited by Wendy Mee and Joel S. Kahn, 2012

Industrialization with a Weak State: Thailand's Development in Historical Perspective, by Somboon Siriprachai, edited by Kaoru Sugihara, Pasuk Phongpaichit, and Chris Baker, 2012

Popular Culture Co-productions and Collaborations in East and Southeast Asia, edited by Nissim Otmazgin and Eyal Ben-Ari, 2012

Strong Soldiers, Failed Revolution: The State and Military in Burma, 1962–88, by Yoshihiro Nakanishi, 2013

Organising under the Revolution: Unions and the State in Java, 1945–48, by Jafar Suryomenggolo, 2013

Living with Risk: Precarity & Bangkok's Urban Poor, by Tamaki Endo, 2014

Migration Revolution: Philippine Nationhood and Class Relations in a Globalized Age, by Filomeno V. Aguilar Jr., 2014

The Chinese Question: Ethnicity, Nation, and Region in and Beyond the Philippines, by Caroline S. Hau, 2014

Identity and Pleasure: The Politics of Indonesian Screen Culture, by Ariel Heryanto, 2014

Indonesian Women and Local Politics: Islam, Gender and Networks in Post-Suharto Indonesia, by Kurniawati Hastuti Dewi, 2015

Catastrophe and Regeneration in Indonesia's Peatlands: Ecology, Economy and Society, edited by Kosuke Mizuno, Motoko S. Fujita & Shuichi Kawai, 2016

Marriage Migration in Asia: Emerging Minorities at the Frontiers of Nation-States, edited by Sari K. Ishii, 2016

Central Banking as State Building: Policymakers and Their Nationalism in the Philippines, 1933–1964, by Yusuke Takagi, 2016

Moral Politics in the Philippines: Inequality, Democracy and the Urban Poor, by Wataru Kusaka, 2017